Leisure Theory

1 WEEK LOAN

Leisure Theory

Principles and Practices

Chris Rojek

First published 2005 by
PALGRAVE MACMILLAN
Houndmills, Basingstoke, Hampshire RG21 6XS and
175 Fifth Avenue, New York, N.Y. 10010
Companies and representatives throughout the world

PALGRAVE MACMILLAN is the global academic imprint of the Palgrave Macmillan division of St. Martin's Press, LLC and of Palgrave Macmillan Ltd. Macmillan® is a registered trademark in the United States, United Kingdom and other countries. Palgrave is a registered trademark in the European Union and other countries.

ISBN-13: 978–1–4039–0569–7 hardback
ISBN-10: 1–4039–0569–X hardback
ISBN-13: 978–1–4039–0570–3 paperback
ISBN-10: 1–4039–0570–3 paperback

This book is printed on paper suitable for recycling and made from fully managed and sustained forest sources.

A catalogue record for this book is available from the British Library.

Library of Congress Cataloging-in-Publication Data
Rojek, Chris.
    Leisure theory : principles and practices / Chris Rojek.
        p.   cm.
    Includes bibliographical references and index.
    ISBN 1–4039–0569–X — ISBN 1–4039–0570–3 (pbk.)
    1. Leisure—Social aspects.   I. Title.
    GV14.45.R659 2005
    790.01—dc22   2005049816

10   9   8   7   6   5   4   3   2   1
14   13   12   11   10   09   08   07   06   05

Printed and bound in Great Britain by
Antony Rowe Ltd, Chippenham and Eastbourne

For Bryan S. Turner, who provided much of the fuel for this fire

Contents

Introduction

We live in uncertain, challenging times, in which the issues of the nature and purpose of leisure are more complex than they were thirty years ago. Old convictions about the capacity of science and technology to solve our leisure ills and produce the leisure society have given way to fresh anxieties about the risks involved in some leisure forms, especially forms which are perceived to be deviant such as the recreational use of illicit drugs, and illegal downloading of music, film and software from the internet. The traditional confidence with which those in paid employment, their dependants and owners of capital asserted their *right* to leisure is now festooned with new worries. These include the casualization of paid employment and its implications for health and pension contributions, the environmental costs of leisure practice, various dietary risks, sexually transmitted illnesses and the persistence of inequality and the role of leisure multinationals in intensifying the development gap. The *Charter for Leisure* approved by the World Leisure board of directors in July 2000 submitted that 'provisions for leisure for the quality of life are as important as those for health and education'.[1] Yet scarcely any government has taken heed in respect of its public spending programme and, at the state level, the relationship between leisure and the quality of life generally remains poorly understood.

There is widespread agreement that the relationship between the individual and the state in respect of civil rights and responsibilities is being profoundly revised in the Western democracies. Ours is an age of ambivalence and anxiety in which many of the traditional postwar beliefs that underpinned leisure forms and practice, such as free education, home ownership, secure employment and environmental stability, have evaporated like castles in the air. The state is either abandoning or reducing many of its traditional functions, especially in the areas of guaranteed inflation-proof pensions, free education, free health care and comprehensive welfare provision. Private corporations have recognized new responsibilities and opportunities in respect of environmental protection and civic virtue. The rise of mass literacy and mass communications has produced a new type of citizen, one who has a longer exposure to institutionalized education than ever before and with unprecedented access to information and policy options via the media. These developments are sponsoring a new version of *active citizenship* based around partnerships between private individuals, voluntary organizations, multinationals and the state.

Active citizenship is based upon an empowered model of the individual to acknowledge and implement civic rights and responsibilities. The model is based upon two levels. First, the requirement of civil society to keep citizens informed about lifestyle options and political choices. Second, the construction of partnerships between citizens, voluntary organizations, ombudsmen and the state to substantiate active participation in rights and responsibilities.

The character of this partnership is still unclear. Moreover, it is resisted by many vested interests that want the world to stay the same. But the trend is unmistakable.

The concept of active citizenship seeks to operationalize a revised notion of citizenship rights and also, crucially, to acknowledge new citizenship responsibilities relating to the voluntary protection and expansion of **social capital**.

Social capital refers to the voluntary investment in community and civic wealth. Whereas wealth is usually defined in economic terms, social capital refers to the social value added by helping and caring. Examples include voluntary protection of the environment, assistance with child care and the elderly and running not-for-profit community leisure and recreation activities.

Post-9/11, it has become impossible to bury our heads in the sand about globalization and its consequences. Or to imply that 'free' time practice has nothing to do with the rest of society. The implications for leisure forms and practice are far-reaching and irreversible. Indeed both the *São Paulo Declaration* of 1998 issued by the World Leisure and Recreation Association and the *Charter for Leisure* of 2000 call upon governments and students of leisure to plan for leisure in a globalized world and to combat the national and international threats posed to leisure.[2] Upon what basis are such bold claims ventured?

In the 1960s, radical theorists bemoaned the mass addiction to consumer culture and the apolitical, compliant attitudes that were held to accompany it. Herbert Marcuse (1964) famously referred scornfully to the onslaught of 'the happy consciousness', by which he meant the introspective and shallow conviction of consumers in the West that increased consumption and productivity were set to march ahead eternally and triumphantly solve the world's age-old problems of ignorance, want, misery and need. At this time, leisure theorists were not numbered among the ranks of radical social theory. After all, Leisure Studies was nothing but a fledgling part of the university curriculum, and leisure theory was in its infancy. Nonetheless, students of the subject typically reflected the complacent, heroic confidence of the day. Writers like Wilensky (1960) and Parker (1983) alluded to the compartmentalization or segregation of leisure from work and the other areas of life, as if these distinctions could be *scientifically* supported. Others, like Kerr and his associates (1973), Bell (1974), Touraine (1971) and Kaplan (1975), predicted the rise of the leisure society. In all of this the notion of leisure as a segmented realm of human experience magically insulated from the rest of life and fated to become generalized in identity and lifestyle became common currency, almost without anyone noticing it.

Arguably, a historical examination of the 1960s would conclude that Marcuse and like-minded others, perhaps acting in the spirit of the times, exaggerated his argument for rhetorical effect. The insulation of Western consumers from problems of Third World poverty, the delusion of using conspicuous consumption as a means of solving personal and collective problems and the environmental risk posed by unregulated consumption and production were never as complete or unopposed as Marcuse's concept implied. As for compartmentalized and segregated models of leisure, and the leisure society project to which they were frequently attached, they were often criticized for woolly or wishful thinking. The notion of compartmentalized and segregated activity runs counter to the concept of 'the whole man' that inspired progressive theory and politics (Mills 1953).

These debates were played out in a world that now seems to have vanished. Globalization, the widening access to education and the expansion of mass communication into every bailiwick of civil society have decisively changed how ordinary people relate to leisure. The old world in which world travel was regarded to be a luxury has been replaced by a world in which travel has been well-nigh elevated to a right of citizenship. We have moved from a type of society in which one or two in ten went into higher education to a society in which four or five in ten go to university. We have left behind a mass communication system based around a handful of terrestrial TV and radio stations and entered a new condition in which hundreds of satellite broadcasting outlets present news and opinions on current affairs around the clock. As a people in the West, more of us have prolonged experience of tertiary education, exposure to media channels of information and world travel than at any point in human history. This has changed things.

Naturally people still engage in leisure practice as an end in itself. However, they do so in a context of mass education, mass communication and mass tourism that presupposes a different relationship between the individual, leisure behaviour and citizenship. Civil society engenders multiple and often discordant flows of information relating to medicine, genetics, environmental hazard, inequality and human rights that has eliminated the possibility of theorizing leisure as a compartmentalized or segregated form of life. On the contrary, it is in our leisure time that we are most exposed to information and policy options regarding the appropriate rights and responsibilities of active citizenship and also to news about the infringement of these conditions. Both directly and indirectly leisure experience supplies the active citizen with data streams on lifestyle options and risks. Leisure never was 'free' time. But a good deal of it is now absorbed in risk aversion, from cutting down on drinking and stopping smoking, to monitoring diet and checking on terrorist alerts when we visit foreign countries, practising safe sex and keeping informed of the environmental hazard posed by carbon gas emissions. Now, it is manifestly not the case that active citizens virtuously devote all of their leisure to being observant about risk. But it is the case that when individuals pursue leisure practices that are known to carry risks to themselves and others, ethical considerations are now automatically invoked.

I was personally made conscious of this in the mid-1990s during a boat trip from one of the islands in Thailand to the mainland. During the course of the trip, a middle-aged Australian tourist with his family began drinking a can of beer. When he tossed the first empty can into the sea there was palpable tension from other tourists on board who cast disapproving glances and dismissive sighs in his direction. As he went on drinking during the trip, and prepared to toss a second can overboard, he was verbally challenged by a young German woman and others joined in. What would have been common practice in the course of leisure a decade earlier, namely littering the sea with non-biodegradable refuse, was now a social pressure point.

In another example, that does not lean upon anecdote, consider the case of smoking. For most of the twentieth century, smoking has been a popular type of mass leisure practice in the West. It used to be regarded as merely a matter of individual choice and conscience. Following the US Surgeon General's Report in 1964, which proposed a clear link between smoking, cancer and cardiovascular disease, this ceased to be the case. Individual choice and conscience in respect of the decision to smoke now carried implications for the health and well-being of the individual and the community in the future. There were social and fiscal implications of this, in that the taxpayer and state would ultimately have to pay for the decision to smoke in the shape of higher taxes to support increased medical provision. Equally, as medical knowledge of the harmful effects of secondary smoking and environmental pollution accumulated, the question of the social and economic cost of smoking for society, that is for *others* (non-smokers) as opposed to the individual smoker, was accentuated. Concerns began to accumulate around the possible effects of secondary smoking. Since 1964 smokers have been repositioned in relation to a formation of scientific and political thought and public opinion that has strongly defined smoking as a harmful leisure practice. In tangible terms, this has resulted in many nations in the West banning smoking in public transport and state buildings, promoting anti-smoking health education in schools and the movement to eliminate smoking from *all* public places. The change has been profound.

Moreover, it is paralleled by a heightened awareness of risk in many other leisure forms, such as drinking alcohol, a high-cholesterol diet, stress in interpersonal relations, driving automobiles with high carbon monoxide emissions, noise pollution and hunting animals for pleasure. If one was asked to provide a general account of these various changes one might perhaps say that they have been shaped by two compelling ethical imperatives – *care for the self* and *care for the other*. Care for the self refers to the various self-monitoring processes relating to achieving physical and mental well-being. Care for the other refers to expanding political participation and exploiting and developing the responsibility for the welfare of the community and natural world as a whole. Both restrict the idea of leisure as mere hedonism. Science is supplying us with more information about the impact of diet, culture and the physical environment on the biomechanics of the human body. It is also educating us about the dangers of some forms of unrestricted leisure practice by, for example, demonstrating that environmental pollution is depleting the ozone layer and contributing to global warming. Genetic engineering heralds the advent of new conditions of embodiment, the life course, disease and illness. In the midst of the immense wealth enjoyed by the West, and our apparent general addiction to commodity consumption, we are developing fresh concerns about overwork and the 'time famine' afflicting leisure and family life (Schor 1992; Hochschild 1989, 1997). Simultaneously, commercialization has colonized much of our non-work activity, making it hard to differentiate leisure from consumption. The question of the multinational manipulation of 'free' time behaviour through advertising, trend-setting and commodity design has become pronounced.

You can test this by using yourself as a resource in a simple experiment. Compile a list of the top five health risks that you associate with leisure practice today. Such a list might include the risks associated with a diet dominated by red meat and high-cholesterol foods, not practising safe sex in casual sexual relationships, smoking and driving without anti-pollution technologies. Now ask your parents and grandparents to make a list of the leisure risks that they recognized when they were your age. If the argument is right, your awareness of the risk to good health and the integrity of the environment of some forms of leisure practice will be much greater. It is not just a question of the ethical imperative of care for the self. The context of contemporary leisure forms and practice is also transformed by the imperative of care for the other.

Improvements in mass communications and travel and rising real income in the economically developed world have vastly expanded our leisure options and experiences. Yet, we are also more conscious than any other generation that many of the leisure goods and services consumed in the West are sourced from developing countries employing low-pay workers often with miserable levels of literacy and life expectancy (Klein 2001). Western exploitation of the leisure and tourist sites of the developing world has accentuated awareness of the commodification of leisure, transport congestion and architectural blight. It has also created a new generation of workers, often employed on part-time or fixed-term contracts, for whom the certainties of full employment and home ownership enjoyed by earlier postwar generations of workers have crumbled. Interrupted patterns of tax and insurance contributions have direct implications on leisure experience since they reduce the rights to pensions and other welfare benefits.

Globalization also brings with it considerations that have less to do with economics and ethics and more to do with a sensitivity to what might be called the etiquette of social interaction. To revert to anecdote again, I was made conscious of this in the course of a trip to Warsaw in 2004. For those who don't know, much of Warsaw, indeed *all* of the old town, was deliberately destroyed by the Nazis as a reprisal for the Warsaw Rising of 1944. In addition, Nazi occupation after 1939 involved a systematic programme of Jewish liquidation. Postwar reconstruction of the city has been a slow business. The Poles decided to build replicas of the main buildings that fell victim to Nazi scorched-earth policy and, of course, to memorialize the Nazi extermination of the Jews. In a reconstructed street in the old town a pile of bricks from the Warsaw Ghetto has been scattered on the ground and the attached vertical banner shows the faces of some of the Jewish victims of the holocaust. Poles and tourists have used the bricks as ledges to place commemorative candles. I happened to be there in September of 2004. Someone, presumably an American tourist, had placed a large cardboard sign in the middle of the monument with the words 'Remember 9/11'. This seemed to me to be tasteless, and offensive. Nearly 3,000 were killed in the attack on the World Trade Center in 2001, while 300,000 Jews were murdered in the Warsaw programme of Nazi extermination. But it is not simply a question of numbers. Every death is equally a cause for mourning. However, beyond this truism, it seems to me morally questionable to attempt to appropriate a monument designed to commemorate one outrage with remembrance of another. We should not conflate memories of suffering as if they are the same thing. In leisure we should be sensitive not only to our own needs and desires, but also to those of others. Care for the other assumes respect for the values of the other. While this is often most potently expressed in recognizing difference in religious practice, it also applies to the other's history of suffering, as is the case with the Polish tragedy of the Nazi holocaust.

These considerations of etiquette and ethics are more pronounced in ordinary leisure practice because multiculturalism offers new leisure opportunities and experiences in our cities and towns. It also threatens some established cultures, whose representatives complain of feeling distracted and engulfed by the possibility of the elimination of native leisure spaces, forms and practices. International terrorism makes us pensive about different lifestyles, religions and leisure patterns flourishing in our backyards. The urge towards social inclusion in leisure policy by embracing excluded or partially excluded cultures, consisting of ethnic minorities, the disabled, the homeless and the poor is tempered by alarms about higher taxation, the public squandering of taxpayers' resources and the withering of national values.

There is also rising disquiet about leisure forms based on the exploitation of others. This embraces both the human and animal worlds. Fox-hunting, bull-fighting, cock-fighting, bear-baiting, boxing and gun ownership have all been subject to moral campaigns that query their continued viability as leisure forms. While the West has experienced the growth in public tolerance for pornography manufactured under consent, sex tourism and the traffic of the under-aged for sexual procurement have become a global *cause célèbre*. The internet offers new opportunities to pornographers and paedophiles that trouble parents and agitate the moral majority.

All societies exist in a condition of scarcity. All must devise institutions and systems to solve the economic problem of legitimating unequal resource distribution and the social problem of establishing social power hierarchies and status ladders that justify the unequal distribution of resources. In addition, all must confront the question of how to regulate aggression and sexuality so as to maintain civil order. The institution of leisure performs an important and increasingly prominent role in managing these issues by acting as the basis for *identity* formation, the *representation* of solidarity, the achievement of *control* and challenging unsatisfactory resource allocation and civic regulation through *resistance*. The changes of the 1960s and 1970s transformed the logic of economic distribution, status allocation and civic regulation that governed our relations to the employment market, to the state and to each other. For one thing, capital and labour resources ceased to be concentrated in industrial and factory production and switched to communication and information. At the same time, industrial production and assembly shifted to low labour-cost economies in the developing world.

In addition, as capital and labour became more global, the central importance of the state in regulating labour markets and dictating public investment diminished. The welfare ideology that dominated thinking about public resource allocation and distribution was weakened. Although the responsibility of the welfare state for basic care of those worst off in terms of health, unemployment and provision for the elderly continues to be acknowledged, it occurs in a context where self-reliance and volunteering (through private health, education, recreation and pension schemes) are strongly recommended as, in many cases, the *preferable* solution to personal and social problems. Similarly, the capacity of the state to regulate economic and social conditions within its own territorial boundaries diminished through globalization. Bilateral and multilateral agreements on trade and human rights have proliferated, but the ability of states to regulate conditions in their own territories has become more conditional. For example, the US Digital Millennium Copyright Act (DMCA) (1998) is a controversial piece of legislation that criminalizes production and dissemination of technology with the capacity to circumvent copyright, and increased penalties for copyright violation. The Act was used by the Recording Industry Association of America (RIAA) in its campaign of litigation against Napster and other file servers which facilitated P2P (peer-to-peer) file exchange over the internet of sound recordings. Napster was the pioneer of this service and, at its height, is said to have claimed upwards of 70 million users (Goldstein 2003: 166). The legal actions of the RIAA eventually compelled Napster to introduce a fee-paying structure. The decision has resulted in the advent of many new online companies providing legal downloads of copyright material such as Apple iTunes, Sony Music Entertainment, Warner Bros, EMI, BMG and even Wal-Mart. Yet companies offering downloads for free, such as Grockster, Morpheus and Kazaa, continue to operate. Why?

The question turns on the First Amendment and the status of the gift relationship in leisure practice. The First Amendment guarantees free speech. Historically speaking, US courts have been extremely reluctant to rule in favour of extending copyright rule to the point at which it may constitute an obstacle to the dissemination of free speech. Now, the internet may be construed as an instrument that widens free speech by expanding access to digital data. If consumers choose to use it to exchange encrypted files of music that has been legally purchased, it does not follow, as night follows day, that the music industry has a right to prohibit the practice. If I choose to give a puppy to my niece for a birthday present, it is generally accepted that the kennel which sold me the puppy has no further rights of redress over what I choose to do with the puppy or, in the event, its offspring. This principle holds good for most commodities that have been legally purchased for private use. If I choose to make a gift of my CD collection by placing it on the internet for others to download, it might be construed that this is my free right over the use of legally purchased commodities, as it is traditionally understood. Indeed, this is what the US District Court ruled in April 2004 in the case of *MGM* v. *Grockster*. MGM sought to enforce the provisions of the DMCA legislation to compel Grockster to cease its downloading service. The Court ruled against MGM by finding that Grockster is not liable for the illegal use of a service made by consumers. To the consternation of the US music industry, the ruling was upheld by the Ninth US Circuit Court of Appeals in August of 2004. The case that a service provider cannot be held liable for the uses made of its operations by consumers is the same unsuccessful defence made by Napster against the RIAA's attempt to close it down and compel it to introduce a legal fee-paying structure. What is different about Grockster's use of this defence?

The pivotal issue turns on the nature of the file-exchanging system. Napster was constructed around a central server in which users deposited and withdrew donated music files. Grockster, Morpheus and Kazaa function through decentralized exchange systems that effectively turn the private computer into a mini-server. The result is that the exchange relationship conforms more faithfully to the traditional gift relationship between peers who elect to exchange legally purchased material for their private use. That is why the American courts have resisted extending the rights of copyright-holders over music file exchange. To do so violates the traditional freedom of consumers to exchange legally purchased items for private use as an ordinary part of the gift relationship.

The P2P controversy in the USA illustrates the difficulties that national organizations have in monitoring and controlling leisure practice in a wired-up world. In effect, globalization has contributed to the deregulation of consumer and labour markets by the deterritorialization of purchasing and investment options. Consumers no longer have to buy a commodity at the price fixed by corporations in their national territory. Instead they can shop around globally via the internet and in many cases involving intellectual property (software, recorded music, film and graphic art) download it instantly in their homes. Similarly, multinationals are no longer compelled to design, manufacture and assemble their products in a single territory. Instead they practise flexible investment policies and allocate functions of design, manufacture and assembly to markets where labour skills and costs are most favourable.

The globalization of labour also has an effect on the capacity for workers to resist corporate practice through collective organization and bargaining as it has been traditionally understood. Today's changes in the employment market compel workers to be more geographically mobile, team-centred and global. All of these factors impede collectivism. Workers who are mobile cannot readily establish secure, integrated common interests. If they work in teams, their system of reward (through performance-related pay) and status mechanisms are typically openly pitted against other teams, rather than the entire workforce. Working globally pinpoints the employer through the employment contract, but tends to render the mass of wage labourers either amorphous or invisible, since most workers only come into contact with them through the virtual reality connections of network links or the mass media. The result is to fragment workers, undermine the principle of common interests that is the foundation of collective bargaining and so weaken trade unionism.

The West has struggled to come to terms with these new conditions. Declining centres of industrial production have fought against the reallocation of resources to the developing world, and have been slow to introduce retraining initiatives in the labour force that would attract investment from the high-tech sector. Many workers have found it hard to adjust to the casualization of the labour market, with part-time or fixed contracts replacing the old order of a 'job for life'. Others have found themselves surplus to requirements.

With respect to consumption, the punitive action of the RIAA in respect of downloading has been used as the basis to reassert traditional rights of copyright, rather than positively examine the Web as an opportunity for revolutionizing retail practice in respect of intellectual property. Public education has adjusted slowly and unevenly to the new skills and consumption opportunities presented by the global, information economy. The retrenchment of welfare state provision has been unpopular, especially in a context of stock market upheaval that has eroded the value of private health, education and pension schemes. Trade unions have moved clumsily from national systems of organization and collective bargaining to the international collectivism, based around international, flexible bargaining, that the new conditions of the global, information economy require. Leisure has become increasingly important in building solidarity and challenging civil and distributive injustice. This is the result of the combination of globalization, mass education and mass communication systems alluded to before, which have arguably created a body politic that has never been better educated and informed. Leisure practice has become more politicized because it is the sphere in which the rights and responsibilities of participating in global civil society are most freely addressed.

If we feel battered, we also recognize new responsibilities of active citizenship. Our traditional civic concepts and the old division between Left and Right seem incapable of addressing, let alone solving, the problems we face in civil society and leisure. Western society is investigating new ways of empowering citizens that avoid the dog-eat-dog solutions of the market and the dependency culture of the welfare state. In addition, there is growing appreciation that many problems of leisure forms and practice require global solutions, not least in the area of environmental pollution, pornography and copyright violation on the internet and illegal drug-trafficking. It is no longer legitimate to conceptualize leisure in terms of carefree hedonism. While hedonism obviously remains an element in many leisure forms and practices, it is indissolubly mixed up with the twin global ethical imperatives of care for the self and care for the other.

The various critical positions on leisure practice – interactionism, Marxism, feminism and postmodernism – have cogently revealed how we are variously *positioned* in leisure forms and practices and how *power* relations permeate our motivation and experience of leisure. They are a necessary and illuminating reaction to the forms of leisure theory that flourished in the tyro departments of Leisure Studies between the mid-1940s and mid-1970s. These writings tended to present rather a sunny view of leisure as a melange of personally life-affirming, wholesome relations that expand social harmony and order. Arguably, the highwater mark of this position occurred in the functionalist and systems publications of the late 1960s and 70s (Parker 1971; Kaplan 1975; Cheek and Burch 1976). Critical theorists of leisure today are right to dispel this optimism as facile and complain that it neglected vital questions of inequality, injustice, domination, oppression and manipulation in leisure forms and practice.

All the same, what is often absent from their criticism is any concession that leisure can be fun; that it can motivate; that it can enable those with a sense of feeling trapped in their work or family relationships to move beyond them; that it can make people happier with their lives and nicer to one another. Leisure theory that fails to recognize the enjoyment, pleasure, exhilaration and sense of belonging that play and travel bring is not worthy of the name. While a central argument of this book is that leisure forms and practice must now be analysed in the context of globalization, risk and active citizenship, the traditional associations of pleasure-seeking and relaxation with leisure must also be defended.

While criticism has a natural role to play in leisure theory, since nothing is ever perfect, its role is sharpest when it takes the form of *constructive* criticism, which is concerned with proposing solutions rather than tirelessly lamenting the existing state of affairs.

To this end, in this book an *Action* approach to leisure analysis is outlined which seeks to consolidate *motivation*, *location* and *context*. Leisure actors are examined as pursuing their chosen motivations of practice. The Action approach has no truck with essentialist perspectives that explore leisure as the reflection of, as it were, 'God-given' individual freedom and choice. Nor does it support approaches that investigate leisure actors as dumb 'bearers' of structural forces of class, gender and race. Competence and knowledge are always assumed to be preconditions of action. Equally, the mobilization and articulation of these resources are always understood to be *conditioned* and *patterned*.

Procedurally, the Action approach begins by examining the *motivations* of leisure actors and, over time, attempts to delineate trajectories of behaviour, that is, lines of leisure conduct which follow regular, predictable directions and rhythms. These trajectories are then connected to *location* factors relating, among other things, to family networks, community forms, gender differences, racial divisions, economic inequalities and religion. Through comparative and historical analysis, location factors are then related to *context*, that is the specific, historically rooted axes of power that condition location and motivation. In all of this, the accumulation of knowledge is itself always understood to be conditional and subject to the discipline of *testing*. The means of testing are twofold: empirical study (including comparative and historical study as well as face-to-face methods) and open, informed, principled dialogue.

The Action approach is inherently critical since it is dedicated to elucidating how power conditions motivation, location and context and therefore how embodiment and emplacement are moulded. However, it knows the considerable danger involved in being *merely* critical. Politically speaking, it seeks to develop and refine the notion of active citizenship by advocating empowerment, distributive justice and social inclusion as the ends of theory. The use of leisure forms as strategies of education in working with young offenders and long-term prisoners and the inhabitants of *favelas* and shanty towns is well-established (Freire 1970; Boal 1979, 1995; Clements 2003; Eames 2003). The Action approach is committed to extending these initiatives by supporting and clarifying the role of leisure in enhancing social capital in everyday life through the strengthening of community networks and encouraging a balanced lifestyle. However, it also recognizes that community and lifestyle are always situated in structures of economic, cultural and political inequality in which ideology strives to mask how power works to advance established interests.

Multinational corporations and state bureaucracies have devised strategies for dealing with uncertainty and challenge. The *mission statement*, which purports to combine clarity of purpose with vision, has emerged as a major weapon in the arsenal of coping. University degrees and modules have followed suit. Were I asked to list the aims of an undergraduate course in leisure theory I would venture the following:

- To develop conceptual clarity about the key issues relevant to leisure forms and practice
- To become familiar with seminal and all important debates in the field today
- To learn how to formulate testable propositions about leisure forms and practice
- To apply theory to the political ends of empowerment, distributive justice and social inclusion
- To learn how to notice the ways in which motivation, action and culture in leisure are influenced by historically rooted relations of power.

Of these, perhaps *noticing* is most important, since it is the prerequisite for all critical examinations of leisure forms and practice. Students of leisure theory should learn to observe that actions have *roots*, and to acquire knowledge that enables them to compare and contrast roots in different locations and contexts. They should also learn to examine how roots are influenced by economic, social, cultural and political forces and to reject theories of leisure which either assign unconditional freedom, choice, flexibility and self-determination to leisure actors or proceed on the basis that leisure practice and forms are structurally determined.

A possible mission statement for leisure theory might be:

To investigate how power and history condition leisure choice and patterns of behaviour in order to enhance the goals of empowerment, distributive justice and social inclusion.

This statement assumes that it is in the nature of actors to define goals, take steps to achieve them and modify them in relation to external conditions. That is, leisure actors do not simply replicate the conditions in which they are located, they modify these conditions as an ordinary part of their leisure behaviour.

This book is an attempt to explore how leisure forms and practice are narrated at the levels of fieldwork and theory. It provides a critical guide to the fundamental contemporary debates. It explores the meaning of an Action perspective in leisure theory and research. It outlines a theory of both the axial institutions that shape leisure forms and practice and the functions of leisure. Finally, it makes an assessment of the central problems that students of leisure theory face in exploiting and developing their craft.

Twenty years ago, I criticized Leisure Studies for coining theories of 'leisure without society' (Rojek 1985: 1). Despite the many important contributions to leisure theory made by others in succeeding years, I find myself maintaining that this criticism holds good. That is one reason why a good deal of this book is devoted to demonstrating that leisure must be analysed as an institution that is inextricably linked to wider, global questions of economic resource allocation, status distribution and civic regulation. The concept of the active citizen is the tool for exploring how the great questions in society today relating to globalization, social inclusion, commercialization, distributive justice, empowerment and the role of science in everyday life pertain directly to the study of leisure.

I regard Leisure Studies to be an interdisciplinary field that has evolved from the established social sciences, especially Sociology, Psychology, Human Geography, Political Science, Social History and the emerging disciplines of Environmental Studies, Business Studies and Management Studies. I maintain that it is at its most intellectually robust and practically stimulating when it engages with the debates in these disciplines by showing what the established social sciences have to learn from the specialized study of leisure and vice versa. However, the social sciences and leisure theory do themselves no favours in disengaging with the public and students by making complex things more complicated by resorting to abstract language and self-referential philosophizing. Simplification is not necessarily a prelude to crudification, not least because it opens questions and controversies to fresh minds uncluttered with the attic furniture of disciplinary-based received ideas and established patterns of thinking.

This book, then, is written for readers who come to the study of leisure theory for the first time. Not all of the questions it proposes will be recognized as relevant to students in year one of their study of leisure theory. But the book has been structured to allow students to return to sections that are found to be tangential or too difficult at level one in later years of study. The opening summaries and concluding key points that accompany each chapter aim to provide students with a checklist that enables them to tailor the contents of the book to their immediate study interests.

Philosophically, the book presupposes that leisure theory is of value to the study of leisure since, for no other reason, to dismiss leisure theory as valueless is itself to make a *theoretical* proposition, worthy of study and testing. Actually, we are all chronic theorists of leisure even if we do not use the term 'theory' to describe what we do. In ordinary life, we recognize patterns of leisure practice and make assumptions and predictions on this basis. We are skilled in 'guessing' what may work or go wrong if certain combinations of factors are present in leisure practice. We all hold beliefs and opinions about the value (or worthlessness) of particular leisure forms. The study of leisure theory is partly about making explicit and systematic what we already know. But it is also about discovering the roots of our beliefs and opinions and comparing how our personal and cultural values are coded and themed in relation to those of others. At its best, it should help us to select the most practical solutions for leisure problems and devise better ways of being 'in leisure' together.

1
Narrating Leisure

In this chapter you will be:

- Introduced to the concept of narrating leisure.
- Appraised of the reasons why individual freedom and choice in leisure are untenable.
- Introduced to an approach that recognizes structural dimensions to leisure form and practice.
- Encouraged to think of how leisure form and practice are *positioned* through ideology.
- Instructed in the basics of A&B analysis.
- Directed to the question of how leisure motivation is consolidated with location and context.
- Guided through the weaknesses of pyschologistic approaches to leisure.
- Directed to the centrality of questions of embodiment and emplacement in leisure.
- Appraised of the importance of a comparative historical methodology and the ethic of cognition for studying leisure.

Leisure is voluntary behaviour. Expressed at the most prosaic level, Leisure Studies is the analysis of voluntary behaviour. Choice, freedom and voluntarism are the basic components in the **narration** of leisure. The analysis of voluntary behaviour must be based in narrative data that can be collected via interviewing, surveys, life history analysis, forms of observational practice and comparative and historical analysis. Narrative

Narration means the native accounts of practice and values. The term 'native' here means member of a recognizable social group. Group membership is associated with generative principles that classify the world in distinctive ways. Because our native status is a condition of birth, we grow up with a world view which, both consciously and subconsciously, we regard as 'natural' or 'universal'. As we shall see more clearly in this study, many errors derive from the native position.

analysis seeks to employ the interpretations, histories and visual recordings of people to analyse leisure practice, but it also aims to place the temporal sequence and continuity of these accounts in a socio-historical framework. This framework is constructed around comparative and historical dimensions of analysis and the elaboration of leisure theory to provide sustainable hypotheses about leisure practice.

Sustainable propositions in leisure theory are always provisional. They must be tested against narrative data that are always and already situated in determinate social and historical conditions that are subject to change, just as the propositions themselves are subject to change. A double spiral between gathering empirical data from the location and context of practice and modifying theory through testing data is therefore the foundation of effective Leisure Studies.

What distinguishes Leisure Studies from anecdote, journalism and literature about leisure is that it is oriented to achieving a *scientific* understanding of leisure forms and practice. It would be rash to propose that we have already achieved this level of understanding. We are still at an early stage in the development of the subject. Nonetheless, our goal is to accumulate knowledge that is more *objective* than political assertion, journalistic conjecture or folklore, *accessible* in the sense of being freely exchanged and debated with others as opposed to being restricted by caste, class and culture, and *testable*. Dogma is the enemy of Leisure Studies. Because we live in a changing, many-sided world we must be ready to test our propositions against the known facts and of course modify propositions and redefine what is factual, if the available scientific evidence dictates.

Species-specific and cultural dimensions of narration

It is important to distinguish between species-specific and cultural dimensions in narrative data. These reflect structural and cultural distinctions in human relations. Thus, all human beings share a species-specific structure of physiological–psychological needs. For example, everyone requires food, drink, clothing, sleep and companionship. It might be said that this is a basic universal set of needs for the human species. The point is worth remembering in an academic and political climate in which the emphasis on the difference and diversity between people is currently ascendant.

However, the satisfaction of species needs varies culturally. For example, the clothing requirements of a Masai warrior are different from those of a Wall Street stockbroker. Even within the same culture there are important variations between cultural strata and settings. For example, the wardrobe of a Chancery Lane lawyer is likely to be different in kind from that of a Hobart taxi driver. Similarly, in some cultural settings, the necessity of eating food assumes the quality of honorific distinction rather than the fulfilment of a bodily need. For example, there is all the difference in the world between eating a cheese sandwich at your kitchen table and taking your friends out to the best restaurant in town. The latter is arguably more about social display and status affirmation than the satisfaction of a physical need, not least because the price of food and drink in the best restaurants is often very high. You are trying to exhibit your cultural knowledge, taste or contact with elite culture in doing so. These are *cultural* considerations which have little to do with the mere satisfaction of physical hunger, and more to do with laying down markers about your status self-image and the impression that you want to make upon others.

The paradox of ethnocentricity

Cultural variation is a fact of life. Yet we often have surprising difficulty in recognizing it. Our natural tendency is to view the world in terms of the conditions that obtain in our own lives and societies, that is, from the 'native perspective'. Thus, as Westerners we assume that the world consists of people who hold similar notions of individual freedom, choice and self-determination. This position is known as **ethnocentricity**.

Ethnocentricity is the habit of projecting the historical and structural characteristics of conditions in one's own life and society as global universals.

The strength of ethnocentricity is that it is based in intimate, 'native' knowledge of the conditions that prevail in our personal lives and societies. Its paradox is that precisely because its strength derives from local characteristics, it impedes our capacity to recognize difference. Typically, codes blinker our capacity to understand cultural difference. Difference may derive from economic, sexual, cultural and religious factors. It is usually a mixture of all of these. As Western societies have become more **multicultural** the issue of difference has become pronounced in the analysis and narration of leisure and society. The analysis of leisure requires us to be conscious of multicultural variation not merely in relation to the society in which we reside but with respect to other cultures and societies.

Multicultural society is a social formation composed of the recognition of manifest and latent economic, religious, ethnic, cultural and sexual difference.

Strictly speaking, neither the trajectory of leisure nor intentions and motivations are autonomous. Rather they reflect cultural and economic *positioning*. For example, wearing a veil in public is a mandatory requirement of religious belief for females in some Muslim communities. Similarly, in some Western youth cultures recreational drug use or alcohol consumption is a condition of peer group membership. It follows that Action analysis requires the student of leisure to map leisure trajectories, intentions and motivations onto a context of cultural and economic positioning.

The individual's leisure is the outcome of the unique combination of elements that make each of us different. But our capacity to recognize difference and develop individuality depends on the recognition of *general* cultural and economic influences upon identity.

Ideology and interpellation

An approach to the analysis of leisure that focuses on the individual's narration of use of time and space for personal enrichment and pleasure is an acceptable starting point for leisure analysis. For one thing it highlights the conscious choice of the individual and recognizes leisure as one of life's primary needs rather than a subsidiary activity, secondary to the fulfilment of the necessities of life.

But there are problems with this approach, the most important of which relate to the question of **ideology**. Ideology equips us with our 'natural' or 'common-sense' view of what it is to be an individual. It shapes our understanding of right and wrong, our 'native' view of identity and order, our associations of pleasure and non-pleasure, and much else besides. Stuart Hall (1985), drawing on the work of the French philosopher Louis Althusser (1971, 1977), argues that ideology **interpellates** subjects. Interpellation constructs our sense of sexual, racial, national and class membership and, by extension, difference. Interpellation operates through **institutions of normative coercion**.

Ideology means a system of representation that legitimates the position of the dominant groups in society. The ideas and values of the dominant groups are portrayed as the 'common-sense' of society. It is most powerful when a particular social and historical state of affairs is represented as 'natural' and the distribution of power and resources in society is regarded to be inevitable.

Interpellation is the process through which a subject is 'hailed' or called into being. A 'subject' may refer to an individual or a topic of behaviour such as a keep-fit regime, a mode of dress or a social attitude.

Institutions of normative coercion are the organizations through which we acquire our knowledge of normal (and abnormal) behaviour. Examples include the family, schools, the media, the police, medicine and the judiciary.

At first sight, voluntary action seems a simple and obvious concept. But when we examine it through the twin lenses of ideology and interpellation its real complexity is revealed. Ideology and interpellation 'position' us in as much as through them we **articulate** our 'natural', 'common-sense' views about the world.

Articulation refers to the expression of ideology through social practice. Interpellation patterns human behaviour and articulation is the realization of patterning. A corollary of articulation is that ideology may be falsified through human practice. In other words articulation allows for the realization of patterning in two senses. First, practice confirms ideological patterning, as when individual subjects unthinkingly replicate the values of the social groups to whom they are attached. Second, practice is the means by which the limitations of these patterns are exposed and acknowledged. Articulation, then, conceives of practice as Janus-faced. It carries the code of social reproduction, but inversely bears the seeds of critical reaction.

If voluntary action is 'positioned' it raises important questions about the nature of individual freedom. For example, if we are culturally positioned to enjoy soccer over baseball, how much is this a question of individual 'choice'? If voluntary choice is inconceivable without the influence of ideology and interpellation, how 'free' is it? By treating ideology as central to leisure practice we foreground the importance of *politics* in leisure theory in general, and Action analysis in particular. Why is this advisable?

Thomas Hobbes: struggle, scarcity and solidarity

To answer the question we need to turn briefly to classical political economy, that is, the theoretical debates about the nature of identity and society that emerged in the seventeenth and eighteenth centuries. For our purposes there is no need to go into detail about the precise, extended nature of these debates. Our aim is simply to illustrate the centrality of politics in leisure practice. To do this the work of Thomas Hobbes (1651) is useful.

Hobbes regards the human condition as based in a struggle for advantage between individuals. Life, he contends is 'nasty, brutish and short'. Of course, that is not *all* there is to life, but it is the context in which we operate. For Hobbes, it follows that the natural propensity of individuals is to accumulate as much as they can so as to make life more pleasant and advantageous for themselves. The problem of unrestricted individual accumulation is that it leads to 'a war of all against all'. To prevent this, society develops contracts that affirm individual rights and responsibilities and lays down cultural taboos and legal prohibitions that prevent individuals from maximizing their own interests in ways that jeopardize the well-being of others.

Hobbes's work highlights three conditions that are indispensable in the analysis of leisure:

- *Struggle*: human life is competitive and revolves around power relations.
- *Scarcity*: the condition in which human beings are situated is marked by scarcity. The condition of scarcity is the pretext for competitive struggles of accumulation.
- *Solidarity*: if the struggle over scarcity is unregulated civilized life is impossible. Agreement around basic rules of human practice is the basis for social solidarity.

From Hobbes we learn that the presence of leisure time and space and access to them are the outcome of political struggles over scarce resources. Politics is a way of managing the problem of scarcity. But the snag about social agreements forged around the distribution of scarce resources is that they are conditional. The growth of economic wealth and technology may result in the increase of surplus time since the necessity to labour can be transferred to machines or, as our wealth grows, switched to various sorts of home helps (Gershuny 2000).

The distribution of surplus wealth, time and space in society is the outcome of political–economic–cultural demands and power struggles. There is nothing 'natural' about the current distribution of time and space between work and leisure, just as there is no guarantee that industrial and scientific development will result in more leisure for all. On the contrary, the allocation of leisure resources is a result of human actions. The primary means through which it is articulated is politics, culture and economics. But this process is itself subject to patterned assumptions about the legitimate goals of work and leisure practice as well as the appropriate balance between consumption and production. One way of opening these issues up in the study of leisure is to examine the question of voluntarism and determinism.

Voluntarism and determinism

In the study of human behaviour action may be located along a continuum between voluntarism and determinism. **Voluntarism** refers to the imaginary condition of absolute freedom in which choices are made without external constraint. **Determinism** is the equally imaginary condition of absolute constraint in which behaviour is governed by external force.

Voluntarism: a condition of free choice, involving:

- No constraints on behaviour
- Flexibility
- Spontaneity

Determinism: a condition of constrained choice, involving:

- Structured behaviour
- Compulsion
- External force

Although human behaviour can be located on the continuum between these two conditions, it is never completely free or wholly determined. Every human relationship involves a balance of power between individuals.

A&B relationships

At first sight, the concept of balance of power may strike you as unexceptional. Consider: if A is physically stronger than B it follows that A possesses a power advantage over B. This is compelling, but it limits the explanation of the balance of power to the immediate physical attributes of A over B and ignores wider issues in balance of power relationships. This refers to what might be called a 'pre-Hobbesian' state in which competitive struggle is unregulated by binding relations of solidarity around agreed ways of managing competition over scarce resources. These wider issues may, and do, neutralize the physical superiority of strength that A enjoys over B, making the relationship between each more equivocal.

Think of it like this: A and B are parts of communities and communities are parts of society. A's physical power over B may be obvious, but operationalizing it mobilizes many political, economic and moral objections. If A physically abuses B, the community to which B is attached may elect to seek restitution on B's behalf. If B is physically injured by A, B may make recourse to the police or courts for reparation. If B is a woman and A is a man, questions of sexism are raised. If A is white and B non-white, or A rich and B poor, questions of race and class are invoked. In short, balance of power relationships are many-sided and possess the latent capacity to mobilize actors that are situated far away from the immediate focus of A's relationship to B. This is what Hobbes meant by the power of contract to regulate human affairs: an individual's sense of injustice possesses the right of public redress.

A&B relationships are a useful mechanism for exploring how balance of power relationships operate in leisure and society. They are partly drawn from the work of the political scientist Robert Dahl (1961). Dahl held a *pluralist* view of society and culture. That is, he regarded society and culture to be a collection of individuals and groups among which no single individual or group possessed sufficient power to achieve domination in the long run. Dahl's use of A&B analysis was designed to investigate how individuals and groups compete for power with each other and to elucidate the consequences of these power struggles. Pluralism has fallen out of fashion in social and cultural analysis. By and large, it is regarded to be an unsatisfactory perspective on power because it cannot incorporate structural dimensions such as class, gender and race. The revision of Dahl's model of A&B relationships adopted here is not intended to be a plea for the renewal of pluralism. The latter is indeed defective in incorporating the structural dimensions of power. In contrast, Action analysis seeks to utilize these dimensions as an intrinsic part of leisure study. However, the Action approach also seeks to overhaul A&B analysis by abanding the notion of individuals and formations as **autonomous agents** and recasting them as consistently and indelibly **social actors**.

An **autonomous agent** is an individual that acts unilaterally to pursue its ends. A **social actor** is a subject that bears social characteristics and is simultaneously both enabled and constrained by them.

The revised form of A&B analysis encourages us to examine relationships of power in terms of the *motivation* of actors, the *location* of trajectories of behaviour and the *context* of action. Actors in leisure practice are conceptualized as possessing social characteristics and are situated in a set of balance of power relationships with other actors. The notions of situated action and the balance of power ratio automatically cancel the validity of pluralist-type approaches based on a version of the proposition that actors are autonomous. The revised form is also a useful defence against 'top-down' models of power that commence from an abstract model of the dynamics of power and so tend to neutralize issues of variation in location. For example, if we read relationships in leisure and society in terms of a dominant class model we may miss important power variations between A and B that relate to location. Variation in location may inflect or moderate the relationship of the individual to his or her class position. The same is true of relationships of leisure and society that are analysed in terms of patriarchy or white power. Thus, a working-class, black woman living in Sheffield or Detroit may occupy the same economic and social position as her equivalent residing in Bethnal Green or Beverly Hills. However, her relationship to class, race and gender inequality may vary according to location factors such as regional bonding distinctions, neighbourhood boundary maintenance procedures, local state policies on housing, health and childcare and many other 'local' factors besides.

The import of this is not that abstract models of the dynamics of power are wrong or valueless. Rather A&B analysis is designed to teach us that location is not the mere reflection of context and that the relationship between context and location is dynamic and interrelational. What occurs between social actors in concrete practice must be analysed first, as it were, *on location*, before moving on to explore wider issues of context. To this must be added the proviso that A&B relationships are always relationships between social actors who bear social characteristics and, further, that these social characteristics can only be revealed through an analysis of the dynamics of location and context.

Individuals acting in immediate locations are always caught up in wider relationships relating to community, race, culture, economics and politics. It is important to state this plainly in order to avoid the fallacy that the dynamics of location are independent or relatively autonomous of context. They are not. However, neither are they determined by context. There is always a dynamic between location and context that implies that some aspects of concrete relations of location may be contradictory to relations of context and vice versa. We can express this more formally (see box). So long as we remember

---

The advantages of A&B analysis

- Questions of difference are immediately raised.
- Questions of location pose questions of context.
- Questions of context suggest problems of economic, social and cultural variation.

- Questions of variation are the seed of moral recognition since they require us to recognize the validity of different positions and the limits of our own 'natural' world view.

The disadvantages of A&B analysis

- Questions of difference may be exaggerated.
- Questions of action may magnify the autonomy of subjects.
- Questions of location may be privileged over questions of context.
- Questions of interest may be expressed only in terms of contraries thus neglecting common issues.

that A&B analysis is a **heuristic device** we can hope to gain most of the advantages and avoid most of the disadvantages.

A **heuristic device** is an ideal concept or mechanism of analysis that helps us to discover relations without getting overwhelmed by problems of complexity.

Of course, as we go deeper into problems of leisure we need to make our assumptions more complex. In particular the nature of the dynamics between location and context will need to be refined. But if we start from complexity we may unintentionally prevent our interest in a given problem of leisure from growing.

The methodology of location and context

Distinguishing between **location** and **context** is as important in the methodology of Leisure Studies as basing theoretical propositions in narrative data and subjecting them to testing.

Location refers to the immediate circumstances of causality that result in a leisure choice and action. **Context** is the setting in which location is situated.

Location is the focal point of leisure choice and action. It is the vector of immediate mental and sensual interaction in which life-option choice is exercised. *On location* is where we consciously seek to pursue the means and ends of our leisure choices.

But it is inadequate to confine the study of leisure merely to the investigation of the dynamics of location. To proceed thus forgets that there is a prelude to location: context. The latter may not be immediately apparent in examining the focus of leisure behaviour. The active and sensuous characteristics of interaction rightly occupy centre stage, so that we forget that action occurs on a wider socio-economic stage and that on-location behaviour articulates rules and patterns that derive from context.

Consider: if A desires to enter the leisure business by opening a computer game software store, it may seem the most natural thing to do in the world. But A's confidence and financial capacity to open a store are very likely related to class. Entrepreneurial spirit is not monopolized by wealthy classes but, for a variety of historical and structural reasons, it is more characteristic thereof. This is one reason why the credit rating of a son or daughter of prosperous parents is higher than that of the offspring of working-class parents. Beyond that, A's decision to try his luck in the software leisure business reflects a market with limited restraints save the financial one. The situation is quite different in a system where the state is more ascendant. For example, A's decision may require a complex bureaucratic vetting process by state officials and strict rules on the range of software to be sold and the rate of profit that accrues.

Questions of class, market and political system are implicit in location, but to fully grasp them it is necessary to bring context into our viewfinder. Like much else in Leisure Studies the distinction between location and context will turn out to be more complex than it seems at first blush.

The mental and sensual aspects of on-location behaviour are important in the study of leisure. Valuable knowledge can be gained through ethnographic studies of the dynamics of leisure practice in pubs, sports grounds, recreation centres, shopping malls and nightclubs (Willis 1977, 1978, 1998; Blackshaw 2003). But these types of leisure interaction are not self-referential. On the contrary they articulate factors from the context in which they are situated. Thus, nightclub, bar or pub interaction bears the markers of class, gender, race, generation and bodily health. These markers do not convey structures that determine leisure interaction but they code and theme behaviour to produce dispositions and propensities in the exercise of individual life options.

A balanced perspective in the study of leisure involves acknowledging mutuality and reciprocity between location and context. Attributing priority to either location or context misses the mutual and reciprocal relationship that one has with the other. Common errors in the study of leisure are either to treat on-location behaviour as autonomous from context or assuming that action on location *follows* context. The first falls into the trap of pluralism by exaggerating the autonomy of actors in leisure conduct. The second deprives actors of freedom. Location activity may reflect dispositions and propensities laid down by context, but mental and sensual activity in on-location behaviour is never completely determined. A dynamic loop obtains between the two. So context may invest the behaviour of actors with constraints and dispositions, but through exercising choice and acting, actors have the capacity to reconfigure the hands they are dealt with.

It remains to make one further important point about location and context: both are forms of *power* relation. We know from the work of Michel Foucault (1970, 1975, 1981) that power is both constraining and enabling. Think of the language that you speak. The Sapir–Whorf hypothesis holds that language is in part a reflection of location and context.[1] For example, the Inuit (Eskimo) people of North America have many more words for 'snow' than we do. According to the Sapir–Whorf hypothesis this is because their physical environment (location/context) requires them to develop a more varied, nuanced vocabulary for the fact of 'snow' than people who live in temperate climates. *Linguistic relativism* means that some aspects of language vary according to location and context so that being equipped with one language constrains one from making the same perceptions that are commonplace in a different language. For example, Westerners will not recognize the various distinctions of snow commonly held by the Inuit if we enter their environment unless we are taught to do so. However, although our language possesses constraints with respect to communicating about the Inuit environment it none-theless accommodates questioning and explanation. Hence, it is enabling since it allows us to exchange perceptions and negotiate rules that help us to live better together. This is what Hobbes's law of contract was designed to do three and a half centuries ago.

We might think of language as belonging to that species of cultural influence that exercises priority, externality, constraint and enablement over us.[2] Thus language exists before individual existence; it is the means through which we make our thoughts and feelings about the world com-municable; it outlasts our individual existence; and while it may constrain perception and communication, it also enables each to occur in the first place. We might extend the point by submitting that most forms of leisure are patterned.

This seems counter-intuitive. To the individual subject, watching television, hill-walking, reading fiction, playing sport, going clubbing or lounging by a hotel swimming pool seem to be a matter of personal choice and individual activity. We do not see ourselves as consciously fitting in with patterns of conduct established historically and structurally, which enable and constrain personal behaviour in various but determinate ways. Yet to view the matter thus is to elevate location above context, and to sweep away the rule-bound, patterned character of leisure practice besides. It is understandable to do so. For while we are subjectively caught up in the dynamics of location, imagining what is happening to us and the actions that we take to be matters of personal volition, it is harder to regard location and choice as the articulation of patterns of causality which have their momentum in the specific balance of power that makes up the context in which location and choice are situated.

Conceptualizing leisure

But how are we to begin to study the relationship between context, location and leisure practice? To bring the matter to specifics, why should A decide to spend her leisure time reading fiction and developing the art of bee-keeping, while B favours watching tennis and nightclubbing? The old Lancashire saying has it that 'there is nowt so queer as folk'. But whatever wisdom is contained in this old saw disguises what we already know about the structural dimensions of leisure choice. Conceptually, leisure may be approached at three contrasting levels (Haywood and Henry 1986). First, it can be investigated in *residual* terms as the surplus time and space left over once the necessities of life have been fulfilled. Second, it can be explored as the time and space that are used consciously for *personal enrichment* and pleasure. Third, it may be examined as *functional activity* that achieves socially defined ends such as social integration, cooperation and mutual understanding or physical and psychological health and well-being.

As Goodale and Godbey (1988) note, the *residual* approach portrays leisure negatively because it privileges the concept of work in the organization of life and consigns leisure to a dependent variable. The second approach places emphasis on the narrative accounts and choices of actors, but arguably neglects to situate these accounts in identifiable power structures. The third approach is based on the analysis of power structures, but perhaps erases the significance of individual choice and narration.

Voluntary activity is only meaningful when the *types* of means and ends informing choice and practice are elucidated. For example, A may voluntarily support a sports team. But A's support may be influenced by

peer group practice that is a function of location. Again the question of the nature of individual choice and the relationship between choice, location and context must be addressed.

Peer groups are belief and opinion-forming groups to which one is attached by reason of generational and institutional location. The students in one's generation at school or university are an example. The workers who labour at approximately the same level in the workplace are another example.

Conforming to the values and beliefs of a peer group is an important attribute of maturing as a citizen, for while we gain a sense of personal identity beyond the family through peer groups, we also acquire a sense of individuality by growing out of them. Personal substantiation confirms A's sense of presence, and assists in separating A's leisure orientation from B's. For example, by supporting Arsenal or the Chicago Bears, A experiences a confirming sense of solidarity with other supporters and distinction from supporters of rival clubs. However, peer group practice may also be experienced as a source of personal invalidation. If A feels overwhelmed or threatened by peers it may provoke a variety of distancing manoeuvres that substantiate A in a contrasting fashion of identity formation or eventuate in outright separation. Hence the positional and ritual importance of the peer group in the maturation of the *person*.

Peer group practice articulates the resources of location. But as we saw in the last chapter, leisure and context are bound together in a dynamic, mutual, reciprocal set of relationships. A may begin to support Chelsea or the Washington Redskins in response to peer group influence, but this practice reflects the wider context of socialization, the commercialization of sport and media representations of sport. Context may not determine location, but it is sufficiently ubiquitous to enable A to develop validating dispositions of choice and propensities for action.

What does this mean for conceptualizing leisure? To begin with, the narration of trajectories of leisure behaviour must never be taken at face value. An individual may tell you that he supports Chelsea or the Washington Redskins as a result of personal choice. But this statement will invariably prove to be an articulation of peer group pressure, family tradition, class position or media sponsorship. Of course, individuals possess choice and can make up their own minds about things. But their choices are always situated in preexisting patterns of leisure that are external to the individual (in the sense of being beyond his or her capacities of control), prior to the individual (in the sense of preexisting him or her) and con-straining–enabling (in the sense of setting the conditions and options for leisure choice). Conceptually, leisure practice is the expression of individual choice made from patterns of behaviour and options of conduct laid down by factors of location and context. These patterns vary culturally, which is why historical and comparative methods of analysis are so useful in elucidating them.

The snare of psychologism

One useful consequence of thinking of leisure relationships in terms of a balance of power between social actors who are the bearers of patterned social characteristics of location and context is that it avoids *psychologistic* tendencies in leisure analysis. These are very common in the study of leisure (Neulinger 1980; Csikszentmihalyi 1997, 1998). A psychologistic account concentrates on an analysis of the beliefs, motivations and perceptions of the individual in a particular location and thus dilutes historical, social and cultural contexts.

For example, Neulinger's (1974, 1980) approach maintains that leisure is a self-enhancing affective state oriented to perceived freedom. Naturally, he accepts that freedom and the cognitive disposition attached to it do not originate in the individual. He (1980) submits that we should distinguish between *intrinsic* and *extrinsic* motivations in leisure behaviour. An intrinsic motivation refers to the individual's own freely chosen leisure choices. An extrinsic motivation refers to the external criteria that predispose an individual to make a given leisure choice. This sounds unobjectionable since everyone is familiar with the idea of the divisions between 'inner' and 'outer' experience, 'individual' and 'society' and 'internal' and 'external'. However, if one remembers the importance of ideology and interpellation in human practice the notion of intrinsic motivation is immediately problematic. If individuals are hailed or called into being by institutions of normative coercion it follows that individual motivations are culturally patterned. If this is the case it is no longer satisfactory to conceptualize them as 'intrinsic' since they pre-suppose 'extrinsic' predisposing factors, notably ideology.

Nonetheless, leaving these points aside, Neulinger's approach emphasizes the centrality of motivation in leisure locations. The individual chooses leisure practice as a way of experiencing more perceived freedom than from obligated activities such as work, family care, bodily maintenance and so on. The focus of this explanation is upon the choices made by the individual and the greater freedom that is perceived as deriving from the realization of these choices.

Similar assumptions are made in Iso-Ahola's (1980, 1989) *motivational* approach. Following Neulinger, he identifies leisure with perceived freedom and self-determination. He adds two further distinctions. First, leisure experience is concerned with achieving intrinsic rewards, the most significant of which is confirming a sense of competence. There is an evolutionary underpinning to this argument. Iso-Ahola presents humans as learning animals. We gain pleasure and substantiation by mastering knowledge and skills (competence) that enable us to shape our physical and social environment. When the selected behaviour is experienced as optimally challenging, individuals maximize their sense of fulfilment in leisure. We move on to new challenges in order to test and enhance our competence and through achieving fulfilment our sense of autonomy is enhanced.

The second distinction is that leisure occurs in a social context. This may seem to be an unremarkable observation but it is peculiar how the general mindset of pyschologism tends towards **solipsism**. Iso-Ahola maintains that individuals search for perceived freedom in a social context and that they gain intrinsic reward by competing with others to achieve optimal satisfaction.

Solipsism is the doctrine that one's immediate experience constitutes the only reality. Radical versions hold that there is no public or physical world outside of individual consciousness. Weaker versions maintain that one's immediate experience is more vivid and true than the experience of others. Either way the crucial point is that personal experience is regarded to be the crucible of consciousness and existence.

Ideas of optimal satisfaction and fulfilment abound in psychologistic approaches to leisure. This is ideologically revealing because it suggests that leisure is widely assumed to be a state of mind or being associated with pleasure, reward and fulfilment. The question is where do those forms of leisure involving self-abuse or outer-directed aggression fit in with this approach? Drug addiction may begin as a search for intrinsic rewards of well-being and personal enrichment, albeit through deviant means, but it ends in an unacceptable state of dependence which nullifies a sense of well-being and personal enrichment. Argyle (1996: 130, 274) stresses that motivation in leisure activity is directed towards social gain, learning, socialization, intrinsic satisfaction (pleasure in the leisure act), disclosure self-image and the management of intimacy. However, he also distinguishes four leisure settings in which the psychological benefits of leisure do not apply. We might categorize these in the following way:

1. *The unemployed* – who are 'time-rich' but lack the means to pursue leisure interests.
2. *The disengaged* – who allow leisure to be dominated by undemanding activities that carry negligible psychological rewards, for example watching television.
3. *The self-abusers* – who cultivate leisure practices that are bad for their physical and psychological well-being, for example drug abusers.
4. *The anti-socials* – who cultivate leisure practices that are physically and psychologically bad for others, for example football hooligans.

The way in which these leisure forms are usually handled in Leisure Studies is to pathologize them. That is, they are presented as deviant activities that do not belong to the field of leisure practice. There are two objections to this. First, the organization of personal and subcultural identity which treats these forms as leisure careers is quite widespread. The disengaged do practice leisure forms that reinforce passivity, disconnection from others and, in some cases, a morbid sense of hopelessness. Similarly, recreational drug use and the use of physical violence are continuous features of drug and hooligan subcultures.

Second, by pathologizing leisure forms that produce no psychological benefits we fail to acknowledge that every individual can drift into, and out of, these states as a 'normal' part of the life course. Unemployment may involve the experience of leisure as a source of *deprivation* since we are unable to pursue our interests for want of money or because we feel guilty about not being employed. Analogously, through overwork or illness we may find ourselves adopting patterns of disengaged leisure activity that kill time and contribute to our sense of estrangement from society.

In the psychologistic approach to leisure there is a curious moral vacuum. It amounts to the failure to recognize that we have the capacity to choose leisure practices that damage ourselves and others over those which add to personal and social well-being. Instead leisure is naively presented as a harmonious realm of personal fulfilment and social integration. We will return to this point later.

Flow

Csikszentmihalyi's (1998) concept of 'flow' or autotelic activity has been widely used because it appears to provide a scientific, testable version of optimal satisfaction. He argues that flow is the optimal interaction between a person and the environment. Some settings involving the matching of motivation and competence to an environment of action may be psychologically frustrating. For Csikszentmihalyi, when the actor's ability is less than the challenge identified in the environment of action, the result may be boredom. Similarly, when the challenge is assessed as beyond the self-defined competence of the actor, the result may be anxiety. Optimal interaction in leisure occurs when the appropriate balance is struck between motivation, competence and the environment for action. He identifies four characteristics of flow:

1. The *freedom* of the individual from obligation.
2. The *voluntary* pursuit of activity.
3. The experience of *pleasure* through participation.
4. The cultural *labelling* of the voluntary chosen activity as 'leisure'.

Flow is the experiential realization of the psychological condition of perceived freedom. The concept is popular with students of leisure because it appears to describe the fusion between the personal motivation to achieve competence and the social situation in which the attempt to affirm or extend competence is made. Csikszentmihayli argues that 'peak experience' arises from challenges in which individuals apply competences successfully in social situations. When individuals push themselves and extend their competences a state of 'optimal experience' is achieved in which individuals become pleasurably immersed in selected behaviours. This is the experience of 'flow'.

The concept of flow is appealing since it appears to capture the positive feedback that accompanies successful leisure behaviour. By expressing this in terms of *experience* it humanizes the meaning of leisure practice through privileging individual cognition. This is a valuable correction to the **behaviourist** undertones that may be exposed in many forms of psychologism.

Behaviourism is the doctrine that human behaviour is patterned by a stimulus–response model in human groups. Good behaviour receives

> positive rewards and is hence confirmed in individual practice. Bad
> behaviour is punished and is repressed in human practice. The import
> of behaviourism is that individual 'choice' is a learned resource that
> accrues from a response to external stimuli.

However, the concept is morally empty since it offers no distinction between selected behaviours that confirm moral well-being
and those forms which violate it. We may gain 'peak experience' by
playing well on a tennis court or singing successfully in a choir. But
the same term was used by the British Home Office psychologist Paul
Britton to describe the motivation of the British serial killers Fred and
Rosemary West who were found guilty in 1995. 'Flow' is only really
intelligible as a concept when we relate it to the *types* of behaviour
that are selected by individuals. Once this moral dimension is recognized the social context in which morality is articulated must be
addressed.

This takes us back to the questions of ideology and interpellation. In
particular, it compels us to examine how notions of the 'individual',
'voluntary behaviour' and 'leisure' are 'hailed' or 'called into being'. As
soon as we follow this logic it is apparent that personal autonomy and
competence are not self-determined. The propensity to be motivated to
achieve them is socially conditioned and subject to moral standards
and sanctions.

Essentialism, embodiment and emplacement

These various forms of psychologistic analysis commit the error of
essentialism. Essentialism is a 'naturalistic' form of explanation that
seeks to explain motivation, location and context in terms of ethnocentric
categories. As such, it is prone to many naturalistic fallacies, the most
important of which is arguably that individuals in the same essentialist

> **Essentialism** is the doctrine that human difference is the expression of
> integral, natural characteristics that cannot be significantly modified.
> Thus, men are held to be *essentially* different to women or blacks are
> regarded to be *essentially* different to whites.

category are fundamentally the same. Therefore, the needs of one can be readily understood because they are the needs of all.

This raises the difficulties of both ethnocentricity and insufficient regard to difference and cultural variation that we described above. Now, one cannot do without *some* essentialist notions, notably the proposition that all human beings are *embodied* and *emplaced*. By the term 'embodiment' is meant that all human beings have bodies and the fate of the body is to grow older and decline. By the term 'emplacement' is meant that all human beings are situated in spatial and cultural locations and contexts. Embodiment and emplacement mean that it is legitimate to consider some forms of the human condition in essentialist terms. For example, all bodies are frail and vulnerable to disease and ageing, and all spatial and cultural contexts are partly precarious in that they are prone to be disrupted by catastrophic events like war or natural disaster. Similarly, all bodies are sensuous and in acting upon the physical and social world we follow common sensual stimuli and responses. These points about embodiment and emplacement might be called propositions of *materialist essentialism* since they submit that the relationship of ourselves to our bodies and environments are the foundation of understanding human behaviour. This is very different from *psychological essentialism* which proposes that humans share universal consciousness about the material facts of embodiment and emplacement. The latter is open to the criticism that needs and wants are socially conditioned and vary culturally and economically. Human beings exist in all sorts of shapes and sizes. A one-size-fits-all approach is unhelpful and will generally be found to rest upon some version of **cultural imperialism** (Tomlinson 1991).

Cultural imperialism is the condition which presents a historically and structurally specific framework of social order as 'natural'. Cultural imperialism operates by striving to naturalize a particular regime of power.

In common with all forms of private and public provision, leisure services today need to be sensitive to multicultural difference and embody a cultural dimension in policy.

The value of a comparative and historical perspective

Although various quantitative and qualitative methodologies may be used in the study of leisure, all should be rooted in a *comparative* and *historical* perspective. A comparative perspective disposes us to analyse the immediate conditions of life and society against conditions that obtain elsewhere. For example, the meaning of leisure in a Western industrialized society is more individualized, diverse and connected to the market than in Islamic or Buddhist society. Western society has witnessed many centuries of social transformation in which community ties based in powerful relations of resemblance and repetition in personal life conditions have been supplanted by ties of association in which positive space is given to individual freedom and diversity. Islamic societies have also experienced social transformations caused by the global revolutions in industrialization and mass communications. However, because the religious base in these societies is more integrated with politics, economics and culture the concepts of the individual and diversity are weaker (Gellner 1981). Western societies have developed relative independence between politics, economics and culture and this translates into the liberalization and diversification of individual conduct, including leisure conduct. A comparative perspective, then, draws attention to the varieties of human experience and offers some degree of insurance against making untenable assumptions of psychological essentialism and ethnocentricity.

Equally, a historical perspective encourages us to analyse the vast differences between the conditions of our lives and societies and those of earlier times. For example, Daniels's (1995) study of leisure and recreation in seventeenth-century colonial New England adroitly portrays puritan intolerance to leisure as a source of hedonism. The puritans accepted that leisure was a necessary part of life. But they required it to be interwoven with scripture, work, family and community and all of the other venerated normative institutions dedicated to advancing the glory of God. Leisure for its own sake, leisure as a set of play activities which gave vent to what the great Dutch historian Johan Huizinga (1948) described as the *homo ludens* aspect of human character, tended to be regarded as aberrant and subversive. Daniels (1995: 217) explains why:

> Play suspended the normal rules of life and substituted its own rules, which allowed violence, deception, destructive competition – even outright lying. Play mocked the community and its moral standards. And, most horrifying of all, formal play had its own rituals, which competed with social rituals for loyalty and time. Play had often given licence to transgress society's values. Players might decline to accept moral responsibility for what they did because they were, after all, just playing.

The main restraints against hedonism in leisure invoked by the puritans were the bible and loyalty to the community. As Daniels demonstrates, both waned in power as social differentiation and social mobility developed among the white settlers.

There are many other historical examples that one might cite, from the Roman practice of feeding Christians to the lions as part of the games, to the development of the animal rights movement in the West which seeks to redefine the 'normal' leisure practice of hunting as a violation of human rights by inciting humans to behave in barbaric ways. Through the historical analysis of human behaviour we gain an understanding of what is unique to our time and what our time shares in common with earlier historical periods. On this basis we can make propositions about human development and regression that are not simply the reflection of the considerations and preoccupations of our own time and place, but which refer to the standard of historical experience to substantiate them.

A comparative and historical method is the foundation of leisure analysis, especially in respect of issues of location and context. If we approach topics in leisure simply from the position of our own time and space, our perspective will invariably be too narrow. We may acquire genuine insights into the leisure forms of our own culture. But in multi-cultural society a narrow perspective is a dog in the manger. It may give us the comfort of believing we really understand what is going on in leisure practice, but by excluding difference and variation it creates analytic problems having to do with validity and verification in the future.

The ideology of voluntarism and determinism

A common assumption in the field of Leisure Studies, which derives from the widespread psychologistic assumptions that still abound in the subject, is that individuals possess freedom, choice and self-determination (Parker 1983). Expressed in terms of A&B analysis, A and B are viewed as agents that possess voluntarism. The subject of how voluntarism is exercised is typically approached in terms of the subjective decisions made by A and B as an ordinary feature of leisure practice. For example, if we assume that A and B live in the same dwelling, A may elect to play a computer game which B may object to because it makes too much noise. Or B may persuade A to go on a beach holiday against A's real wishes, and this may spoil the holiday by producing conflict. Our natural, common-sense way of explaining the actions of A and B is to do so from the standpoint of the individual. This appears to be consistent with intuition. Everyone knows what it is to choose to go for a walk, see a film, split for a dance or stay at home. We might think that it is as 'natural' and 'obvious' as breathing, eating and sleeping. It is nothing of the sort.

Consider: A might wish to go for a walk, but cannot because she has to be at work, or look after children or go to the doctor to get treatment for an illness. A's capacity to participate in non-work time may be functionally dependent upon time spent in paid employment or childcare. B might wish to see a film, but this depends upon having the money to enter a cinema and the film that B wishes to see may be subject to legal restrictions on sexual or political content imposed by the government. A may have a yen to stay at home for the evening, but this may not be possible because A's housemate B has decided to have a party or because A's children need childcare.

On close inspection most of our freedoms are confidence tricks. Two points need to be made. First, our leisure choices depend upon the labour of others. For example, A is only free to download free digitalized music on the internet because suppliers have provided and maintained websites and workers maintain electricity power. Second, and to bring the issue to the subject of global inequality, leisure activities in the affluent Western societies are often resourced by the low-wage, high-work economies of the developing world. For example, Ritzer (2004: 17) notes that the leisure multinational Nike employs over 100,000 in Indonesia to manufacture shoes. The wages of these workers is in no sense comparable to that of Nike's workers in the West, which of course is the main reason why the company decided to transfer manufacturing to the region. Further, Ritzer notes that the income of most Nike employees in Indonesia is insufficient to support a family. Moreover, working hours would be regarded as severe in the West: as much as 15-hour days, for six to seven days a week.

Leaving aside the key question of global inequality for a moment, one might express this differently by proposing that individual freedom is the expression of *webs of interdependency*. The concept of webs of interdependency derives from the writings of Norbert Elias (1978a, 1978b, 1982). It refers to the economic, cultural, political and social interconnections between individuals that make individual choice and self-determination subjectively meaningful. Think of webs of interdependency in terms of a cat's cradle. Movement in one corner of the web causes the whole structure to reconfigure and establishes a new equilibrium of relationships. Of course, in one respect human behaviour is quite unlike a cat's cradle, namely it is *conscious*. Similarly, unlike a cat's cradle, human relations *develop* often in ways that we find surprising and unplanned. Nonetheless, the idea of webs of interdependency conveys very powerfully the important insight that conscious human behaviour often has *unintentional consequences* and further, that we are always and already *interdependent* actors.

The ideology of voluntarism operates to privilege autonomy and location in the analysis of leisure and society. In reacting against it, leisure students must not succumb to the fallacy of determinism. The ideology of determinism operates to privilege constraint and context in the analysis of leisure and society. It erases the dynamic between location and context and the capacity of agents to make choices. In trying to steer a course between the analytically void polarities of voluntarism and determinism it is necessary to emphasize again the dynamic relationship between location and context and the interdependence of social actors.

Leisure and life satisfaction

In the 1980s some students of leisure argued that the subject should be renamed 'Life Satisfaction Studies' or 'Emancipation Studies'.[3] Given the positive connotations attached to leisure in Western culture this is understandable. Most of us associate leisure with the expansion of **life options**, the self-regulation of time and space and commitment to activities that possess intrinsic interest, the accumulation of intrinsic pleasure and the integration of society. Still, there are good reasons for objecting to renaming Leisure Studies as either 'Life Satisfaction Studies' or 'Emancipation Studies'. Three points must be made. First, to do so commits the ethnocentric fallacy of ignoring the immense inequality in the international division of labour. The growth of leisure time and space in the Western-type democracies is in part based in exporting labour-intensive, low-pay functions to the emerging economies. Many writers now point to the accentuation of the development gap and the

---

Life options refer to the chances that an individual possesses to realize creativity and potential. The concept emerges from the sociology of Max Weber who argued that life options are conditioned by structural factors such as class and status. Weber was a brilliant thinker, but he was also a man of his time. So today most of us would add factors of gender and race to his list of structural factors.

growth of multinational product-sourcing from sweatshop workshops in the developing economies. Leisure multinationals like Nike, Gap, Levi Strauss, IBM, Adidas and Wal-Mart assemble their products in the Philippines, Mexico, China, Indonesia, Taiwan and Thailand (Castells 1996, 1997, 1998; Klein 2001).

The second point is that the attempt to conflate Leisure Studies with Life Satisfaction or Emancipation Studies reveals a shallow understanding of the politics of difference and inequality in the Western-type democracies. Gender, ethnic, generational and health inequalities stratify life options in highly visible and more subtle ways. The balance of power between established and ascendant groups may have shifted in some important respects in favour of the latter, making the old divisions between Left and Right untenable (Giddens 1998, 2000, 2002). But it is very far from being equal.

Third, to return to Daniels's (1995) historical account of leisure and recreation in colonial New England, the individual pursuit of pleasure is often condemned and opposed by the community. Even today, doing what you want in leisure can be a source of censure in others. If part of your diet of life satisfaction comes from smoking, taking drugs, drinking too much and hunting animals you are likely to conflict with the ethical imperatives of care for the self and care for the other which have colonized so much of the climate in which leisure forms and practice are now developed. The moral of all of this is that one person's pleasure is often another person's pain. In addition, globalization and the greater awareness of interdependence have, so to speak, brought the articulation of pain out of the closet. In contemporary society people are not afraid to speak out against smoking, animal rights and the defence of the environment. The twin ethics of care for the self and care for the other have made living anachronisms of those who continue to pursue hedonism as a total and self-sufficient goal of leisure practice.

The ethic of cognition

If context and location elucidate the trajectory of leisure choice, how can they contribute to determining the *value* of options, both for the individual and society? There is a very real dilemma here that Ernest Gellner (1998: 183–4) called the **ethic of cognition**. We need to understand this for two reasons. First, because it reinforces the point made by Hobbes that being and choice always involve political and moral dimensions. Second, it preempts psychologistic approaches by insisting on *ethical* connotations in leisure choice and action.

The **ethic of cognition** is the recognition of the inalienable right of the individual to scrutinize rules, precedent and hierarchy. In traditional societies organized around tribal, monarchical or religious structure rules, precedent and hierarchy are not highly flexible. Challenging tradition may result in punishment. The acknowledgement of the ethic of cognition constitutes a dramatic leap in human history because it liberates criticism and innovation from hidebound obedience and servitude.

Gellner submits that individual choice is riven between two models of individual and society that dominate modern social thought, and have done for at least three centuries: **atomistic individualism** and **romantic organicism**. What does he mean by these terms?

Atomistic individualism

- The judgement of the individual is sovereign.
- The aim of individual life is self-sufficiency which is achieved through personal endeavour.
- Cooperation with others may be necessary but it is secondary to the individual enterprise of developing a coherent sovereign cognitive world.

Romantic organicism

- The judgement of the community is sovereign and the individual is subject to its law.
- The aim of individual life is to contribute to the collective remaking and improvement of the community.
- Cooperation with others is the necessary condition of social membership and belonging.

These models are based on contradictory visions of man that correlate with a contrasting set of beliefs and values. Romantic organicism views man as a group animal, who finds fulfilment and self-substantiation only through participation in the community. Group values are organized around a monoculture that is hostile to pluralism and difference. Individual leisure activities must therefore operate to reinforce the central values of the group.

Conversely, atomistic individualism holds that man is essentially an individualist, who is a member of the community on the basis of contract agreement but finds optimal satisfaction in the pursuit of self-interest. Pluralism and difference are recognized as attributes of the human condition. On this account, restrictions on the pursuit of self-interest in leisure choice are apt to breed dissatisfaction and resentment and thus promote tensions and rifts. Further, the freedom assigned to leisure practice is held to produce innovation and development in personal and cultural life. Each model offers a perspective on the nature of human beings, a set of role ideals and guidance on 'free' time behaviour. Atomistic individualism proposes that true solidarity will only be found in the recognition of individualism, while romantic organicism takes the view that solidarity is only possible in some version of collectivism.

These models are so deeply engrained in culture that we have already encountered elements of them in the discussion. Voluntarism, pyschologism and pluralism are related to atomistic individualism. Determinism, moralism and socialism are part of romantic organicism. Moreover, versions of each model are evident in the split between Republican and Democrat and Conservative and Labour in politics and the division between market and control in economics. We have a common language that enables us to describe and comprehend each model. But how are we to choose between them? Should we place individual freedom in leisure as a value superior to reinforcing the central values of the community? Must the attempt to legislate around freedom in leisure always mean social control or is legislation actually the *precondition* of our individual freedom?

While it is common to present leisure choices thus, Gellner holds that it is too stark to do so. Each model misrepresents our real situation. Hence, atomistic individualism argues that 'there is no such thing as society'.[4] What we call 'society' is simply the aggregate of all individuals pursuing self-interest, for the most part with due observation to contract and legal restraint. The best example of this argument is Robinson Crusoe, an observation that incidentally illustrates the fundamental defect of the model. For Robinson Crusoe was a *fictional* figure. Real human beings do not live for, or follow, self-interest alone. As we demonstrated in the discussion of ideology and interpellation, the very notion of the *individual* carries profound ideological connotations. There may be important functions that derive from proceeding as if atomistic individualism accurately described the world, but the model is fundamentally a **myth**. Moreover, undiluted and unchallenged it is a hazardous myth, since it points towards plural, ethical codes in individuals that have no necessary

> **Myth** is a psychological and social activity which reconciles contradiction and unifies individuals into a sense of collective identity. An ideology is generally articulated by a dominant social and political group and is therefore imposed upon a community. A myth is a general feature of collective identity that applies to all social strata organized within this category.

reference to the good of the community. Atomistic individualism in its pure form does indeed result in the Hobbesian nightmare of the war of all against all.

If there are problems with atomistic individualism, is romantic organicism preferable? Not quite. Although individuals live in communities, the subordination of personal interest to community values is unduly restricting and damages the quality of life. Sentimentally, we may think of ourselves as patriotic members of the community who are actually no more than loyal foot soldiers in the wider social organism. Indeed, there are many examples of this altruistic attitude in society. The decision of the solider to fight and die for his country or that of Hamas or al-Qaida terrorist suicide bombers to kill themselves and others for their ethnic–religious beliefs are examples in which individuals voluntarily subordinate their personal interests to what they perceive as a greater cause. But these attitudes derive from individual choice, and the majority acknowledge and observe a legitimate difference between individual and community interests. Atomistic individualism and romantic organicism may be myths but they fulfil important functions in real life. For Gellner (1998: 183–4) the myth of atomistic individualism is a mainstay of the ethic of cognition. This is the prerequisite for projects of cultural, political and economic **transcendence**. For it permits individuals to query convention, habit and power. This is not quite impossible in societies organized around romantic organicism. Even in Nazi Germany and Stalinist communism, individuals challenged the authority of the command state. However, it is much harder than under atomistic individualism. In romantic organicism stepping out of line, defying the values of the group and attempting to pluralize life options are dealt with punitively.

> **Transcendence** is the attempt to move beyond perceived socio-political–cultural limits to impose new principles of governance in a community.

In Gellner's sociology, the ethic of cognition is a social value that enables us to compare and contrast different societies and take new steps in social development. However, there are good grounds for holding that it is *concentrated* in the spheres of leisure and science. For if leisure is the sphere of voluntary behaviour and science is the realm of open enquiry they must, by virtue of these facts, be that area of life in which the relaxation of necessity and responsibility is maximized, allowing one to critically scrutinize the limits of culture and civilization with the greatest candour and sobriety.

If we examine life under romantic organicism we do indeed find much evidence that leisure functions as a catalyst for innovation and pluralism. To be sure, some historians of Western civilization, such as Johan Huizinga (1947) and Louis Mumford (1967, 1970), contend that the *homo ludens* aspect of mankind has been more significant in human development than the *homo faber* aspect. *Homo ludens* is associated with an 'as if' quality of lateral thinking in human existence which leads to innovation and transcendence. *Homo faber* is also a crucial element in human development but it is subsidiary to the leaps of imagination, invention, science and poetry associated with *homo ludens*. Since the play function is concentrated in leisure, it follows that leisure is identified as the switch-point for enlarging and enriching human life. The leisure educator Charles Brightbill (1961: 177–8) made the same general point in insisting upon the transformative capacity of play and leisure in individual and social development.

Homo ludens means 'man the player' and refers collectively to the various forms of imagination, invention, science and poetry that change the character of human perception. *Homo faber* means 'man the worker' and refers collectively to the various forms of labour expended in the service of imagination, invention, science and poetry.

According to Gellner (1997: 183; emphasis in original), the ethic of cognition has been supremely important in transforming religions, cultures, economies and political systems:

> It was when [human beings] begin to think as individuals, and to break up their world, as an intellectual exercise, that they also burst through the erstwhile limits on cognition and production. It was then that the great scientific and economic revolutions took place. It was then that

cognition and productive growth, which are *essential* not contingent elements of our world, became possible. The separation of issues and data, the imposition of a standard and descriptive idiom, the exclusion of claims to special and privileged status (either for sacred data, or for sacred sources of information) – all this is almost certainly an important element in any genuine understanding of the distinctive world to which we belong.

This appears to nail Gellner's colours to the mast of atomistic individualism and a regime of leisure that treats pluralism and difference as intrinsic social values. With the proviso that undiluted, unchallenged forms of atomistic individualism end in the Hobbesian nightmare, this is indeed the conclusion drawn by Gellner.

What of the myth of romantic organicism? Can any positive functions be attributed to it? In view of the major claims that Gellner advances on behalf of atomistic individualism, and if we grant that the two models are competitive alternatives, our first inclination may be to provide a negative answer. However, a moment's thought helps us to view the situation more constructively. Romantic organicism is based upon social belonging. Social belonging is necessary if we are to recognize mutuality and reciprocity in human groups. Mutuality and reciprocity are the foundations for developing notions of individual rights and responsibilities in leisure and society.

Social belonging is not necessarily a virtuous concept. Belonging articulates principles of social inclusion and because of this positions some individuals and groups as *excluded*. Social exclusion is the cause of much bitterness and strife in human communities. Romantic organicism can certainly solidify the divide between social inclusion and exclusion. Yet its strongest, most ecumenical version recognizes interdependence as the human condition and allows for pluralism and difference as a prerequisite of social membership and growth.

But as with all types of myth, there are dangers with romantic organicism. The clue to this is embedded in Gellner's use of the word 'romantic'. A romantic world view is by definition passionately felt. Passionate positions are often exclusive since they are the articulation of beliefs and perceptions that are not necessarily shared by others. These beliefs and passions may be used as militant principles of inclusion and exclusion. This happened during the Bolshevik revolution in Russia and in the Nazi rise to power in Germany in the 1920s and 30s. Bolshevism and Nazism defined anybody who was located outside these political belief systems to be part of the problem. Bolshevism led to the purges of political opponents and the creation of the Gulag; Nazism produced the victimization of anti-Nazis and the Holocaust. Romantic organicism is by no means extinct. In our own day the activities of terrorist groups like Hamas and al-Qaida, in part, make use of principles of militant inclusion and exclusion. The lesson seems to be that romantic organicism is capable of producing passionate solidarity, but that in its pure form it also generates human stereotypes that sponsor belligerent anti-human values.

The lethic of cognition, then, imposes on the individual the responsibility of questioning leisure life options and choices and considering their consequences. It calls upon us to maintain a watchful eye on authority and defend human rights against violation. Programmatically, this extends beyond the confines of the national boundaries in which we happen to be situated. If we believe in social membership as a precondition of webs of interdependence, we must acknowledge the responsibility of individuals to be vigilant about human rights throughout the globe.

Key points

- Leisure is voluntary behaviour.
- The meaning and practice of voluntary behaviour are situated in the context of processes of ideology and interpellation.
- Leisure practice, ideology and interpellation involve a struggle over scarce resources.
- Scarcity is a basis for competition *and* solidarity.
- Attempts to analyse leisure practice are often focused too narrowly on the motivation of actors. To prevent this, analysts of leisure should always remember that location is in a dynamic relationship with context.
- Common problems with leisure analysis are ethnocentricity and universalism. The methodology of comparative and historical analysis is a useful defence against these problems.
- Leisure relationships always and already involve power. Power is simultaneously constraining and enabling.
- Models of atomistic individualism and romantic organicism are pervasive in the ideology of leisure and human life. They involve contrasting presuppositions about the provision, allocation and value of leisure resources.

2
Action Analysis

In this chapter you will be:

- Introduced to the principle features of Action analysis.
- Presented with an outline of 'life politics' and its relation to leisure forms and practice.
- Offered a map of the central non-pscyhologistic/voluntarist positions in leisure theory, namely the systems approach, the interactionist approach, Marxism and feminism.
- Given a critical audit of each of these positions.

Action analysis is based on the grounded investigation of leisure practice. Grounded behaviour is conditioned by the interplay of factors of personal choice, location and context. The foundations of the Action

---

Action sociology developed in industrial sociology as a way of understanding workers' orientation to work in terms of extrinsic factors such as family and leisure. In Leisure Studies I propose to use the term 'Action analysis' to refer to grounded research that is committed to working with actors to understand leisure trajectories by exploring the interplay between location and context, and formulating leisure policies designed to achieve distributive justice, empowerment and social inclusion. Action analysis is committed to generating evidence based on testable propositions and using knowledge to elicit a scientific understanding of leisure forms and practice.

---

ach are the recognition of the **embodiment** and **emplacement**
leisure actors and the consequences thereof.[1] Both embodiment
and emplacement are decisively formed through ideology, culture, economics and politics, that is, both articulate relations of *power*. Action
analysis proceeds methodologically, on the presupposition that leisure
practice involves *situated* actors. The basic characteristic of the body is
defined as *vulnerability* and of the environment as *precariousness*. As such,
the Action approach may be classified as a version of Hobbesian contract
theory, since it proposes that vulnerability and precariousness are the
pretext for recognizing mutuality and reciprocity and developing
solidarity. Because all of us have bodies that are vulnerable and live in
environments that are precarious, we share a common predicament.

Core traits of the situated actor

- **Embodiment**: everyone's actions are influenced by their genetic
  composition, mental–physical attributes, stage in the life cycle,
  gender, class, race, status and other relations of power.
- **Emplacement**: everyone is spatially and culturally positioned, and
  their position is associated with distinct beliefs, values and networks
  of relations.

This is the pretext for recognizing universal citizenship rights and
responsibilities, of which leisure is a major constituent (Turner and
Rojek 2001). Leisure is a particularly significant component of civil society and citizenship since it typically explores voluntary mutuality and
reciprocity in informal settings. By playing, singing and dancing together
informally we develop strategies for recognizing and acting upon the
universal predicament of embodiment and emplacement and the elaborate common citizenship interests that override divisions of class, gender,
race, status, religion and associated distinctions of status. Of course, it is
also necessary to note that all of these activities may be the basis for
aggression and conflict. But a positive view of leisure must focus on the
cooperative, integrative potential of leisure forms and practice.

The Action approach does not regard leisure as merely the accumulation of voluntary actions. On the contrary, leisure is analysed as
a cultural, economic and social *force* that *positions* actors in determinate trajectories of leisure practice. These trajectories also differentiate
actors. Hence, leisure trajectories are understood not merely to reveal the

individual's personal investment in the pursuit of intrinsic satisfaction, but also to classify individuals by class, cultural, gender, racial, religious and status criteria.

The subject's leisure life choices on location, and the narration thereof, constitute the initial point of analysis. These data are approached descriptively and interrogatively, through examining embodiment and emplacement by means of observation, interviews, group work, questionnaires and the comparative and historical analysis of location and context. The behaviour of the subject and the subject's narrative accounts of embodiment, emplacement and motivation are the building blocks of theory. They enable the researcher to map leisure trajectories and to compare and contrast patterns of behaviour with other individuals and groups.

Leisure trajectories consist of the paths of leisure activities followed by individuals. Because subjects are situated in locations and contexts that are independent of personal choice, it is not enough to rely on narrative data alone. The analysis of **time-series** leisure trajectories aims to consolidate leisure choice with location and context. The researcher correlates the leisure options exercised by the actor with data on gender, class, race, nation, generation, subculture and other components of location and context. These are used to construct a dynamic model that combines narrative data on location with the various issues of context that condition leisure trajectories.

Time-series analysis accumulates narrative data in order to establish sequences and directions of behaviour. Sequences of behaviour can be systematically related to issues like the life course, class, gender, race and status to show how leisure operates as a social force at the levels of individual and cultural experience.

Action analysis is a collaborative approach to investigating leisure that involves working with the subject to acquire an understanding of leisure positioning and options. Ethically, research is directed by the principle that body and place are *resources* rather than *objects*. Elucidating narrative data is part of an active process designed to broaden the individual's consciousness of positioning, enabling him or her to invest in leisure options as a change agent. Improvement is understood to apply equally to the intrinsic satisfaction gained from leisure trajectories and the ethical imperatives of care for the self and care for the other and their relation to leisure forms and practice. By stressing the ethical dimension, the significance of leisure conduct in sponsoring self-respect and respect for others is underlined.

The Action approach aims to balance individual pleasure with ethical imperatives of **empowerment, social inclusion** and **distributive justice**.

Political dimensions of the Action approach

- **Empowerment,** increasing the individual's knowledge of mechanisms of resource allocation and leisure life options. Stimulating a proactive stance to issues of bodily health, environmental balance and the affirmation and development of rights in civil society.
- **Social inclusion,** extending civil rights and responsibilities to all members of society, by developing a framework of citizenship that recognizes bodily frailty and environmental precariousness.
- **Distributive justice,** promoting a civil and legal system that strengthens social capital, guarantees citizenship rights and widens opportunity for the underprivileged without imposing fiscal restraints that constitute a disincentive for entrepreneurship and wealth creation.

It therefore involves a political, interventionist component because it is committed to changing behaviour to fulfil these imperatives.

Methodologically, the Action approach is committed to the evidence based testing of theory on location against leisure practice. Theoretical propositions may be predicated upon well-documented data but they must always be regarded as provisional. Testing is accomplished through open debate and the controlled application of propositions in the field. Action analysis aims to be anti-dogmatic and anti-doctrinal. It rejects the old view that political considerations can be neatly divided into traditional categories of Left and Right. It supports a *cumulative* approach to science whereby knowledge is accumulated through the intergenerational efforts of researchers and subject to *testing*.

Since the collapse of the socialist alternative in Eastern Europe in the late 1980s and early 90s, globalization has become a signature theme in debate and research in the social sciences. The Eastern European 'command' economies collapsed for good reasons. Generally speaking, they were not economically dynamic, they practised human rights violations and they were politically stagnant, ritually glorifying the party apparatus and party leaders while signally failing to generate a form of politics capable of addressing local, cultural and environmental issues. However, as long as they existed they constituted an alternative to market-based systems organized around multinationalism, competitive acquisition and the celebration of self-interest. Command economies certainly did not *transcend* commodification and rationalization. Alienation from monolithic state bureaucracy and urban–industrial gigantism was certainly common in the former Soviet system. In addition, a black market that utilized conventional market strategies of competition, exploitation and the achievement of quasi-monopolistic control of demand and supply flourished. Nonetheless, ideologically speaking, command economies were programmatically wedded to the goal of attaining a morally and economically superior version of urban–industrial society. With their collapse a tangible society-wide alternative to capitalism has disappeared.

Life politics

What has replaced them in the West as an alternative to pure capitalism is what Giddens (1998) terms 'life politics'. This is associated with a widespread revitalization of the debate about the rights and responsibilities of citizenship and the limits of nation-state power. Life politics is a conscious attempt to avoid the snares and delusions of atomistic individualism and romantic organicism. It involves a combination of elements that

---

Characteristics of life politics

- Rejection of old Left/Right divisions.
- Focus on the politics and ethics of embodiment and environment.
- Acceptance of new civic responsibilities in caring for others and preserving the planet.
- Emphasis on social inclusion not exclusion.
- Recognition of globalization and cosmopolitan citizenship.
- Commitment to a mixed market with a flourishing third sector (for example voluntary organizations and charities).
- Scepticism about large-scale bureaucracies and multinational autonomy.
- Rejection of political clientism.
- Support for multilateral solutions to global problems.
- Recognition of the social transition to multicultural society and respect for difference.

used to be appropriated exclusively by either the Left or Right. This is evident in various aspects of social, economic and international relations. For example, there has been an evident shift from national interventions into global problems designed to advance the values of either atomistic individualism or romantic organicism towards a multilateral approach. This was dramatically symbolized in the Allied war against the Taliban in Afghanistan; and multilateral peacekeeping in post-Taliban Afghanistan and Iraq after the demise of the dictatorship of Saddam Hussein. Multilateralism is also pursued in the campaign to deal with the environmental effects of global warming, the campaign against the spread of HIV and Aids and G8 summit and WTO economic and trade talks. It seeks to create a new space in international relations in which dialogic relations that avoid the traditional colonial–subaltern power model of traditional Western foreign relations policy are delineated and in which all parties accept a stakeholder relationship with multilateral initiatives predominant (Linklater 1998).

Multilateral cooperation is far from being a bed of roses. Under George W. Bush's presidency, American exceptionalism in respect of controlling carbon monoxide emissions and balancing world trade arrangements, notably in respect of steel production, have been prominent counter-trends. Similarly, despite adopting many aspects of market organization in recent years China remains ideologically fixed to a communist solution to national and global issues. In addition, the thrust towards globalization is resisted by local religious, political and cultural formations that fear being engulfed or eradicated by the process. International terrorism is partly a reaction to globalization. Even so, the machinery of multilateralism and the commitment to finding multilateral solutions to global problems are more advanced now than at any point in the postwar era. A significant caveat that must be added here is that multilateralism is being developed in the context of the emergence of clear global power blocs. Clearly, the United States is now the world's only superpower. However, its global ascendance is counterbalanced by the emergence of the European Community as the expression of European economic, political and cultural interests, China and Japan with weaker but nonetheless influential power blocs in South East Asia, the Middle East, Australasia and Canada.

The implications of life politics for leisure practice run deep. Under the old politics of Left and Right in the West, leisure was treated as a private resource. Although formally defined as separate from work it carried no obligation to extend participation in civil society. The most powerful expression of private leisure was hedonism, that is, the individual's pursuit of pleasure for its own sake. Left-wing approaches following the principles of romantic organicism sought to harness private leisure for collective benefits. Yet, in general, they recognized the ultimate, *personal* character of leisure choice and practice.

In the context of life politics leisure is no longer treated as a private resource because the effects of private practice are acknowledged to have ethical and functional consequences for the self and others. Hedonism remains a prominent cultural value. Yet unbridled hedonism, pleasure-seeking as an end in itself, is scorned because it leaves no space for exercising and enlarging citizenship rights and responsibilities, with respect to the self, others and the environment.

At the heart of life politics is the concept of the informed, active citizen. A corollary of this is that leisure is now concerned with both intrinsic satisfaction and equipping individuals to play an informed active role in social and environmental protection and enhancement. Informed, active citizens need to be briefed about the dynamics of socio-economic inequality, racial injustice, sexual exploitation, disability rights and environmental risks. Mass communications provide a conduit for these data and their role under leisure in life politics is pivotal. Through mass communications citizens gain the information that enables them to be active and productive in social intervention. Local networks of information through schools, universities, workplaces and neighbourhoods provide a significant supplement of information and knowledge.

Ideologically, active citizenship is presented as good for the citizen and good for the society. Leisure partnerships between citizens, corporations and the state are presented as more fulfilling and enriching than the donatory models of leisure provided by either the market or the state. This is especially important at a moment when the state is scaling down the doctrine of the universal provision of education, health and care enshrined under the welfare state. Instead, the state is encouraging a 'do it yourself' attitude, albeit crucially within the ethical circumference of care for the self and care for the other. New Labour's policy of making students pay higher tuition fees to attend university is a good example of this. The policy was presented as an example of responsible citizenship that utilized the ethical principles of care for the self and care for the other. For New Labour it is acceptable for students to pay higher tuition fees since their university education is likely to confer substantial benefits upon them in the employment market and to create opportunities for others to have access to the same resources. Of course, many political questions are raised by this policy. They do not concern us here, because the key point is that New Labour rejected both market and state solutions to the problem of underfunding in higher education in favour of a redefined version of the rights and responsibilities of the active citizen.

From a radical standpoint, one defect of life politics is that it proposes reform *within* capitalism. Market organization and state administration are subject to *ethical* imperatives to achieve care for the self and care for the other. However, the old Left idea of transcending capitalism is not on the agenda. For radicals, this compromises the project of active citizenship since it means that reform must accept the dehumanizing premise of the system, that is, that labour is generally replaceable. Two points must be made in response to this.

First, while the transcendence of capitalism and the development of mutuality and reciprocity are attractive aims, there are no sustained examples of post-capitalist organization. The Soviet experiment disintegrated and China's road to communism embraces many aspects of market organization. Those radicals who maintain that the goal of politics should be to transcend capitalism are short on empirical examples that support their case.

Second, under an ethical imperative that combines care for the self with care for the other, it does not necessarily follow that **generic replaceable labour** translates into generic replaceable citizens. Active citizenship proposes a variety of new ways to consider the value of labour and leisure, notably in respect of exploring how voluntary

---

The term **'generic replaceable labour'** derives from Marxist sociology. It condenses several tendencies in capitalist production: (1) the replacement of human labour with mechanized functions; (2) the deskilling of labour through automation and the restructuring of management systems; (3) the periodic redundancy of human labour through the business cycle; and (4) the generation of a 'reserve army' of human labour in the underclass (of long-term unemployed or semi-employed labour) and the Third World. The term 'generic replaceable citizen' is newly coined here. It also condenses several meanings: (1) citizens who are procedurally defined as consuming more economic resources (through welfare rights) than they contribute (through fiscal regulation); (2) citizens who are permanent or long-term members of the underclass or the Third World; (3) citizens who can no longer contribute to the labour process through chronic ill health.

activity designed to enhance collective wealth and well-being can be rewarded.

At this stage in the discussion, it may help to summarize the main features of the Action approach:

Action analysis

- Based on the subject's embodiment and emplacement.
- Defines vulnerability and precariousness as the universal predicament of actors and applies this for the elaboration of a framework of citizenship rights.
- Consolidates leisure choice, location and context in explaining leisure practice.
- Treats propositions as provisional and subject to testing.
- Politically committed to empowerment, social inclusion and distributive justice.
- Supports the ideal of active citizenship and identifies leisure as a resource for self-directed learning and action.

We can gain purchase on what is distinctive about the Action approach by considering it in relation to the social systems approach. The latter was a reaction to psychologistic approaches that tended to cast the actor as an atomized individual. It sought to reconcile the exercise of leisure life options with context. The main exemplars of this approach in Leisure Studies are Cheek and Burch (1976).

The social systems approach

Cheek and Burch (1976) advocate a social systems approach to leisure that is theoretically derived from the sociology of Talcott Parsons. They define leisure as a social institution that fulfils specialized functions that contribute to the stability and growth of the social organism. 'Leisure activities', they (1976: 156) propose, 'serve as an expression of social solidarity and norms to reaffirm the larger social order.' According to this approach the main challenges facing social systems are the maintenance of order and reproduction. Primary groups have evolved to resolve these problems. Primary groups are intimate settings in which nurture and support are provided for individuals, enabling them to participate fully in the maintenance and growth of the social system.

The pivotal primary group is the family. Through the process of family socialization individuals learn to acquire roles and perspectives on social hierarchy and sift through leisure life options that are internalized as 'natural' or 'appropriate'. This process is fundamental in identity formation. If society is a social organism the family is a cell transmitting the central values of the system to individuals. The school is another setting that both extends the experience of family socialization and provides critical counterpoints to it by acquainting the individual with contrasting role models and types of identity.

Cheek and Burch contend that voluntary behaviour is another setting in which primary groups emerge and influence identity formation. Through leisure experience individuals acquire systems of symbolic communication, role models, expressions of commitment, trust relations and social bonding which are indispensable in the life course. Voluntary behaviour typically allows for more expressive experience than formal settings of school and work since leisure often involves the relaxation of restraint. It is compatible with high levels of affection, humour, self-disclosure, playfulness and other forms of emotional intensity that are associated with intimate knowledge and affective cohesion.

One important example of this is taste. According to Cheek and Burch (1976), voluntary behaviour is at the heart of acquiring and internalizing taste. Taste is a mark of social distinction and as such offers a collective basis for identity formation and the recognition of social membership. Cheek and Burch (1976: 130) define taste in donatory terms as a 'preference exercised in response to normative pressures'. Taste cultures are in effect versions of primary groups, providing standards and values that transmit standards of identity, continuity and stability. Taste cultures are mediated through ethnicity, peer group and social stratification, but they are grouped around the central values of the nation. They are enormously significant in the acquisition of personal identity and the representation of public belonging. For example, national sports competitions override social divisions and symbolize the nation.

Primary groups are presented as the decisive influences in identity formation and social bonding. They include the 'significant others' who mould our attitudes and values and substantiate identity. Through them we learn the concepts of freedom, choice and self-determination that are so important in leisure practice. For Cheek and Burch, leisure provides relative freedom for the formation of deep affective and expressive bonds. The requirement for this freedom does not originate with individuals but with the social system that requires individuals to develop affective, expressive bonds in favour of the social system as part of the socialization process. The social systems approach exerted a widespread influence in the study of leisure, especially in the early days of the discipline. Evidence of it can be found in the work of Dower (1965), Dumazedier (1967), Rapaport and Rapaport (1975) and Parker (1983), particularly in the strong emphasis they place on the functional, integrative action of leisure practice in maintaining social order. As multiculturalism has become more pronounced in contemporary society, the ethnocentricity of the social systems approach has been sharply exposed.

Action approaches differ from systems approaches in holding that the condition of scarcity and difference involves struggle in identity formation. Normative order is explained as a function of the institutions of the normative coercion rather than the socialization of the individual into the central values of the social system. Accordingly, more emphasis is assigned to the role of ideology in identity formation and variation in cultural reproduction. The centrality of the notion of struggle in the Action approach to leisure is reflected in the prominence given to multicultural difference and variation in analysis. Embodiment and emplacement are investigated as conditional phenomena. Factors of location and context may elicit the reformation of embodiment and emplacement. Feminism and multiculturalism are examples of social and political movements that have transformed popular consciousness about questions of embodiment and emplacement. The recognition of sexism and racism has impacted upon leisure life options in making some leisure choices ethically tenable and others ethically problematic.

The Action approach holds that identity is not fixed, nor is it singular. A may support Arsenal or the Chicago Bulls, but he may also be a son, a father, an orchid grower, a Republican and a cineaste. Individuals move between identities and maintain more than one front of identity at any particular point in time. Identity is connected to social membership and changes as we move through different locations and also through the life cycle. The identity facets that you display in the gym are different from those you exhibit in the classroom; just as the identity facets that you are recognized by at 20 are different from those which apply at 50. It is wrong to propose that identity is simply the reflection of location since this would necessarily ignore biography, which one might think of as the conscious accretion of a trajectory of experience and the absorption of the unintended consequences that arise therefrom. The Action approach regards social experience as inherently dynamic and flexible.

However, this does not mean that there are no solid elements in identity or membership. On the contrary, the Action approach regards social membership through relations of context and location as producing particular types of *identity balance* in the individual. Identity balance refers to the formation of elements that make the individual distinctive as a person. In the course of biography and the associated trajectory of leisure, identity balance may undergo significant changes. These may derive from the expression of individual choice to become a 'different' person, the location of the individual in the life cycle, the edicts of central authorities, or a mixture of all of these.

Main strengths of the systems approach

- Produces a comprehensive, holistic analysis of society, culture and leisure.
- Opposes a psychologistic perspective on leisure.
- Attempts to determine tenable functions of leisure in cultural reproduction.
- Seeks to transcend cultural relativism.

Main weaknesses of the systems approach

- Provides an inadequate perspective of individual freedom and social diversity.
- Exaggerates the universality of the central value system and fails to encapsulate the enabling and constraining effect of power.
- Fails to address the problems of ideology and interpellation.
- Offers an unsatisfactory account of diversity, change, deviance and conflict.
- Overestimates the importance of the family as a primary group, and underestimates the role of media and subculture in socialization.
- Presents identity narrowly as the *reflection* of the values enshrined in the primary group.

The interactionist approach

The most significant contribution to elucidating the plurality and dynamics of identity in Leisure Studies is the work of John Kelly (1983, 1987). Drawing on the symbolic interactionist approach in sociology, especially the thought of Erving Goffman, Kelly interprets leisure as 'a state of becoming'. His approach privileges experience but also stresses its situated character. The main influence on situated character is the mix between personal and socio-cultural orientation.

Personal experience is the axis of the interactionist approach. Individuals are defined as beings that react to external stimuli, but also have the capacity of reflecting on the nature of stimuli and transfer their reflections into actions which impact upon external stimuli by seeking to moderate, intensify or, in some other way, control them. The approach reproduces the stock sociological distinction between agency and structure. Agency refers to the active capacity of the actor to pursue voluntarily chosen goals. Structure refers to the conditions of restraint that allocate resources and rules for individual action. However, interactionism collapses these distinctions by proposing that leisure is a state of *becoming*. That is, in the voluntary actions of leisure the individual develops identity ideals which demystify structural influence and relate agency to the constraints of location and context.

According to Kelly (1987: 229), the chief characteristics of leisure experience are twofold: the sense of relative freedom and immersion in activity. Experience is always conditioned by situational factors that influence the meaning that individuals attribute to leisure experience and regulate the duration of experience. Kelly presents orientation as a function of the life goals of actors in the life course. These goals and their realization are bound up with factors of location. The latter enable action in the sense of supporting the quest for the realization of life goals. However, they also obstruct orientation by presenting closure to subjective motivation or generating experiences of inauthenticity. For Kelly, inauthenticity in leisure experience is a condition in which the creative exercise of freedom is blocked and immersion in a selected activity is impeded.

Becoming in leisure is portrayed as a **dialectical spiral** in which motivation for relative freedom and immersion in an activity engages with and responds to situated factors. This requires us to view leisure as both an act and an environment for action. The balance between the motivation behind an act and the environment of action is the decisive

---

Dialectical spiral refers to the process of contradiction and resolution in which motivation impacts upon the physical and social environment and achieves a balance. The concept is designed to highlight the conditional nature of leisure experience and the process character of leisure forms.

element in determining the quality of leisure experience. If the balance is conducive optimal leisure experience is achieved and the individual experiences a sense of freedom, immersal, pleasure and enrichment. If the balance is skewed the motivation behind optimal leisure experience is thwarted and the individual will experience frustration, anti-climax and inauthenticity. In Kelly's work, optimal leisure experience is a highly significant component in social becoming. Work and family relations often fasten the individual down to obligations and responsibilities that are experienced as demanding and self-estranging. These obligations and responsibilities are reconciled in optimal leisure activity, albeit temporarily; they therefore provide milestones in personal growth.

Kelly's interactionist approach provides a sophisticated reading of the conditionality of leisure experience and the plurality of leisure identity. Although personal biography is the anchor to personal engagement with interaction settings, it is compatible with flexibility in the presentation of the public face. The focus on the centrality of face-to-face interaction means that this approach is extremely adaptable. Role improvization and innovation are essential features of social becoming. The dialect-ical spiral is pivotal in the transmission of experience and the emergence of knowledge. Leisure practice is conceived as connected to institutional roles, but carries the potential for the experience of relative choice and freedom.

One difficulty with the approach, fully acknowledged by Kelly (1983: 19), is that location tends to prefigure over context in analysis. While the emphasis of analysis is on identity balance and the generative perception of the relationship between action and environment, the configuring influence of context is understated. This produces a shallow reading of power, particularly in respect of questions of ideology and interpellation. Although embodiment and emplacement are implicit in interactionist analysis, the problems inherent in the ideology of embodi-ment and emplacement are not directly confronted. Embodiment and emplacement are treated as exclusive concepts, since in interactionist analysis you have your own body and you are situated in your own space, whether it be conceived of as dwelling space, city space, nation or culture. Yet the question is: what forms of identity are marginalized and rejected by the attribution of bodily and spatial exclusivity? This opens up a whole front of complex political questions, having to do with the representation of identity and the distribution of scarcity that are not examined in interactionist accounts. While the approach does lead to ethical questions, the development of a general ethical position on leisure is not central to its purpose.

These various conditions limit the application of the approach, especially in a cultural landscape where notions of bodily and spatial exclusivity are regarded as old hat (Butler 1990; Haraway 1991; Hall and Du Gay 1996). 'Post-identity thinking' has emerged from the debates around postmodernism and post-colonialism. It has made inroads into Leisure Studies through work influenced by notions of hybrid geography and liquid modernity (Aitchison *et al.* 2000; Blackshaw 2003). Because it poses a variety of challenging issues about the coherence representation of identity on location and in context it needs to be addressed fully in a separate chapter (pp. 110–24). However, the challenge it presents to interactionist readings of leisure may usefully be briefly reviewed here.

Post-identity thinking stresses the ideological moorings of concepts of embodiment and emplacement. As we shall see in more detail in the final chapter, these concepts are regarded to be in an irretrievable state of crisis. In particular, they are viewed as fatally compromised by issues of post-colonialism, multiculturalism and globalization. In so far as we know more about the operation of interpellation, ideology, power and difference in culture, our confidence in the notion of autonomous, integrated identity diminishes. Stuart Hall (1993a: 360–2) puts his finger on it when he proposes that post-identity thinking obliges us to regard identity as 'irrevocably...an open, complex, unfinished game – always under construction'. Unlike interactionism, Hall's cultural studies approach holds that there is no dominant identity. Identity balance is redefined as a process of slippage through which repressed aspects of identity in the self, and marginal identity in the culture, are deliberately accentuated through political action. The result is that old forms of authority that are based in the notion of dominant identity are reconceptualized as being in a state of permanent crisis.

Diminished confidence in the old categories of identity does not necessarily produce a general lack of faith about issues of action and solidarity. On the contrary, it may be the spur for new thinking in these areas to develop notions that are more compatible with the recognition of multiculturalism, post-colonialism and globalization. Post-identity thinking lays down the gauntlet of many difficult problems for interactionist approaches to leisure. Centrally, it rejects the notions of grounded embodiment and emplacement. Accordingly, our identification with integrated categories of masculinity and femininity in leisure roles and cultural–spatial categories of community, race and nation is disrupted. Analogously, the categories of choice, freedom and self-determination, which are so prominent in psychologistic approaches to leisure, are vitiated. The questions are: what do choice, freedom and self-determination in leisure mean, if in exercising them as embodied and emplaced actors we exclude or preempt difference? How do postulated leisure communities construct mythical notions of 'Otherness' by stereotyping, stigmatizing and even scapegoating other cultures?

The interactionist approach in Leisure Studies partly began as an attempt to overcome social systems approaches to leisure which give pronounced importance to the stability of leisure function and leisure roles. For example, as we saw above, Cheek and Burch (1976) maintain that the function of leisure is to provide the interaction context to enable social integration between intimates, friends and family. On this account, leisure merely reproduces the central values of the social system and, in doing so, strengthens stability and order. The social systems approach is a version of romantic organicism. Interactionism is closer to the model of atomistic individualism in assigning greater importance to the interpretive capacities and knowledge of individuals. However, in adopting this course the structural influence of factors like class, gender and race on the dialectical spiral tends to be erased. In turn, this neutralizes the significance of ideology and interpellation in configuring both individual motivation and the composition of environments for action.

Main strengths of the interactionist approach

- Allows for knowledge and innovation in the behaviour of the individual.
- Recognizes a dynamic between structure and agency.
- Uses the experience of the subject as the focus for testing theory.
- Has a non-dogmatic perspective on theory.

Main weaknesses of the interactionist approach

- Fails to embrace an adequate view of interpellation and ideology.
- Crudifies the division between structure and agency, for example by failing to distinguish a politics of difference and location from context.
- Ignores the challenge of post-identity thinking.
- Allows interaction on location to dominate analysis and so develops a weak comparative and historical perspective.

Marxism

Marxism emphasizes the *political*, historically *constructed* character of leisure forms and practice. By positing class struggle as the key to understanding leisure conduct it at once wrong-foots both systems thinking, with its complacent account of leisure as a mainstay of social reproduction, and interactionism with its ill-defined, woolly endorsement of the role of leisure in the process of social becoming. At the height of its influence in Leisure Studies, in the mid-1980s, Marxism appeared to be far more concrete, pointing to the role of class inequality in the distribution of leisure chances, the influence of class domination in the regulation of leisure forms and the historical roots of ideological manipulation in leisure relations. It is also worth noting that, at this time, the Marxist contribution constituted a challenge to American intellectual and research leadership in the subject, since the main proponents hailed from Western Europe, Australia and Canada (Andrew 1981; Van Moorst 1982; Brohm 1978; Rigauer 1981; Clarke and Critcher 1985). American leisure theory tended to replicate the ideology of American civil society in holding fast to the centrality of individualism, liberalism and pluralism in explaining leisure forms and practice (Kaplan 1960, 1975; Brightbill 1961; Neulinger 1974, 1990). Against this, Marxism submitted that inequality, power and ideology are the keys to understanding leisure forms and practice.

To begin with, the Marxist contribution followed classical Marxist principles in stressing the crucial importance of economic property relations in allocating leisure resources (see Rojek 1985). Economic power is explained as the ultimate source of political and cultural domination. For Marxists, the struggle for changing leisure practice is presented as a struggle for controlling the economy and state. The state is understood in Althusserian (Althusser 1971, 1977) terms as comprising *ideological* and *repressive* components. The ideological institutions of the state include schools, universities, social work, the judiciary and the media. They operate to interpellate conformist docile citizens. The repressive institutions of the state include the police, the military and traditional mental health organizations. They function to control popular conduct by the use or threat of violence. Both components of the state are dedicated to reproducing the conditions of capitalist domination. Marxists regard the state to be the central lever of economic power, moral regulation, cultural influence and the legitimate use of physical force. Of course, corporations and multinationals are recognized as crucial in the organization of global capitalism. However, their autonomy is conceptualized as a dependent variable of the state, not least because the state has the capacity to seize ownership of private assets and set them to public ends.

With hindsight, this position on corporations and multinationals is very unsatisfactory. It attributed a monolithic role to private business and peculiarly neglected globalization. For example, Clarke and Critcher's (1985) important study of leisure is almost exclusively based on an analysis of the British case, and this at a time when global leisure multinationals like Nike, Disney, Microsoft and Sony were developing new forms of global cultural manipulation in leisure practice. Already in the 1980s the old doctrine of 'socialism in one country' was in turmoil by globalization and the economic distinctions of class were giving way to new cultural ambiguities of class.

Accordingly, as the 1980s drew to a close the Marxist tradition in Leisure Studies assigned more importance to the significance of *culture* in processes of consumption and leisure. Interest began to transfer to the question of how economic inequality is *culturally* represented and negotiated in leisure practice and cultural relations (Clarke and Critcher 1985). This allowed for more variation in the analysis of location, context and leisure trajectories. Following Bourdieu (1984), **cultural capital** was analysed as the passport for acceptance in social networks

---

Cultural capital is a term introduced by Bourdieu (1984). It refers to non-material types of wealth such as access to knowledge, networks of influence, trend-setting taste cultures in leisure and consumer culture. Bourdieu argues that prestige and success are functions of gaining access to cultural capital. For the economically disadvantaged the education system is the key institution of normative coercion that confers access to cultural capital. For the economically advantaged, the family plays this role.

---

that produce life advantages and solidarity in education, work, marriage and leisure (see Thornton 1995). Class characteristics such as accent, dress, housing, friendship networks, available free time, access to space and knowledge of specific leisure forms like soccer, art, the theatre and the cinema were theorized as the key to shaping relationships and generally channelling people of similar class backgrounds together. Class differentials in cultural capital were regarded to operate in innumerable ways to position individuals together as people of the 'right sort' and sift out representatives of different class formations. But within this positioning various cultural differences were recognized. Bourdieu's (1984) concept of taste formations was an attempt to decipher this in relations of culture and leisure.

At one level, his approach is quite orthodox. For example, he reproduces the standard argument of the Left that class formation is finally based in the ownership and control of economic property. However, he also argues that serious errors derive from neglecting cultural and symbolic dimensions of class or treating them exclusively as a dependent variable of economic power. According to Bourdieu, the struggle over taste in art, fashion, music and cuisine and the value assigned to speech forms, accent, leisure and travel choices and education reflect class distinctions, no less than the contest over wages and the control and ownership of the means of production. Indeed, he follows conventional Marxism in maintaining that there is no set of relations in society that is outside the fundamental structure of class. However, taste cultures possess contradictions that are marked by specificity and they cannot be reduced to the class contradiction.

For Bourdieu, then, there is a loosening of the traditional Marxist emphasis on the ubiquity of class. For example, he maintains that the family, schools, universities, the judiciary, social work and the mass media are simultaneously instruments of class reproduction *and* generative of specific taste cultures that operate as sites of resistance.

Bourdieu's work suggests a more complex model of class relations than the dichotomous dominant/subordinate model propagated under classical Marxism. Bourdieu's taste cultures are a shifting kaleidoscope of power formation that permeates and complicates class boundaries in ways that are anomalous with traditional class analysis. He submits that class distinctions organize the context of taste cultures, but specific, aesthetic, political and play elements on location are not bound by these distinctions. On the contrary, they arrange themselves in ways that cross-cut class boundaries, rendering economic divisions ambivalent and requiring new ways of thinking about political alliances that transcend the dichotomous class model.

Bourdieu's work on class, culture and leisure should be regarded as an attempt to move away from dogmatic, essentialist models of class and class struggle. The same ambition is evident in the work of Stuart Hall and the Birmingham School (Hall *et al.* 1978) that introduced the notion of 'resistance through rituals'. The Birmingham tradition also parallels Bourdieu's analysis in proposing a duality of function in the institutions of the state: schools, universities, the judiciary, social work and the mass media. That is, these are understood to be simultaneously instruments of social and cultural reproduction and cultural fronts of resistance. Hall and his associates raised the important question of the prosaic use of leisure practice to challenge class domination. School subcultures, racial formations and youth formations were analysed as constructing cultural space in which identity, representation and solidarity creatively resisted the signature categories of capitalist rule. Just as in leisure markets there are informal markets where leisure commodities and services are exchanged at a more advantageous price or where illegal forms flourish, the Birmingham approach proposed layered subcultures of resistance and opposition within national leisure cultures. The cooption of these subcultures into what Hall (1979) called 'the law and order society' is conditional. The shift in Britain during the late 1970s towards what Hall (1985, 1988) called **authoritarian populism** was analysed as a deep-rooted historical process in which dominant class formations operate from cultural specificity to make alliances and deals to control the state. Authoritarian populism condenses a wide range of popular discontents and mobilizes them around a 'get-tough' policy for the nation's ills. The 'permissive society', with its relaxed perspective on leisure forms and practice, is denigrated for its alleged softness on crime and individual responsibility. The state is used to make concessions to the subordinate classes in relation to distributive economic justice and the extension of citizenship rights. However, the battle to win hearts and minds is also conducted throughout civil society, especially in the area of public opinion that is outside the realm of the state proper. Beguiling the majority with specious moral arguments that countermand their economic and political interests is the core of authoritarian populism. The arguments of the New Right in the 1980s, which assigned ethical

---

Authoritarian populism is usually based around an autocractic leader who articulates a set of policies that damage the interests of the subordinate class but nonetheless achieves significant popular support. The policies of Margaret Thatcher in Britain and Ronald Reagan in the USA during the 1980s are examples. Presented as a heroic project of revitalizing the market and setting the people free, the policies amounted to a cavalry charge against the values of the welfare state and permissive society. The thinly veiled aim was to reassert the traditional role of capital in governing economic, social and political policy.

imperatives to individualism over collectivism and the market over the state, are examples.

The capacity of the dominant class formations to control the state is regarded to be intrinsically provisional. Hall took over Antonio Gramsci's concept of **hegemony** and used it in preference to the traditional Marxist concept of class domination. The battle for hegemony is decisive in asserting the political, intellectual and moral leadership of ascendant formations. It predisposes debate and action to follow approved directions. However, it seldom operates through naked domination or assertions of power. Typically, it functions through insinuations of 'common-sense', 'natural justice' or immemorial ways of national life (heritage) that must not be jeopardized through change. Besides, since agency can never be wholly controlled, hegemony is subject to counteraction. Circumstances may alter its capacity to persuade populations and regulate behaviour. The concept therefore allows for the positive power of resistance and struggle to transform the hegemonic order of things. While it originated in a very different tradition, the Birmingham approach mirrors Bourdieu's cultural sociology in proposing that class is compatible with various and multidimensional cultures that cannot be finally reduced to an economic base and also insisting that politics is at the heart of relations of leisure, consumption and culture.

> **Hegemony** refers to the engineering of voluntary, popular 'consent' by delineating the terrain of economic, political and cultural debate and struggle. It does not deny difference or opposition, but rather positions them in a subordinate condition by redefining 'common sense'.

Similarly, more recently, Aronowitz and Culler (2003: 10–11) propose that it is no longer tenable to confine the study of the class divide to the economic line of power. In addition, analysis must examine what they call 'immaterial production'. By this, they means the diverse and various *cultural* ways in which access to and ownership of property influences representation, identity, control and resistance. This involves abandoning traditional models of class based around divisions between a ruling class of property owners, a middle class of managerial, information and knowledge workers and a proletariat of unskilled or semi-skilled wage labourers (Clarke and Critcher 1985). For Aronowitz and Culler, this old Marxist approach to class is obsolescent. Instead, drawing on various aspects from the work of Mills (1956), Gramsci (1971), Bourdieu (1984), Laclau and Mouffe (1985) and Hardt and Negri (2000), they emphasize the importance of *the power bloc* in capitalist society. This is a conglomerate of the political directorate and the decisive groups of owners of multi-national capital. The bloc operates on a divide-and-rule principle to create tensions and rifts between oppositional social formations – wage workers, elements of the knowledge–information class, women, blacks and other racially oppressed groups. This is done by a variety of means including media stereotyping, scapegoating, state sponsorship of unequal patterns of redistributive justice and political indoctrination.

What emerges most forcefully is the capacity of the power bloc to influence the means of representation through ideology and interpella-tion. Through shaping the agenda and time allocation of news items, the division of entertainment space (pubs versus private clubs), con-sumption space (Fortnum and Mason or Bloomingdale's versus Toys 'R' Us or Wal-Mart), cuisine space (the Savoy Grill or Gordon Ramsay's at Claridges versus pub food or the local café) and, of course, housing space (Hampstead or the Upper West Side over Brixton or the Bronx), the power bloc summons and regulates class identity.

While class analysis may have been recast in recent years, Marxist accounts continue to emphasize the segregation of classes by economic capital in sport, leisure forms, the arts, politics, the labour market and dwelling space. For example, despite postwar moves to dismantle class barriers, a blue-collar worker is likely to feel immediately out of place in a power bloc leisure setting such as an exclusive club, or the highest-priced seats in sport and the opera. Although class boundaries and the maintenance mechanisms associated with them are becoming more fuzzy, class distinctions are still significant in positioning individuals in relation to access to economic and cultural resources and the distri-bution of prestige.

Much of the recent work in class analysis can be regarded as expressing a preoccupation with the question of how consumption reinforces and elaborates polarities of identity, solidarity and opposition that derive from production. Class background is portrayed as the pivotal influence in the social and economic division of labour. Access to the ownership and management of economic resources, high-status employment, quality leisure time and consumer culture reflects class membership. However, as Bourdieu's (1984) own work richly demonstrates, within class formations taste cultures organized around leisure and consump-tion constitute significant schisms in class membership and action. On this reckoning, class continues to define relations of context but does not standardize cultures of location and the leisure forms and practice they sustain.

Much of the appeal of Marxism in the 1980s and 90s lay in its articulation of alternative leisure forms and practice based in overcoming capitalist domination. Marx (1977) himself distinguished between a *realm of necessity* and a *realm of freedom* under capitalism. The former comprised the various obligations and responsibilities required for individuals to reproduce themselves and their dependants. All known systems of production and consumption require a realm of necessity since labour and consuming the fruits of production are the basis for economic and social preservation, growth and prosperity. According to Marx, under capitalism, the realm of necessity is subject to the interests of the dominant capitalist class, for the well-being and wealth of this class is predicated on the exploitation of subordinate classes and the appropriation of surplus value. However, even capitalism allowed workers time away from work to replenish their energies and stimulate personal growth. This is the sphere of leisure relations. Marx argued that under capitalism working-class leisure forms and practice are driven down to replenishing energies exhausted by the demands of work. Any excess assumes the form of an 'animal' level of play. He (1964 [1844]: 111) writes:

> Man only feels himself freely active in his animal functions – eating, drinking, procreating, or at most in his dwelling and dressing-up, etc., and in his human functions he no longer feels himself to be anything but an animal. What is animal becomes human and what is human becomes animal. Certainly eating, drinking, procreating etc., are also genuinely human functions. But abstractly taken, separated from the sphere of all other human activity and turned into sole and ultimate ends, they are animal functions.

In this passage, Marx attests that hedonism under capitalism, as an end in itself, merely flatters the imagination of the individual. It conveys a fleeting sense of satisfaction. Conversely, because it is alienated from what we would now call the ethical principles of care for the self and care for the other, it is simple motor pleasure.

Leaving aside the prevalence of alcoholism, drug abuse and pornography under capitalism, Marx's words about the 'animal' character of leisure seem now to be rather passé. However, it should be noted that a later generation of Marxist scholars revived this connotation in their analysis of leisure and consumption under capitalism. Adorno and Horkheimer (1944), Marcuse (1955, 1964) and the early work of Kracauer (1995) argued that the capitalist culture industry, consisting of film, television radio and other branches of the mass media, tends to reduce consumption to the lowest common denominator. Hollywood feeds consumers a diet of stereotyped action thrillers and soft-core pornography that functions to 'distract' consumers from political mobilization and the extension of solidarity. These writers argue that the development of consumer culture takes capitalism into a new, more sophisticated stage of domination over the masses. Under it, control is accomplished through the 'free' choices made by consumers in leisure and consumption activity. These 'choices' are directed by the culture industry to achieve conformity, docility and the reproduction of capitalist hegemony.

However, while Marx and his followers have cogently stressed the realm of necessity under capitalism, they also submit that the oppressive nature of this realm generates an antithetical realm in which intimations and practical examples of freedom can be glimpsed. The *realm of freedom* consists of relations that support the free and full development of the individual. These relations are only generalized with the development of a society in which the associated producers succeed the capitalist class in controlling the means of production. In classical Marxism this stage of human development is identified with the rise of genuine communist society, a social formation that even Marx beheld as a long-term objective in human evolution.

One should immediately note that the types of statism achieved by the Soviet model in Eastern Europe after 1945 have little to do with genuine communism as envisaged by Marx. These types were structurally more akin to the Marxist–Leninist model of 'the dictatorship of the proletariat', that is, a state-centralized system of domination designed to equip economy and society with the means of production, information and socialization compatible with genuine communism. The fact that the Soviet model was unable to transcend this stage exposes the structural unpreparedness of these societies for a smooth transition to communism. It does not necessarily invalidate Marxism, since the latter predicted that this transition is most likely to be accomplished smoothly in the most culturally and economically advanced societies. Having said that, the absence of this transition anywhere in the West constitutes a significant problem for Marxists that we cannot go into here.

According to Marxism, intimations of the desired general state of affairs are evident in cooperative relationships under capitalism, especially in the relations of mutuality and reciprocity achieved in community self-help, leisure forms and practice and sport. The whole relationships constructed in some aspects of capitalist leisure therefore constitute a harbinger of the generalized form that supports the complete free and full development of individuals. The *utopian* payload of Marxism is extremely important in accounting for its longevity. The prospect of free and full development is what unites Bourdieu, Hall, Aronowitz and other neo-Marxists in making the case for socialist transformation. Under capitalism, leisure forms and practice are on one side dehumanized by the capitalist imperative of expanding commodification as the condition for the reproduction of the system. But they also signal forms of livelihood and practices of self-actualization, mutuality and reciprocity that offer resources of hope for the future of mankind.

Main strengths of the Marxist approach

- Produces a holistic account of leisure, culture and society that incorporates a consistent view of power and ideology.
- Constructs a cogent theory of the interpellation of individuals as subjects in civil society and leisure forms and practice.
- Applies a comparative and historical perspective as a defence against psychologism and the functionalism of the systems perspective.
- Perpetuates a utopian model of free and full development that mobilizes strategies, choice and action in trajectories of life and leisure practice.

Main weaknesses of the Marxist approach

- Overstates the significance of class in the development of leisure, society and culture.
- Fails to incorporate a multidimensional perspective on power that acknowledges the specificity of gender, race and status influences on soicety culture and leisure forms and practice.
- Exaggerates the determinism of individual forms of choice and practice.
- Perpetuates a monolithic view of ideology and consumption.

Feminism

Feminist approaches to the influence of gender in leisure follow class approaches in stressing the centrality of ownership of and access to property (Green *et al.* 1990; Shaw 1994; Henderson *et al.* 1996; Wearing 1998). However, property here is not understood principally in terms of ownership of economic or cultural capital but the more material level of *embodiment*. The construction of gender correlates with a sexual and social division of labour in which women are positioned as domestic labourers and emotional managers par excellence. In this way gender operates to allocate economic and cultural capital resources appropriate to consolidating the regime of male power.

The role of women in the family, especially the significance placed upon child-bearing and child-rearing, places barriers on equal participation in leisure between the sexes. Gender construction operates with an internal and external system of constraints. Internally, the identity formation of women in relation to leisure privileges importance of physical appearance and presupposes a sense of a lack of equal entitlement to leisure with males. Externally, women's participation in leisure is constrained by a lack of time and money compared with men in the same class formation. Symbolically, women are interpellated in a relation of dependence to male culture, which assigns accentuated importance to female sexuality and impedes women's access to public space such as bars and pubs and freedom to move freely through public nocturnal spaces.

The context in which the embodiment of gender is constructed and reproduced is **patriarchy**. Through patriarchy women's confidence in entitlement to leisure is impeded and repressed. Patriarchy reinforces capitalism by privileging child-bearing and nurturing in the construction of female gender, hence the significance assigned to the physical appearance and health of women in male culture. The family remains the principal mechanism for transferring economic capital intergenerationally;

Patriarchy is a system of social, cultural and economic male domination over females and younger males. The primary unit of patriarchy is the household which is predicated in the assumption that the male is the chief breadwinner and source of ultimate authority. Feminism has contributed to the obliteration of many legal restrictions on the participation of women in public life, for example, the right to vote, unequal rights at work, unequal opportunities of education. However, while the formal power of patriarchy has been diminished it remains as a system of prejudicial male beliefs about women which informally restrict women's opportunities in work, politics and leisure.

the ownership of property logically implies the male attempt to control women, for the female body provides the destiny for all capital in the form of producing children with recognized rights of lineage to the inheritance of capital.

Of course women participate in leisure forms and feminist leisure practice is sensitive to, and critical of, male power. But gender construction is pervasive and its sexual inequalities are evident in the many expectations and dependencies, both stated and implied, concerning women's leisure that go with it. In the words of Clarke and Critcher (1985: 160):

> Women are expected – and come themselves to expect – to partici-pate in those leisure activities defined as appropriate for women, at those times and in those places compatible with established female roles.

Although critical theorizing of patriarchy under capitalism is well-established, there are many difficulties with the approach (Eisenstein 1977; Barrett 1980). Initially, the main problem was the perceived drift towards analysing patriarchy as a transhistorical formation. This con-tributed to the underestimation of differences *between* women deriving from divisions of class, race, status, health and ethnicity. There are also problems in constructing female gender as dependent, not least in undertheorizing the roles of female collusion with, and manipulation of, sexual inequality. However, feminists have argued powerfully for the retention of patriarchy as an 'umbrella' term (Wearing 1998: 33) in the analysis of leisure and culture.

Since the mid-1990s, the accent in feminist work on leisure has been upon criticizing essentialism in its various forms (Wearing 1998; Scraton and Watson 1998; Aitchison *et al.* 2000; Fullagar 2002). The concept of the 'Other' has emerged as an important rallying ground in this type of analysis. For Aitchison (2000: 135), the concept of the Other has three important characteristics:

1. The construction of 'Other' presupposes the construction of 'same-ness' on the part of the invoking authority.
2. 'Otherness' is always based in power relations because it assumes an invoking authority.
3. That which is defined as Other is assigned a gender and under patri-archy this gender is always feminized.

What might be called 'post-feminism' aims to extend the feminist turn in various ways. Traditional feminism regards the 'Other' as the female subject/agent which male power constructs as passive and secondary. The task of feminism is therefore to dismantle male hegemony. Destabilizing male discourse is central to this project since it is male hegemonic language and the concomitant 'symbolic economy' that it generates which positions women as the Other in relation to men.

Drawing extensively on post-colonial theory, post-feminism maintains that old-style feminism is too parochial. The question is not how male power relates to feminism. It is how *all* types of identity thinking reproduce the notion of a fixed, integral subject that is independent from others. Identity thinking is regarded as operating through untenable binary oppositions such as male/female, mind/body, culture/nature and work/leisure. While these oppositions are held to privilege 'transcendent male reason', they encompass a range of identity thinking that cannot simply be reduced to the topic of male hegemony (Fullagar 2002: 63). This can be difficult to comprehend, especially in versions of post-feminism that condense the traditional feminist attack against male hegemony with a more far-reaching sally against all forms of essentialism.

Think of it in terms of A&B analysis. A is a woman and a feminist. But the notion of female gender within which her personal identity is inscribed is a product of male hegemony. Since women's identity as the Other is based upon male authority, A's identity as a feminist involves overcoming male power. However, the result of this is to replace one untenable version of fixed, integral identity with another. The procedure of post-feminism is to demystify essentialist thinking by exposing the traces of male authority in the construction and practice of feminist identity. But A is not merely a woman and a feminist. She is also Caucasian, a Midwestern American, able-bodied, middle-class, childless and unmarried. Each of these conditions connote distinctive forms of identity that connect up in complex ways with the concepts of woman and feminist. By seeking to expose these traces and to reveal how they interconnect with each other, discursively, institutionally and subconsciously, post-feminism seeks to destabilize the authority of *all* forms of fixed, identity thinking. So, A's identity as an able-bodied person is conditioned by traces of positions that define the able-bodied from disabled; her identity as a Midwestern American carries traces of the repression of and opposition to regional and non-American forms and practices; her position as a childless woman is based upon traces of separating herself as different from women with children; and so on. The effect is somewhat like a move in chess, where the position of a piece is understood to be conditioned by its difference to other pieces on the board, yet the identity and actions of each piece can only be understood by considering the relationships between all of the pieces on the board. Post-feminism proceeds by isolating how identity is imposed and inter-pellated upon subjects and destabilizing the slippage between identity and its traces. This has raised the question of heteronormativity and white power as dominant forms of sexual and Western identity.

Recent post-feminist work on leisure and gender has examined how regimes of power deploy discourse to position women in relations of domination and subordination (Aitchison 2000; Aitchison *et al.* 2000; Fullagar 2002). Male power is portrayed as assigning women to the margins of leisure by constructing them as a species category designated by innate dependence and frailty. The discourse of male power defines women as the 'Other'. The construction of the 'Other' as a category pre-supposes various economic and cultural relations of subordination. The discursive strategies of the male regime parallel those of the colonial regime. Indeed, Aitchison *et al.* (2000: 124) coin the term 'post-colonial feminism' to refer to approaches in leisure and culture which (a) focus on the global rather than the Western local; (b) challenge the masculinity of leisure and cultural theory; and (c) elucidate the role of socio-historical discourse in positioning subjects.

Women's 'Otherness' in leisure is evident in the coding and theming of female gender in advertising and the media. The objectification of the female body and its subordination to male authority are prominent themes in feminist literature. True to its anti-essentialist colours, recent feminist work dismisses foundational notions of masculinity and femi-ninity, heteronormativity and desire in favour of an approach that privileges the discursive regulation of embodiment and emplacement. Male accounts of alienation, commodification and rationalization are castigated for allegedly 'universalizing' experience and eradicating different desires and gendered subjectivity (Fullagar 2002: 60). Yet this does not explain why women feel 'different' and how they express this in their identities and the forms of leisure they develop.

All of this points to post-binary ways of conceptualizing identity, association and practice that once again have close parallels with recent tendencies in post-colonial and cultural theory. However, the stress on the discursive character of identity leads to a new set of problems about action in feminist politics. The post-colonial feminist approach proceeds on the basis that identity is always provisional and always predicated upon the Other. So male identity is expressed by positioning itself as superior to female identity, white power adopts the same mechanism with respect to non-whites and the able-bodied follow suit in relation to positioning themselves in relation to the disabled, and so on. Recognizing this is held to reveal how much power is based upon assertion, imposition and interpellation.

Yet it is not clear that unmasking power in this way results in a politics of emancipation. By accentuating identity crisis as a catalyst in social and political change, the post-colonial feminist approach contributes to the destabilization of the male power regime, but it is elusive about the preferred social–cultural formation that 'post-identity' practice will support. However, the reconfiguration of power in Leisure Studies and much else besides that will follow the successful dismantling of male hegemony is not elucidated. True, Fullagar (2002: 63) gives some clues in her championing of the recognition of 'multiple desire', the end of 'the self's desire for mastery' and the opening of the self to 'the immanence of the world'. Yet, leaving aside the question of how propositions concerning the immanence of non-human forms are to be objectively investigated (how do we know what lava or a tree feels?), let alone tested, this type of analytical poetics seems to rely upon a version of romantic organicism (Gellner 1998). It is one that is welcome in recognizing solidarity in living with and through difference. But it does not show how the Hobbesian problem of seeking to maximize one's interests in a war of all against all will be surmounted in post-feminist, post-colonial society. Unless one relies upon the implausible proposition that human rights will be *spontaneously* honoured, the questions are what forms of contract and what new types of institution will be necessary in what might be called 'post-identity' society.

Post-feminist approaches to leisure have become more ecumenical. They continue to emphasize the pervasive character of gender inequality, but they are notably more open to exploring the positioning of gender inequality in relations of class, race, nation and collateral dimensions of power. But in destabilizing identity thinking a gap has been created between existing political institutions, practices and forms of identity and what is destined to replace them.

Main strengths of the feminist approach

- Highlights the pervasive character of gender construction
- Emphasizes the positioning of Otherness in identity thinking
- Assigns gender inequality as a basis for political solidarity
- Locates sexualized embodiment as a primary characteristic of leisure forms and practice

Main weaknesses of the feminist approach

- Slides into transhistorical untenable generalizations about gender construction and inequality
- Has produced an unhelpful 'them and us' binarism in Leisure Studies which is now receding
- Post-colonial feminism produces a penetrating critique of identity thinking, but an elusive politics of action

Key points

- Action Approach: grounds the behaviour of the actor in factors of personal choice, location and context.
- Analyses actors as vulnerable and locations and contexts as precarious.
- Aligns with life politics as an attempt to avoid the traditional polarization between Left and Right.
- Seeks to avoid the conservatism and determinism of the Social Systems Approach.
- Seeks to avoid the relativism of Interactionism and retain and develop a political economy of leisure.
- Aims to avoid prioritizing class, gender or race in the analysis of leisure conduct, but instead analysing the constant interplay and changing balance of power between them.

3
Primary Functions

In this chapter you will be:

- Introduced to a model that holds that the condition of scarcity creates problems for all societies in respect of the distribution of surplus and the legitimation of inequality.
- Invited to consider the political dimensions of leisure forms and practice in respect of *representation, identity, control* and *resistance.*
- Guided through the relationship between these functions in leisure and the management of the ratio between scarcity and surplus.

Prosaic treatments of leisure tend to portray it in an undifferentiated way as fulfilling, good and pleasurable. For example, Kaplan (1960: 22) sought to rationalize the common-sense view by connecting the notions of pleasurable expectation or pleasurable recollection with leisure. By way of elaboration, he identified seven essential elements of leisure experience:

- The psychological recognition of activity that is the antithesis of work.
- The identification of leisure with pleasure.
- Minimum involuntary role obligations.
- The psychological perception of freedom.
- The inclusion of an entire range of responses from inconsequence and insignificance to weightiness and importance.
- The general psychological recognition of play.
- The identification of activity as being close to the values of culture.

This amounts to a peculiar mix between psychologism and systems theory. On one side, it is difficult to envisage tenable criteria for measuring 'inconsequence', 'weightiness', 'insignificance' and 'importance'; on the other side, the presumption that there are unambiguous central values of culture to which leisure conduct must be oriented is questionable. Fulfilment and pleasure cannot be disassociated from location and context. The questions are; pleasure and fulfilment for *whom*, according to what *criteria* and in which *location/context*?

For example, A may take pleasure in being bound and gagged in sexual activity. Indeed, several studies suggest that the popularity of sado-masochism as a leisure and lifestyle option is growing (Thompson 1994). A's activities may readily be shown to fulfil the values of individualism in respect of freedom of choice, voluntarism and private satisfaction. In other words, it articulates the values that are often presented as characterizing Western society.

Be that as it may, sado-masochism is still on the World Health Organization list of 'mental disorders' (Presdee 2000: 98). As such, B might object to A's predilection, and may affirm the superior values of eating out, reading, foreign travel, the pub, cookery, gardening, fashion, DIY, the cinema and the gym – which, incidentally, researchers submit constitute the top ten leisure pursuits in the UK[1] – sado-masochists beware!

Social psychologists of leisure purport to have discovered a strong correlation between leisure and freedom of choice, enjoyment, intrinsic motivation and relaxation. However, there is considerable slippage between regarding motivation as a cause or effect of participation. Furthermore, meaning is generally used as a multidimensional category making it difficult to generate useful analytic observations or hypotheses (Osgood and Howe 1984; Horna 1994).

One solution is to situate questions of meaning and motivation at the level of the individual into the wider context of the functions of leisure. Function here is understood to refer to a determinate orientation in leisure practice that arises from the condition of individual embodiment and emplacement in relation to location and context. It is not a 'system property', but an attribute of conscious choice and the position that individuals occupy in relation to the allocation of economic resources and the distribution of prestige. As such, it is not satisfactory to examine whole societies in terms of leisure functions. Societies are composed of too many diverse elements and factions for that. For example, one cannot propose that leisure practice in the UK or USA operates exclusively to enhance social harmony. Indeed, this may be the *intention* of bodies like the Sports Council or the Arts Council in England

and Wales who have the task of sponsoring leisure activity approved by the state. But a given state leisure policy, such as, say, more money for ethnic theatre or gay and lesbian films, will have different functions for distinct social groups and these functions will change in relation to their position *vis-à-vis* different social groups and the responses of these groups. In studying these various and diverse relations the emphasis must be on the embodied, emplaced character of actors in concrete leisure settings of location and context. The position of these actors in relation to the balance between scarcity and surplus, and the regulative mechanisms that condition this balance, are prerequisites of analysis.

At the same time, the function of activities cannot simply be investigated as a matter of individual choice or determination. Societies do not merely exist, they also *reproduce* through economic, cultural, political and social regulative mechanisms. As has been emphasized several times now, in studying the functions of social action, then, it is not enough to focus upon the narrative data supplied by social actors. These data, and the experience that gives rise to them, must be situated in relation to location and context.

Indeed, we can go further and propose that the pursuit of leisure functions is always a mixture between the reflexive choices of actors and the logic of cultural reproduction. Following Bourdieu (1984), a key concept in cultural reproduction is **habitus**. Habitus equips individuals with leisure dispositions that link individual trajectories of leisure practice with collective trajectories.

Habitus means the values and forms of practice associated with the origins and membership of individuals with specific social strata. The term is most closely associated with the sociology of Pierre Bourdieu. It is the basis for his theory of cultural reproduction which holds that institutional forms and patterns of practice are transmitted between generations to signify solidarity and difference *vis-à-vis* other structures. Leisure is one of the most important types of social reproduction in Bourdieu's sociology.

With these caveats in mind, there is still much merit in applying the concept of function in respect of leisure forms and practice. It enables researchers to examine leisure trajectories in a comparative and historical perspective that goes well beyond narrative data. Through it we can acquire a better understanding of how we are *magnetically* pulled into

SCARCITY

REPRESENTATION   IDENTITY
CONTROL   RESISTANCE

SURPLUS

Figure 3.1   Functions of leisure

making leisure choices and why the choices we make provoke reactions in others.

I submit that leisure practice performs a range of functions, the central four of which are representation, identity, control and resistance. Through *representation* leisure practice *themes* behaviour and constructs *markers* of action and belonging. Through *identity formation* leisure practice functions to establish boundaries of inclusion and exclusion that support recognition and relations of belonging. Through *control* leisure practice functions to regulate conduct and lifestyle options. Finally, through *resistance* leisure practice mobilizes resources against agents of control and their associated power regimes.

In most cases, it is probable that leisure practice will involve a mixture of these functions. Moreover, the pursuit of functions will be tracked in relation to leisure functions pursued by other actors positioned in relation to the balance between scarcity and surplus and the regulative mechanisms thereof.

These functions operate in the context of the balance between scarcity and surplus in society (Figure 3.1). If regulative mechanisms service the twin circuits of production–consumption and the management of aggression and sexuality, the primary functions of leisure are concerned with ascribing, contesting and negotiating resource allocation in the field of leisure practice.

Before coming to these functions, it is necessary to justify the use of the concept of function, since the term has become so closely associated with the systems approach that it connotes conservatism and complacency.

Reclaiming the concept of function

Within the twin axial circuits, leisure forms are bound up with order and change. The systems approach has been much criticized for making *functionalist* assumptions and therefore presupposing that leisure practice always achieves social integration. To wit, leisure is presented as operating to maintain order by accomplishing correspondence between system goals and personal behaviour. Conflict, dissent and change are either marginalized or altogether left out of the picture.

This has resulted in a degree of scepticism over the value of the concept of function in leisure analysis, since it is held to always privilege order over change and integration over conflict. The Action approach retains the concept of function, since it is at the heart of many aspects of leisure behaviour. For example, historically, the growth of leisure in industrial society is a function of the development of surplus and collective bargaining. Similarly, the popularity of going to the gym is a function of the combination of increasing medical knowledge about the physical benefits of bodily fitness and stylized cultural/media representations of the desirable body.

It is difficult to see how any form of leisure conduct is intelligible if we discard the concept of function. However, the Action approach overhauls the systems approach meaning and use of the concept of function and transforms it into something else. For the Action approach, the relationship between order and change is always one of balance. At particular moments in history, the balance may weigh in favour of reproducing order, at others it may tilt towards promoting change. Moreover, functions are not theorized as abstract properties of the social system, but attributes of social groups who develop them as conditions of collective membership and social action. The function of using leisure to maintain order may fulfil the interest of dominant groups to maintain control. For example, orchestrating nationalist arts and sports events, festivals and parades is a common mechanism of cementing national consciousness and obedience. By the same token, for subordinate groups it may be experienced as oppressive and generate the function of resistance. For example, in multicultural society the notions of national leisure values and heritage are often experienced as alienating by groups who do not share dominant cultural values. This conflict of values has several functional consequences. It may result in dominant and subordinate groups negotiating a *modus operandi* between national leisure values, heritage and multiculturalism, so that values of difference are coopted. It may elicit a social reaction among subordinate multicultural groups so that they break from national leisure values and heritage to boost the distinctive leisure forms and practice that distinguish their own community. It may precipitate an attempt by dominant groups to extend national leisure ideals and heritage as a test of citizenship, so forcing dissenting multicultural groups to capitulate.

In each case, a balance of functions between order and change, reproduction and conflict come into play. This power balance is the articulation of conflicting and dynamic social, economic and cultural interests. Functions cannot be assumed to perform the goals that groups assign to them. On the contrary, the assignment of functional goals by dominant groups elicits many complexes of action and reaction in which functions may be fulfilled or resisted. Adequate analysis of the balance of functions always necessitates, first, a mixture between theoretical propositions and on-location investigation and, second, a commitment to understanding functions as *processes*.

Leisure forms and practices are not separate from the twin circuits of production and consumption, and aggression, sexuality and civil order. Analysts of leisure who urge students to dwell only on the values of autonomy and voluntarism in leisure behaviour have done a great disservice to the task of properly appreciating how leisure functions in the balance between order and change. Analytically speaking, leisure operates between the poles of surplus and scarcity. That is, it operates in the condition of *inequality* and produces four functions associated with a variety of tension balances between order and change, harmony and conflict: representation, identity formation, control and resistance. These functions are not unique to leisure forms and practices. However, leisure is an ideologically significant element in maintaining and challenging the power groups associated with the twin circuits of regime power, because it is presented as the sphere of voluntarism par excellence. Hence, the commitments one makes through leisure are generally understood to be more authentic and meaningful than undertakings that derive from external force, whether it be the diktat of schooling, work or some other normative institution.

1. Representation

Representation involves theming and manipulation to influence voluntary behaviour. Regulative mechanisms generate principles of desire and censure in leisure forms and articulate them through habitus. For example, membership of racial groups comes with a variety of stereotypes about leisure forms and practices in other races. The work of bell hooks (1983) on Otherness and race argues that white images of non-whites commit the fallacy of assuming that representatives of the racial Other are more worldly, sensual and libidinous because they are marked as 'different'. Cultural appropriation of racial categories channels desire and fantasy. This permeates the whole relationship between whites and blacks and vice versa. However, because desire and fantasy are aesthetically concentrated in leisure forms, through, for example, film, television, popular music, dance clubs, fashion and sport, they are conspicuous in leisure behaviour. According to hooks, especially for young white males, the non-white female body is a significant feature of desire and fantasy in leisure practice and fantasy relations. Regulative mechanisms therefore channel desire in leisure conduct just as they channel access to material resources. They are gatekeepers in representational culture as well as material culture.

In respect of leisure forms and practice, representation works to legitimate the allocation of economic resources and distribution of prestige by placing a well-nigh totemic significance on the ideal of respectable, earned free time (Rybczynski 1991). Representations of the weekend and the vacation are popularly bracketed with a break from routine and repression. They are the occasion for ritualized types of leisure practice that celebrate excess, physicality and the suspension of responsibility. That is why leisure ritually licenses forms of transgression such as drunkenness, taking chemical stimulants and violence (Blackshaw 2003).

Yet, while it is tempting to read the return of the carnivalesque in ritualized forms of weekend and vacation leisure practice, it is also shallow to do so. The break from work routine is more pronounced among young males than either middle-aged males and women at all stages of the life course. Moreover, it is performative in the sense of dramatically *displaying* freedom from the regime of work, rather than constituting a genuine departure from it. In the end it should be regarded as enhancing social conformity.

Interestingly, most studies of contemporary work orientations to paid employment show that the work ethic persists as a major factor in the motivation of labourers. Historians of leisure have shown that when workers are given the option of more free time or working longer to earn more money, they overwhelmingly choose the latter (Schor 1992; Cross 1993). This is generally explained as evidence of the addiction of workers to consumer culture, since surplus income is spent on home improvements, luxury commodities and exotic holidays (Schor and Holt 2000).

This suggests substantial convergence between leisure and participation in consumer culture. In Western civilization free time is dominated by the desire for commodities and buying things. The representation of free time as an arena of conspicuous consumption is a marker of social distinction. Working harder to earn more disposable income that is spent on consumer commodities fulfils the circuit of production and consumption. In addition, the instinctual drives of aggression and sexuality are sublimated by competing for commodities in the marketplace and wanting and owning. The appropriation of leisure space and time by consumer culture strengthens the power regime because it distracts consciousness from alternative or oppositional forms of leisure and politics. Appropriation is organized in highly sophisticated ways. For example, representation of the good life and leisure role models used to be developed and mediated through the community. The family and school continue to exert influence in this respect, but it is vestigial because mass media are now central. Putnam (2000) portrays mass media as inexorably colonizing private life, precipitating the radical decline of civic meetings and action and operating as the focus of information and entertainment. Arguably, he underestimates the variety and resilience of local leisure forms. Stebbins's (2001) work reveals surprising continuities in the use of leisure as a means of social integration and activism. Yet Putnam's conclusion that media-sponsored 'infotainment' culture dominates private life, community and leisure is confirmed by many other studies (see, in particular, Gitlin 2002; Kellner 2002).

Representations of leisure practice have always been part of the *moral regulation* of society. In the sixteenth and seventeenth centuries, the Puritans sought to restrict theatre, singing and dancing on the grounds that these leisure forms were sources of distraction from contemplating the glory of God (Daniels 1995). The rational recreation movement in the late nineteenth century also propounded a variety of leisure role models and images centred on abstinence from alcohol, monogamy and self-help. However, both Puritanism and rational recreation demonstrated the profound difficulties involved in regulating voluntary behaviour. Moral precept and example positioned leisure on the horizon of human activities and undoubtedly made some leisure forms desirable in the sight of ordinary people. Representation is much less successful when it assumes a legal form. For example, moralists succeeded in outlawing the sale and manufacture of alcohol in Prohibition America. The result was the immediate emergence of illegal underground drinking venues and a priceless business opportunity for the newly emerging American Mafia.

The balance of historical evidence suggests that the community, religion and the family are no longer the key institutions of normative coercion. The community, family, the Church, schools and workplace continue to play a local part, but the triumvirate between the market, the state and mass media is now decisive in establishing the context of the circumference of moral regulation. Of course, individuals and groups play a significant role in petitioning the market, the state and the mass media for change. However, it is social, cultural and economic interests in this triumvirate, and not the community, family, schools and workplace, that establish the ethical ethos of care for the self and care for the other.

We should be wary of attributing general good or bad consequences to the representation of leisure in the market, state and mass media. The question of whether representation is good or bad depends on *what* is being represented and by *whom*. There is a *market* in representation, just as there is a market in goods and services. Social, economic and cultural interests in corporations, the state and the mass media encode and decode representations of leisure. Because encoding and decoding are interwoven with the public domain, correspondence between the intentions and consequences of social, economic and cultural interests can never be assumed. It is also a question of balance and correspondence between intentions and consequences depends upon factors in the market, state and mass media which are beyond the control of any single individual or group.

Finally, the function of representation may be exposed as an aspect of the *control* of leisure practice. As such, it may be the focus of counter-reaction in the form of new *identity* formation and the development of leisure forms and practice as weapons of *resistance*.

2. Identity

Leisure practices and forms are markers of social inclusion and exclusion. In some cases participation is tribal. A supports Manchester United or the Washington Redskins because he was born in the city and his father took him to the games as a child. Tribal fans pledge their allegiance by dint of bloodline and they are frequently contemptuous and dismissive of Johnny-come-latelies who *voluntarily choose* to be a fan of *their* club. In our kind of society where achievement, aspiration and upward mobility are valued highly, tribal or ascribed forms of identity in leisure are in decline. Historically speaking, there has been a general movement from **ascribed** status to **achieved** prestige (Rojek 2001a).

Ascribed status is where prestige, honour and privilege follow bloodline. Kings, queens and the aristocracy possess distinction in the sight of others by reason of their exalted lineage.

Achieved status is where prestige, honour and privilege accrue from personal accomplishment. Distinction is attached to tangible, demonstrable practice.

Leisure forms that demonstrate active choice have more *cachet*. When we engage in fine eating at the best restaurants in town, go hill-walking or sailing, play golf or work out in the gym, we participate in status-placing activity. These leisure forms are practised not merely for the intrinsic mental or physical enjoyment that accrues from them, but for what they represent about us as connoisseurs of modern life. Leisure is *declarative*. It says something to others about our self-image, aspirations and judgements about what is of value. Through these declarative articulations we manifest ties of belonging and markers of difference. By extension, leisure practice is an important indicator of social inclusion and exclusion. It represents to others the kind of person you are and the kind of persons with whom you choose to associate.

Veblen's (1899) classic study of the leisure class pioneered our understanding of the significance of identity and status-placing activity in leisure forms and practice. Today, it remains a richly suggestive resource in leisure analysis. In his terminology, the upper class constitutes a *leisure class* who enjoy massively greater access to economic capital. Anticipating work on leisure and class conducted nearly a century later (Bourdieu 1984; Clarke and Critcher 1985), Veblen argued that the identity of the leisure class is solidified through cultural capital. Thus, he recognizes that wealth alone is not a sufficient basis for acceptance as a bona fide member of the leisure class. The latter requires the display of cultural criteria and codes of behaviour. At their core is the consistent display of freedom from the need to engage in paid employment. Since, by definition, the leisure class does not work, the display of their exclusive social status is concentrated in leisure pastimes. Veblen's examples of leisure forms in this category included equestrianism, hunting, learning and speaking 'dead' languages such as Latin, observing codes of etiquette and organizing lavish society balls and parties.

By the standards of the industrial nouveaux riches and the rising working class, these activities have virtually no economic value. Indeed most of them manifestly squander wealth rather than contribute to its accumulation. According to Veblen this is the secret of identity formation in the leisure class. For the cultural value of these non-economic practices is inestimable. They instantly *represent* in the eyes of the world liberty from the squalid cares of wage-labour and membership in the upper echelons of refinement, prestige and influence.

Incidentally, in highlighting the coded nature of leisure behaviour in the leisure class Veblen successfully countered the popular misconception that wealth always delivers freedom. In Veblen's view, wealth in the leisure class imposes obligations of cultural practice that restrain freedom in transparent ways. Members of the leisure class are not free to do as they please. In order to maintain their status they are required to pursue heavily coded leisure forms and practices. If they neglect to do this, their cultural standing is placed at risk.

Veblen's work chiefly addresses the role of leisure in the identity formation of the leisure class. However, his theory acknowledges that the forms of leisure practised by the leisure class influence forms and practices in other classes. The core concept here is **conspicuous consumption**.

Conspicuous consumption is the extravagant display of wealth through gratuitous forms of expenditure. Consumption activity is not based upon the satisfaction of physical need but the exhibition of status superiority.

Veblen intended his analysis of the leisure class and conspicuous consumption to be a warning to society. By affixing high cultural value upon the display of excess and waste, the leisure class established a dangerous code of emulation for the lower orders. Veblen reasoned that if style and glamour are associated with leisure, excess and waste, national economic competitiveness is bound to decline in the long run.

Veblen's worries about leisure and the culture of waste have been partly confirmed. Many of our most popular leisure forms such as smoking, fast food, drinking alcohol and taking recreational drugs are literally wasteful in that they use up the resources and resilience of the body. Similarly, petrol-based transport and the use of spray perfumes are leisure-related forms that contribute to environmental pollution. By participating in these leisure forms might one subconsciously signal one's freedom from the cares of the world? The smoker who relishes his habit may reflect on the burdened life of those who seem to worry about *everything*. The popularity of the conspicuous consumption of idle time, getting drunk or smoking suggests that the celebration of waste has indeed become a characteristic of leisure practice, just as Veblen predicted. Various forms of identity can be traced through these leisure trajectories, which are usually attached to casual forms of leisure (Stebbins 2001).

By the same token, Veblen failed to foresee the emergence of political formations that, partially at least, owe their identity to criticizing the culture of excess. Examples include the Green movement, anti-smoking groups, anti-car groups and gym subcultures. To be sure, Stebbins's (2001) category of serious leisure may be studied as both the reproduction of cultural values and the counter-culture to casual forms and practices that pursue leisure as waste. Leisure identities are therefore not merely formed through emulation. They also arise from criticism and differentiation from dominant or mainstream practices.

In a society in which the triumvirate between the market, state and mass media plays the decisive role in representing and regulating leisure behaviour, **branding** is a significant platform upon which identity and lifestyle are constructed and exchanged. The purpose of branding is to automate desire and attach it to a commodity. Nineteenth-century rational recreationists who preached the virtue of abstinence, monogamy, prudence and self-improvement were engaged in a branding exercise, although they would not dream of labelling it as such at the time. It was based in oral and written culture and resorted to respectable example to engender desire and ambition in the lower orders.

Branding is a form of theming. It imprints symbols upon commodities to increase consumer desire for them. For example, Jean Paul Gaultier clothes are sexy, Coke is effervescent, Apple Mac is cool, Virgin is trustworthy. Branding is usually sponsored by corporations and seeks to bundle a calculated set of automatic wants and expectations with a commodity.

Today, corporations have radically trimmed oral and visual culture in the mobilization of desire in favour of visual culture. Advertisers use bold, emphatic, unambiguous images to sell us the latest Jaguar car, holiday in Jamaica or Sony MP3 player. Increasingly, these images are calculated to convey not merely desire for a product but for the lifestyle that goes with it (Klein 2001; Smart 2003).

The TV ad campaign for Jaguar cars in the summer of 2003 is a case in point. The ads showed an attractive well-dressed couple located in a high-tech office whose peace is enigmatically disrupted by a sleek, fast-moving jaguar. The response of the couple is 'I must buy that silver Jaguar' and the ad closes with them speeding off in the car and the written invitation: 'Unleash One Today'. A number of subtle and automatic condensations of desire are at work in this ad:

1. The physical power and beauty of the animal translates into the lines and acceleration of the car.
2. The purchase of the car is associated with daring and superiority.

3. The high-tech lifestyle of the office is rendered portable through the appearance and moment of the car.
4. Ownership of the car is associated with a desirable sexual relationship.
5. The enigma of the jaguar suddenly appearing from nowhere in the office translates into the symbol of the car owner as intriguing and breathtaking.
6. Having the car bestows limitless power and freedom that the office curtails.

We know from repeated studies that branding automates desire and channels visual culture to condense complex sets of meanings into overpowering purchasing wants (Ewen 1988; Goldman and Papson 1998; Schor and Holt 2000). But we are less accustomed to thinking of this process as colonizing our leisure and regimenting leisure lifestyles.

The market has a strong tendency to turn leisure into a satellite of consumer culture. Because what we do *for fun* is attractive, it alerts commercial interests who seek to commodify it. This is one reason why so many leisure forms that begin as play forms, such as soccer, baseball, popular music, cooking and drinking, now carry the hallmark of extensive and systematic commercialization.

Ritzer's (2000, 2004) work shows how the globalization process standardizes identity. The spread of global commodities and locations, such as shopping malls, car parks, airports and fast-food outlets, creates uniformity, predictability and the regimentation of desire. Critical reactions to globalization are always short-lived, because their fate is to be recommodified. Identity becomes 'McDonaldized' so that national and local variations become insignificant. Ritzer's work lays down a number of challenges for understanding contemporary leisure and culture and we shall come to them in the final chapter of the book. Here, it is enough to note that his diagnosis of globalization as a process of standardization and regimentation is very reminiscent of mass society theory in the 1940s and 50s. The onslaught of 'hidden persuaders' tempting us to adopt the same emotional economy and follow routinized work, consumption and leisure practices made no allowance for compassion or resistance (Riesman 1950; Packard 1957). But it did highlight the common dilemma of the powerlessness of individuals in the face of pulverizing social, economic and cultural processes that they did not invent and which they cannot control. This brings us to the third function of leisure in contemporary society.

3. Control

Leisure forms and practice are always connected to regimes of power. Undoubtedly, freedom and voluntarism are two of the most common and powerful characteristics popularly claimed for leisure conduct. We only have to think of the longing that people attach to the weekend, public holidays and vacations to recognize the potency of the association with freedom, choice and leisure. Yet the pretext of this claim is the ideology of neoliberalism in the West which insists that society is nothing more than a collection of individuals pursuing their self-interests. On this account, the only form of control that the individual needs to address is self-control, because neoliberalism has a heroic perspective of individuals as masters of their own destinies.

Leaving aside the structural influence of regulative mechanisms of class, gender, race and culture, a moment's thought will establish that there are many restraints over public leisure behaviour, notably in respect of the body, assembly and incitement:

(i) *Body*: if, following Freud (1936), the body has natural instinctual desires to discharge aggression and sexuality and pursue hedonism, these natural drives are subject to many controls. For example, the public appearance and activity of the body is regulated. Public drunkenness and rowdiness may lead to censure and in some instances incarceration. Public nudity is confined to controlled spaces such as approved bathing beaches and nudist camps. Heavy petting and sexual intercourse in public are prohibited. Representations of the body on the internet and through print are subject to obscenity laws, especially in respect of sexual torture and child pornography.

(ii) *Assembly*: public assembly for play or protest is subject to notification and policing. Spontaneous public assembly and 'loitering' are categorized as a threat to the peace. The New York City power black-out in August 2003 involved increased police surveillance because the authorities fretted that increased numbers stranded on the city streets under cover of night might resort to looting and riot. In the event, people were remarkably calm and law-abiding, but the example illustrates the minatory attitude of the authorities to non-sanctioned public assembly.

(iii) *Incitement*: the use of leisure to incite religious, racial and sexual intolerance is unlawful. In America the racial harassment perpetrated by the Ku Klux Klan of white supremacists, which reached peak membership in the 1920s and resurfaced during the civil rights movement in the 1960s, targeted blacks, and also Jews, Catholics and foreigners. Indeed, the ambivalent attitude to KKK activity shown by white police officials in the South was one of the *causes célèbres* of the civil rights campaign. Of course, KKK membership expressed a commitment to land and lifestyle and therefore extended much further than the sphere of leisure activity. Nonetheless, leisure was a decisive focus for meeting, preaching and organizing incitement and harassment.

In the UK during the 1980s, the support of Muslims for the *fatwa* issued against Salman Rushdie for his book *The Satanic Verses* was officially condemned. Public burnings of the book in Muslim city communities was monitored and censured. The book dramatized the question of what constitutes legitimate reading in leisure.

Sanctions on leisure are a privilege exercised by dominant groups intent on retaining decisive influence over the twin axial circuits of power, relating to relations of production and consumption and the economy of aggression and sexuality. They have a long history. In the Middle Ages English monarchs encouraged bowmanship, running, wrestling and physical sports as a method of keeping the population fit for time of war. Later in the sixteenth, seventeenth and nineteenth centuries Puritan leaders in both Europe and America preached encomiums to industry, thrift, moderation and temperance. Daniels (1995: 217), writing of New England puritan settlers in the seventeenth century, makes a telling observation about the Puritan position on leisure *in toto* when he writes:

> Leisure and recreation posed a special threat to the ideal of a unity of experience. Puritans were acutely aware that much play historically occurred outside the normal bounds of society...Play had often given licence to transgress society's values. Players might decline to accept moral responsibility for what they did because they were, after all, just playing. What they were doing was not real. Additionally, the play community did not always end when the activity was over. Participants brought back to regular society appreciations, feelings, and beliefs that adhered to other aspects of life.

Puritans sought to make leisure forms and practice comply with the totality of life as expressed in the central values of the community. This paved the way for the rational recreation movement of the late nineteenth century which was essentially a class-based programme for standardizing leisure conduct.

Sanctions on leisure behaviour are often associated with religious belief. For example, Sunday observance groups still deplore leisure and consumption activities on the Sabbath. Until quite recently it was illegal in the UK to sell alcohol beyond designated hours on Sundays. Devout Christian, Jewish and Muslim believers impose restrictions on the appearance and movement of the female body in public and emphasize that a woman's highest calling is home and family.

In societies organized around versions of romantic organicism, leisure is an important lever of social control. For example, both Nazi Germany and Soviet communism are interesting for students of leisure because they were the first movements of romantic organicism to have access to mass communications as a means of propaganda and to use them to shape leisure conduct. Practically speaking, they invented the technology and political culture of using the mass media to drill leisure behaviour and ensure compliance between the values of the individual and the values of the masses. Hitler's Nazi party sponsored the 'Strength Through Joy' leisure movement that offered organized rural retreats, sports facilities and subsidized vacations. The Nazis used the 1936 Olympic Games in Berlin as a device for aggrandizing National Socialism both in the sight of the domestic population and in the eyes of the world. Stalin's Communist Party also recognized leisure as a transmission belt for communicating group values and promoted organized rambles, sports, festivals and a subsidized Youth movement to enhance popular adhesion to the ideals of communism. Soviet sponsorship of sport, especially athletics, was in part designed to demonstrate the ideological superiority of the Soviet system over the capitalist alternative. The Olympic Games became a showcase that pitted the Soviet system against the American way. Both the Nazis and Soviets combined mass political rallies with elements of folk festivals. Hitler's speeches used a variety of cinematic and theatrical effects to create the aura of mass hysteria (Kershaw 1998: 452–3). The idolatry that was organized around Hitler and Stalin borrowed much from the cult of the idol developed by the Hollywood film industry.

Both Nazism and Soviet-style communism treated leisure as a public asset for advancing propaganda through mass communications. The *Volksempfanger* or 'the people's radio' flourished through Hitler's decision to provide cheap radio sets for the workers. They soon generated the colloquialism 'Goebbels' blasters', named after his minister of information and propaganda. Although the Western media are attached to a very different set of political and ideological values, they also understand the propaganda value of mass communications in colonizing leisure practice.

The Voice of America, the BBC World Service, Sky and BBC World supply a mixture of entertainment, sport and news to advance the capitalist alternative to non-capitalist countries. These organizations were particularly important tools of propaganda in the recent Allied conflicts with the Taliban in Afghanistan (2001–2) and Saddam Hussein's regime in Iraq (2003).

In general, the nineteenth and twentieth centuries have witnessed a clear trend from the imposition of external controls on leisure behaviour to self-policing. Rational recreation was a forerunner in this process. It sought to regulate leisure behaviour on principles elaborated from the bible and self-improvement. Foucault (1975, 1980) notes that science and professionalization built on Christian belief systems to apply a secular regime of power which externalized, problematized and critically evaluated one's being, action and thoughts. One became one's own watchman or censor, a category that Foucault's sociology identifies as 'the critically reflective self'. Foucault's work focuses on the influence of medicine and penology in constructing the critically reflective self. But arguably his work thereby glosses over an equally penetrating form of self-policing: consumer culture.

What does it mean to hold that consumer culture is a penetrating form of control in leisure conduct? After all, we all know that nobody *forces* us to buy commodities. We are free to ignore advertisements as well as heed them. Businesses can go out of business as well as prosper. This train of thought leads free-market gurus to propose that consumer sovereignty is the *actual* condition in which we live under capitalism (Friedman 1980, 1984; Hayek 1944, 1976, 1979).

Two general arguments are used to expose this argument as a mirage. First, consumer sovereignty assumes a level of perfect knowledge about actual or potential commodities that is absent in reality. All consumers live in imperfect markets in which knowledge on the supply side is partly structured by the self-interested actions of corporations. Through advertising, marketing and pricing policies multinationals channel consumption to fulfil the interests of capital.

Second, on the demand side, all consumers live in imperfect markets because there are patent economic, social and cultural inequalities between the wealthy and the poor. The wealthy possess a higher propensity to consume. So long as this is the case their power to influence the distribution of commodities will be greater than that of the poor. The main implication of these arguments for the study of leisure and consumption is that current patterns of leisure and consumption behaviour are not necessarily an accurate guide to people's real wants (McGuigan 1998).

Notwithstanding this, apprenticeship to consumer culture impo. deep obligations on the distribution of leisure practice. How to live with credit, how to behave in a shopping mall, the advantages and disadvantages of internet shopping over other retail forms, the psychology of discount warehouse shopping, haggling in markets, especially in the Third World – all of these are consumer *rites of passage* and formations of identity. Unlike forms of religious control, they make no reference to an afterlife but instead offer rewards in this world. They are moral, but only superficially so. For example, consumer culture pays lip service to the values of sobriety, moderation, industry and thrift, but tolerates credit, pornography and alcohol. It laments poverty in the developing countries, but at the same time instils and rewards a general bargain-hunting mentality. More and more leisure activity is devoted to wanting, spending and buying. Consumerism has colonized leisure time and space so thoroughly that leisure forms that involve no level of commercialization seem culturally anomalous.

Consider: A responds to media messages about the physical benefits of keeping physically fit by considering a schedule of daily exercises. This *can* be done without commercial transactions. For example, it costs nothing to walk or run every day. However, what possesses cultural *cachet* is buying the *right* running gear, taking out membership in the *best* gym, owning state-of-the-art exercise machinery and buying the latest CD-ROM exercise programme. If A elects to do none of this, his friends are apt to decry his sincerity in keeping physically fit. He will be castigated for not being sufficiently serious about the task.

Similarly B decides that she will spend her spare time writing a novel. It is *possible* to do this without reading any other novels or attending creative writing classes. However, this is widely presented as the road to failure. The way to write well is to *learn* how to do it, and this involves reading widely and attending classes. Nor does commercialization end there. When B finishes her novel and sends it to a publisher, she is *statistically* likely to have it sent back, unread, by return of post. Mainstream publishers do not generally read unsolicited manuscripts unless they arrive via the recommendation of an agent.

Arguably, the foremost example of the marriage between mass production and mass consumption in the twentieth century was Fordism-Keynesianism. This was a system that also stimulated the colonization of leisure by consumer culture. It was part of a vast process of **rationalization** that either eliminated, marginalized or coopted and redefined folk forms of play.

⌐ is a term used by the classical sociologist Max Weber to
ᴉeral tendency in capitalist society for life to succumb to
ᴉtional–legal control. Weber associated the process with
bureaucracy and what he called 'the disenchantment of
the world'. The concept has recently been extensively revised and
updated by Ritzer (2000) in his 'McDonaldization' thesis (see the final
chapter for more details).

Fordism-Keynesianism dominated economy and society in the West
between 1945 and 1973. The premise of this system was that mass production requires a mass consumer market of predictable, relatively
homogeneous wants and leisure forms. The solution, pioneered by
Henry Ford of the Ford automobile company, was to create a rapid, efficient flow of production by automating the production process and
simplifying manual assembly tasks. Automation reduced the price of
the automobile, but Ford realized that the growth of the business
required high product turnover. This was accomplished by two means:
keeping the wages of workers relatively high and brand innovation. By
using branding to school consumers into the habit of discarding their
cars for a new product every three or four years, and paying workers
enough to afford this luxury, Fordism achieved exponential growth and
a model for other entrepreneurs to emulate. Two factors were at work:
existing car owners developed the habit of disposable consumption

Fordism-Keynesianism is the regime of organizing production and
consumption around mass production, the mass market and the
interventionist state. The mass production system developed by Henry
Ford in the manufacture of automobiles assumed high wages for
workers which in turn strengthened the propensity of the mass
consumer market to absorb new products from the assembly line. The
Fordist system of mass production defined industrial and business
strategy in this period and its success was reinforced by high-spending
state policies in industrial investment and welfare. Keynesianism is the
doctrine of high public spending and the manipulation of aggregate
demand by public spending in excess of taxation developed by the
British economist John Maynard Keynes.

that followed the track of brand innovation, and as kudos became culturally attached to car ownership, more and more new buyers entered the market.

David Gartman (1994) has cogently argued that mass consumption of automobiles revolutionized leisure in the West. A new commercialized mass leisure form – driving and the various preoccupations and protocols of car ownership – was introduced virtually overnight. But this was as nothing compared with the impact of fast, reliable, private *mobility* upon leisure time and practice. Long-distance travel into the countryside became practicable. So did out-of-town employment. Supermarkets gradually made the local grocery store obsolescent, as shoppers shifted to a weekly rather than a daily mode of buying household food and provisions. Even relations in the family were transformed as children could take jobs in other towns and cities without breaking up the extended family.

Fordism was based on the dual standardization of production and consumption. Inevitably, leisure became more standardized as a result. In Britain, the term 'affluent worker' (Goldthorpe *et al.* 1968) was coined to describe the new, well-paid assembly line workers. Affluent workers were theorized to be 'other directed'. That is, unlike craft workers they sought no *intrinsic* reward from their labour. Instead, the accent for them was upon gaining high wages that financed wider participation in consumer culture and mass leisure commodities such as television, package holidays, fashion and pop music. Students of leisure could confidently theorize about 'mass leisure' because the circuit of production and consumption was programmed to cater for the needs of 'mass society' (Nosow and Form 1962; Wilensky 1964).

However, by the late 1960s theories of mass society and mass leisure looked increasingly beleaguered. The inflexibility and rigidity of the regime of mass production and consumption became exposed. In particular, the principle of relative homogeneity in consumer wants and leisure forms and the Keynesian commitment to high levels of welfare funding were gradually either relaxed or abolished. Higher levels of education and more flexible systems of mass communication made consumers more discriminating. Niche marketing, in which commodities are directed at particular income and lifestyle groups, gained the initiative. Outwardly consumerism and leisure form became more diverse and changeable. At the same time the mechanisms of branding to signify distinction and difference became more refined. The use of irony in advertising and marketing gave consumers a false sense of seeing through the social control processes of consumerism. In fact, what became transparent is the organized sales process of particular commodities. Irony was used by Nike, Apple, Calvin Klein, Smirnoff Vodka, BMW and others to screen the subtle packaging of an entire lifestyle with the consumption of the commodity (Klein 2001). For example, Apple responded to the problem of declining market share by aiming their output at niche markets in the communications, information, education and entertainment sectors. Consumers of Apple Macs found in the advertising campaign slogan 'Think Different' confirmation of their maverick, renegade status. The use of irony in advertising makes consumers complicit in decoding the process of **commodity fetishism** but leaves them relatively defenceless against market incursions.

Commodity fetishism is a term coined by Karl Marx. It has two levels of meaning. First, it refers to the irrational devotion to commodities which Marx saw as akin to the primitive devotion to totems and magic. Second, it refers to the 'naturalization' of the commodity world so that consumers treat it as a 'given' of social and economic life and become oblivious to the labour process and exploitation in creating commodified goods and services. Klein (2001) gives examples of commodity fetishism in the leisure sector today when she refers to the consumption of commodities from leisure multinationals like Nike, Toys 'R' Us, Gap and so on which neutralizes the sourcing of production to the low-income developing countries.

If the argument of consumer sovereignty has little to commend it, arguments that analyse consumption in terms of social position and habit are more tenable (Bourdieu 1984; Hebdige 1988). This approach maintains that leisure and consumption reflect habitus. Individuals possess freedom and choice but they express it in leisure and consumption to make their trajectories of practice consonant with the social collectivity of which they are a part. This regime of consumer culture and leisure is a corollary of models of romantic organicism. It presupposes that the behaviour of the individual is always directed to the reaffirmation and therefore strengthening of the social and moral fabric.

The consumer habit model is pronounced in societies in which individual choice is subject to strong, centralized religious or political edict. In societies based in a one-party state or where a prescriptive religion is ascendant, such as Islamic fundamentalism, patterns of behaviour in consumption and leisure tend to be homogeneous. In the

Western capitalist-type democracies greater heterogeneity in consumer and leisure behaviour prevails.

4. Resistance

If the colonization of leisure by consumer culture suggests an inexorable encroachment of commercialization and commodity fetishism upon 'free' time it is as well to note that resistance is also a prominent function of leisure. Resistance is also a basis for the formation of leisure identity. In the late nineteenth and early twentieth centuries workers campaigned successfully for the progressive shortening of the hours of labour. At this time, expansion of leisure time was explicitly presented as freedom from the control of capital (Hunnicutt 1988, 1996; Cross 1993). Trade unions advocated leisure for culture and progress. The question of how leisure hours should be usefully spent was influenced by the didacticism of the rational recreation movement that emphasized the value of physical exercise and self-improvement. However, strata within the working class were well-aware that the rational recreation movement was dominated by the middle class. This inspired a determination among some working-class groups to develop their own versions of cultural progress and improvement which, for the most part, reinforced and privileged values of collectivism over individualism (Yeo 1976; Bailey 1978; Gray 1981; Yeo and Yeo 1981). Working men's clubs encouraged a variety of leisure pastimes than can be read today as embracing the rational recreation ideology of progress and improvement, while at the same time resisting the mantle of middle-class leadership: brass band-playing, model-building, allotment cultivation, folk-singing and pigeon-racing. These developed in conjunction with working-class practices: snooker, billiards, darts, skittles, whist, shove ha'penny, dominoes and bingo. These practices were typically concentrated in the pub, which operated as a key focal point of community leisure in industrial cities (Hill 2002: 133).

Notwithstanding the significance of these examples of class resistance in leisure it is salutary to note two things. First, historians of leisure are unequivocal in concluding that the movement for shorter hours began spluttering out in the late 1920s and collapsed after the Second World War. Initially, this was in response to the exigencies of the economic depression. Those without work spent a good deal of their time travelling to find it, while those in work sought to retain their jobs and increase their job security by volunteering for longer working hours. In the post-war period workers appear to have become more integrated with the core values of consumer culture. So much so that, faced with the choice of increasing leisure time or working longer to increase income, workers have consistently chosen the latter option (Schor 1992).

Second, capital has made considerable inroads in commercializing working-class leisure pastimes. Clarke and Critcher (1985) point to the decision of the brewing industry in the 1970s and 80s to engineer the decline of the traditional working-class pub and replace it with theming designed to attract a younger, more affluent clientele. Similarly, while games like snooker and darts continue to be played in British pubs, they have been appropriated by television and turned into prime-time spectator viewing. Modern pubs are most likely to offer satellite broadcasting on a large plasma screen rather than traditional bar games as an attraction.

Arguably, the most dramatic example of commercial appropriation is football. Long held to be the 'working man's game' in Britain, the sport experienced a middle-class putsch in the 1990s. This was a result of a combination of soaring admission prices, the new cosmopolitanism in the game produced by importing foreign players and the emergence of Sky Television's quasi-monopoly status in broadcasting live games (King 1998). Soccer grounds became gentrified and the cost of attending matches soared. The traditional fan base struggled to keep up with the rising cost of attendance. They were forced into rationing attendance at live matches and resorted to watching broadcasts on satellite TV as a second-hand form of participation.

The conclusion is inescapable: withstanding the colonizing logic of consumer culture is formidably difficult. Consider the recent case of P2P file-sharing. P2P technology is shorthand for the peer-to-peer communication technology that became a serious threat to the music sales of record companies at the start of the twenty-first century. P2P is a communications model in which participants share their communications files and permit free downloading. The P2P concept is not new. For many decades, ham radio networks used the concept to communicate analogue voice signals. The DARPANet system in the 1970s, which was the crucible for the internet, was based in a free peer-to-peer system of communication exchange between government and university mainframes. However, the internet pioneer for producing free communication of intellectual property under copyright for the masses was Napster.

Started by a 19-year-old college drop-out, Shawn Fanning, in June of 1999, Napster was an MP3 (digital music) search and delivery service that searched for record holdings on computers linked to the system and enabled their transfer to individuals through downloading. This was a clear form of leisure *resistance* since it defined leisure identity in response to a system of leisure control that was widely perceived as unfair and authoritarian. At its peak Napster provided as many as 1 billion music files (Van Hoorebeek 2003: 143). Napster promoted itself as a populist alternative to the excessive profits of both recording companies like EMI, Time Warner and Sony and the greed of major pop stars. It offered music for the people at no more than the cost of an internet connection. In terms of the commercialization of leisure Napster was a clear attempt to challenge commodification and rationalization by decentralizing power and choice to the consumer.

Within six months of trading Napster was sued by the Recording Industry Association of America (RIAA) who alleged copyright infringement and demanded a fee of $100,000 each time a digital file was downloaded on the system. Three months later in February 2000, US universities initiated an attempt to ban Napster due to overwhelming student use of the system. In April of 2000 the heavy metal band Metallica sued Napster for copyright infringement asserting that the free exchange of intellectual property in copyright is illegal. After a prolonged and complex legal battle, in which the Ninth Circuit US District Judge Marilyn Hall Patel denounced Napster as a 'monster', the company suspended operations in May 2002.

However, this did not put an end to net downloading of free digital files. Second-generation P2P-trading commercial quality services like Kazaa, XoloX, Gnutella and iMesh took over. Van Hoorebeek (2003: 143) estimated that 81 companies now exist. In May 2003 the Kazaa network was the most in-demand software with 230.3 million downloads and an uptake of 12 million a month (*Guardian*, 23 July 2003). Moreover, second-generation companies making full use of new broadband internet systems have diversified, offering perfect digital file shares of music and film.

Arguably, the difficulties of policing P2P internet communities are insoluble. Although the technology is still in its infancy, it offers the potential of a fully decentralized mechanism for downloading digital music files. Higher bandwith, low-cost storage and the provision of powerful desktop storers are likely to facilitate wider use. The system is as wide as the number of users which is theoretically uncontainable, is not dependent on a central server and organically responds to attempts by copyright holders to block exchange. Copyright-holders have concentrated their efforts on attempting to develop encryption technologies that prevent downloading without payment. The RIAA has subpoenaed consumers offering new download material on networks like Kazaa, claiming violation of copyright law. However, devising an effective mechanism of policing and stopping them is formidably difficult. To

tral platform has been invented and fee structures for
ʒ are variable.

ɛ appears to be a mix between self-regulation on the part of
ner and some form of licensing system for downloading.
Doubtles. the institutional and behavioural parameters will take several
years to work out. Notwithstanding that, the determination of copyright-
holders to retain control and a secure flow of pecuniary reward for
ownership of intellectual property has been reasserted. It is unlikely to
be significantly abated by the attempts of renegade search engines to
decommodify music by neutralizing the regulation of digital file-sharing.
The efforts of Napster and second-generation music-sharing internet
companies to liberalize access by making the consumer king have been
thwarted by the assembled forces of intellectual copyright control who
insist on maintaining a commodity relation between the output of the
artist and record company and the public. The decommodification of
popular music through the P2P technology has prompted copyright-
holders to recommodify and extend intellectual property rights over
digital downloads on the internet. The de-rationalization of popular
music by seeking to lever control from the record companies and artists
and pass it to the consumer has been met by re-rationalization under
which service providers are forced to comply with legal restraints and
the record companies move to a licence form of P2P downloading.

The corporate coopting of folk and popular forms of leisure and commercializing them for pecuniary gain is a cornerstone of contemporary
consumer culture. Various studies demonstrate the power of record companies to appropriate the music, construct youth markets and 'commodify
rebellion' (Sanjek and Sanjek 1996; Goodman 1997; Seiler 2000). They
argue that mergers and acquisitions have boxed in development opportunities for independent companies. The cultivation of new recording
stars by independents immediately attracts the acquisition interests of
the major companies like Time-Warner, Thorn-EMI, Sony and Polygram.
Of course, independent record companies beat the game and produce
successful performers from time to time. But their capacity to exploit
and develop the product is limited. The commercialization and commodification of popular music are evident both in the recording and
marketing process and the sponsorship of major live acts by corporations.

Although it is tempting to adopt a functionalist reading of the cooption
of leisure forms, stressing *à la* Cheek and Burch (1976) the integrative
function of consumer-leisure patterns of behaviour in solidifying
social order, or Ritzer's (2000, 2004) thesis that the fate of alternative
and critical forms and practice of leisure is to be 'McDonaldized', it is

wrong to do so. *Some* patterns of consumption and leisure succeed in resistance.

For example, recreational drug use is a complex phenomenon. There are tensions in the literature between writers who stress the dependency of subcultures upon ascendant values of hedonism and freedom, and those who dwell on the politics of addiction and its relation to poverty (Moore 1990; South 1998; Wilson 2002). However, Becker's (1953) classic argument that recreational drug use involves the formation and mobilization of oppositional identity is broadly confirmed. Of course, what is meant by *oppositional* identity depends on what recreational drug users perceive they are opposing. The accentuated significance that Willis's (1978) hippy subcultures place upon challenging the values of 'straight' society carries over in contemporary youth subcultures. However, recreational drug use also involves creating spaces of escape from routine, standardization and conformity. Escape areas may not constitute an oppositional culture, but they coexist in some dissonance with the values of 'the American way' or 'respectable society' (Rojek 1993). Loophole drug cultures engineer escape vectors in existence that offer the experience of freedom, power and spontaneity that formal leisure settings frequently fail to deliver. In these loopholes individuals may exercise and explore the ambivalent relationship that they have with the dominant value system of conformity, possessive individualism and rational self-control. Drug subcultures exploit and develop Hall and Jefferson's (1975) argument about cultural practice that allows for 'resistance through rituals' as an everyday occurence. The covert, ceremonious procedures of taking marijuana, cocaine, heroin and ecstacy tablets 'write over' the inscriptions of ideology and interpellation required by social order. Lyng (1990, 1991) has helpfully referred to this as 'edgework' by which he means activities that test the boundaries of conventional identity, practice and association. By going beyond the boundaries, loophole drug subcultures create private, ritually sanctioned spaces of cultural ambivalence. While ambivalence in loophole recreational drug subcultures is intrinsically much more equivocal than oppositional drug subcultures, it nevertheless departs from convention and celebrates social values that contrast with sobriety, thrift and self-control.

Resistance can take the form of subcultures that adopt deviant means to achieve generally sanctioned ends. Robert Merton's (1968) famous analysis of crime and the American dream argued thus. Merton held that the end of personal wealth is a universal goal of the American dream. The means to achieve this end are not equably distributed.

Following Weber, Merton held that the wealthy enjoy superior life chances over the poor. In these circumstances, some elements among the disadvantaged resort to illegitimate means (crime) to achieve the end of wealth.

Anton Blok (1974), working in a very different tradition of historical anthropology, points to similar mechanisms in the formation of the Mafia. Incidentally, his work demonstrates how homogeneous consumption and leisure patterns are crucial in the recruitment and solidification of the Italian Mafia. In particular, he highlights the role of village feasts and fairs in providing opportunities for males to engage in 'contest struggles' of physical strength which are not only leisure forms but play an important political role in establishing Mafia leadership patterns in the village.

Likewise, Maloney (2002) provides a compelling account of how leisure forms in Northern Ireland, especially the working men's club and pub and religious–community parades, contributed to identity formation and practices of resistance in the IRA in the 1960s and 70s. While, for obvious reasons, we do not yet have studies of the role of consumption and leisure patterns in establishing identity formation in terrorist organizations like al-Qaida, we know enough about the role of consumption and leisure in forming transgressive and oppositional forms of solidarity to predict a strong correlation.

Mass communications and leisure practice may also be a means of resisting propaganda and developing oppositional identity. Neither the Nazis nor the Soviets succeeded in controlling the airwaves. The radio broadcast party propaganda, but it also transmitted anti-fascist and anti-communist material from the West. In the post-Stalinist period, in the Eastern European command economies, radio and television played a crucial and still largely undocumented role in providing data about Western lifestyle, popular music, art, diversity and affluence that exposed the poverty of life under the communist regime and contributed to popular resistance against party rule.

The exploration of resistance through leisure, the internalization of the politics of resistance and its relation to the attempt of the state to impose order are keynote themes in the Birmingham School approach to the study of contemporary culture (Hall and Jefferson 1975; Hall *et al.* 1978; Clarke and Critcher 1985). Although alive to the role of leisure in cultural reproduction, it stresses the affinity between culture and leisure as forms of resistance. By developing leisure and play forms that, so to speak, are *inscribed* over the requirements of consumer culture, individuals and groups position themselves in alternative or oppositional space that challenges the rule of capital and the state (Hall and Jefferson 1975;

Hall *et al.* 1978). Resistance through leisure by forms of music, fashion, sport, trespassing, petty theft, writing and drama generates cultural and political capital that acts as a bulwark against capitalism. This extended the use of violence as a political response in leisure forms and practice. The example of mugging was examined at length since, at the time, it dominated media agendas (Hall *et al.* 1978).

There were two stages to the argument. First, the popular connotation of mugging with idleness and irrational behaviour among young males was rejected. Most people equate mugging with mindless violence. It is often bracketed with leisure in the popular press as a phenomenon associated with leisure since muggers are portrayed as people with too much idle time on their hands. The Birmingham approach turned this argument on its head. It examined mugging not as an isolated type of illegal and mindless behaviour, but as a response to the contradictions of relations of inclusion and exclusion in the British nation state. The *positioning* of sections of society in time-rich/economically poor identities unintentionally generates the propensity to use violence as a means of breaking routine, redressing inequality and marginalization. Thus, mugging is ultimately related to the crisis of citizenship and moral regulation in the nation state.

The second stage of the argument developed this proposition to elaborate a powerful historical analysis of how the dominant economic and political groups in society fight a complex 'war of manoeuvre' to incorporate protest and resistance. The pressures 'from below' to extend civil liberties and achieve redistributive justice redraw the boundaries of civil society. The provision of public education, health, pensions and recreation facilities signalled the recognition of the state that it has a duty to improve general conditions. The stimulus to improvement is not simply dictated by humanitarian impulses. In the British case, the construction of the welfare state was bound up with new relations of dependency with respect to the state and civil society which were designed to incorporate the people under the rule of the hegemonic power bloc. Hall and his associates (1978) present economic redistribution and the revision of civil rights as strategies to tie individuals into social order.

Positioning is intended to soothe social tensions. However, over time, it has the unintended consequence of stimulating new tensions as individuals realize that they are mis-positioned by the state and the welfare and state care system is failing them. Mugging is interpreted as one response to this structural contradiction.

The Birmingham approach demonstrated how the *representation* of mugging operates as a means of controlling culture and leisure practice.

Quantitative analysis of incidents of mugging over several decades established that the rate of mugging in the 1970s when the media panic was most extreme was actually *lower* than in previous postwar decades. By enlisting the concepts of **media amplification** and **media spiral** the Birmingham team attempted to show how the state sponsored anxiety about 'unruly behaviour' in order to discipline a whole way of life that is perceived by the governing echelons of the power bloc as threatening to the status quo.

> **Media amplification** is the exaggeration of popular anxieties and state fears about particular forms of practice which are labelled in negative terms. **Media spiral** is the process of sucking more and more media outlets into the vortex of generating popular anxiety by amplifying the threat to society posed by particular forms of negative practice. Both concepts illustrate Cohen's (1972) idea of 'moral panic' which is an exaggered, media-amplified social reaction to relatively minor acts of social deviance.

Already in this (Hall *et al.* 1978) work an important shift in the Birmingham School approach to the analysis of culture and leisure is evident. Identity and resistance are interpreted not simply at the level of the intentions and will of actors. In addition, the forms of cultural *signifying practice* that positions actors are also central. By the term 'signifying practice' is meant the system of representation that positions actors through coding and theming.

It was a bold but controversial line of analysis. For one thing, it invited the inference that mugging should be investigated as a *creative* response to structural inequality. Of course, Hall and his associates were not advocating a pro-mugging argument. Their concern was to elucidate how mugging was *positioned* in the structure of economic inequality and processes of inclusion and exclusion in civil society. The failure of the state to achieve redistributive justice made the state-sponsored ideology of welfare and equality appear fraudulent. Mugging was interpreted as a *political* response to the bankruptcy of the state's 'war of manoeuvre'.

The Birmingham approach also illuminated how moral debate conditions behaviour. Most of the media portrayed the rise of the 'law and order' society in Britain in the 1980s as a response to popular anxieties about crime, racial tension and overgenerous welfare provision. Hall and his associates demonstrate how politics amplifies media recognition of sensitive issues and translates it into the domain of everyday life. In turn, popular anxieties are used as the basis for 'get tough' policies on crime, unemployment, idleness and political forms and lifestyles that are regarded to pose a threat to 'normal, family life'.

The use of leisure to break laws and expose oppression has a long history. Marches, rallies and other forms of peaceful process have political objectives, but they also include ludic elements. Indeed, pouring scorn on political figures and heaping derision upon unpopular laws is part and parcel of the democratic process. The recent disturbances at World Trade Organization economic summits and the coordinated May Day protests against multinational domination in London ritually use play elements to destabilize power regimes.

Key points

- Leisure performs functions of representation, identity, control and resistance for social groups within society which contribute to the dynamic of order and change.
- Leisure functions reflect shifting balance of power relations between individuals and groups. *Contra* the presuppositions of the systems approach, leisure does not necessarily function to enhance the social system.
- Leisure functions reflect the twin circuits of production and consumption and the management of aggression and sexuality that constitute the primary regulative mechanisms in society.
- Mass communications, the market and the state have displaced the Church, the family and the community as the decisive institutions of moral regulation. They set the context for representation, control, identity formation and resistance in leisure forms and practice.
- The control of leisure practice has shifted from external restraint to self-policing. Representation and identity formation are crucial in constituting 'the critical, reflective self' and resistance.
- Leisure forms show a strong tendency to be colonized by corporations. In the nineteenth and twentieth centuries leisure practice converged with consumer culture.

4
Coding and Representation

In this chapter you will be:

- Introduced to the concepts of leisure forms and practice as types of coding and representation.
- Presented with an explanation of the difference between encoding and decoding.
- Appraised of MacCannell's concept of 'markers' and Gottdiener's of 'theming'.
- Invited to explore the relationship between mythogenesis and leisure.

Leisure is not simply a set of behavioural trajectories, identity types, structures of power, forms of practice and a nexus of institutions. It is also a system of representation. In the West, leisure carries strong connotations of freedom, choice and self-determination. The options that we possess in our leisure choices and the resources that we spend in pursuing them relative to non-capitalist countries legitimate the worth of the entire social, economic and political system. The connotations are so pronounced that it is reasonable to present leisure as one of the mainstays of the ideology of Western individualism and liberty.

There are many ways in which the political implications of this may be investigated. For example, the ideology of freedom in leisure reinforces the work ethic. For by identifying leisure as the reward for work, Western ideology articulates a powerful rhetoric of work-centred existence. Paid employment or marriage to an income-earner or owner of capital is presented as the *a priori* of leisure. By extension, those who elect to centre their life around leisure or reject paid employment in favour of some version of state-sponsored subsistence are classified as anomalous citizens. In extreme circles, they may be classified as generic replaceable citizens whose right to entitlement is suspended by their decision *not* to engage in paid employment. Leisure is thus redefined as an entitlement of workers and owners of capital, but its status among the unemployed is ambivalent. Indeed, there is a strong tendency to moralize about the leisure of the wageless, notably by twinning it with idleness or crime.

Similarly, the powerful positive connections between leisure and freedom in the West result in strong inhibitions to reform the system. The liberty granted under the regime of capitalism thus becomes understood as an inherent social virtue, so that attempts to extend liberty by steering behaviour beyond the boundaries of capitalism are rendered intrinsically suspect. In this way, Western forms of leisure and sport become ideologically positioned as the desirable global norms, and non-Western forms are represented as marginal and transient.

Picturing leisure as a system of representation that advances the ideology of the West lifts the analysis of leisure from naive libertarianism. It recognizes leisure as a channel of social conditioning. The question of the rhetoric of freedom, choice and self-determination in relation to the representation of leisure is then identified as a focal point for enquiry. Once this issue is made transparent the question of the representation of leisure forms as a type of power becomes salient.

Encoding and decoding

Stuart Hall's (1973, 1993b) famous encoding/decoding model is an attempt to explain how ideology cuts into behaviour at the levels of culture and politics. In so far as leisure is a form of culture, the model is also relevant for exploring the relationship between ideology, representation, form and practice in leisure studies. The question that Hall sets himself is to examine how public communication structures everyday life. The model postulates that mass communications is the fulcrum for ordering public discourse. However, this claim for mass communications tacitly reinforces Habermas's (1962) argument concerning the **public sphere**. According to Habermas, in the nineteenth century public space emerged in civil society that recognized the rights of citizens to debate and change the normative institutions of power (the monarchy, the state, political parties, the law, policing, schooling). The public sphere was established as an arena in society in which universal rights and

The **public sphere** is the network of discourses and institutions in civil society in which issues of citizenship are communicated and subject to interrogation. This network includes the various branches of the mass media (radio, television, the press) and also the legal system, education, social work and policing. This network establishes principles of normative order in everyday life and is fundamental in regulating subjective behaviour.

responsibilities of citizenship were examined, interrogated and developed. For Hall, the public sphere has been colonized by the mass media which, together with the state, set the agenda for debate and propose the parameters of what is legitimate in respect of citizenship rights. For example, in relation to the question of leisure, the mass media representation of pornography, the dangers of unemployment, the rights and wrongs of cannabis use, to name but a few issues of the day, shape the popular discourse about leisure conduct. The mass media present data that inform the public about issues and influence judgements. Of course, data in the public sphere are tested against local knowledge. But the authority of the BBC, Fox News or CNN compared with folk knowledge is outwardly superior since it has access to wider on-location, comparative and historical data than, say, family or community folklore or wisdom. The absorption of mass communications data in leisure is therefore a type of moral regulation since it carries judgements about desired forms of identity, association and practice. According to Hall, mass communication is encoded with a variety of presuppositions regarding legitimacy, rights and duties that operate in conscious and subliminal ways to shape individual behaviour. Hall's concern is to elucidate how encoding operates and to expose its political functions and objectives. Decoding is the accomplishment of an objective reading of encoding processes so that the political dimension and subliminal messages are fully exposed. Encoding and decoding operate at a variety of conscious and subconscious levels.

Communication may have an overt ideological purpose, but it also operates to elicit 'preferred readings' in the audience. A *preferred reading* is a desired response to coding that arises from the *loading* of media communication with prompts, symbols or other suggestive devices. The equilibrium between encoding and decoding is inherently unstable, making transformation through exposure a legitimate objective of counter-cultural politics.

Hall's theoretical intention is twofold. First, he seeks to reveal the constructionist role of the mass media in putting a gloss on social reality. Second, he seeks to reject behaviourist and determinist readings of individual behaviour as a blank subject by proposing the notion of the active audience.

While there have been many criticisms of the encoding–decoding model, not least from Hall himself (1993b) (see also McGuigan 1992; Rojek 2003), the perspective remains useful to apply to leisure as a system of representation. Theoretically speaking, the ways in which we use leisure time and space are infinite. The fact that trajectories of leisure behaviour are regular and predictable imply that conduct is patterned and, further, that that pattern follows networks of power which operate at many levels in everyday life. Representations of leisure through advertising, television, film, popular music, medical models of healthy behaviour or criminological constructs of deviant behaviour are seminal in organizing our 'natural', 'common-sense' perspectives with respect to legitimacy, value and responsibility in leisure conduct. For example, through images of 'the body beautiful' we formulate masculine and feminine identity ideals and allow our behaviour to be influenced by fashion. Celebrities like David Beckham, Brad Pitt, Jennifer Lopez and Kylie Minogue function as identity objects and role models that shape our leisure behaviour.

Similarly, representations in the Western public sphere of life and leisure in Islamic countries establish models of the 'Other' which may be used to legitimate domestic forms of leisure over 'foreign' alternatives. These representations often operate through myths and stereotypes to generate preferred readings of Western superiority. Images of public stoning or amputation of adulterers in Islamic fundamentalist countries, combined with representations of correlative dogmatic policies on female dress, alcohol consumption and 'respectable' behaviour, produce a one-dimensional view of liberty, leisure and Islam against which the West is made to seem intrinsically more rational, tolerant and progressive. In the Islamic world a counter-ideology operates in which Western liberalism in matters of alcohol and sexuality is branded as decadent.

Encoding and decoding are central in the organization of leisure identity and public responses to leisure forms and practice. Our leisure choices are stamped with representations of leisure role models and idealized life options that are perpetuated in the mass media, the advertising campaigns of multinationals and state public communications policies. Methodologically, leisure practice, in the sense of mental and physical choices and actions, is co-determinate with representations of leisure. Leisure Studies should therefore apply a two-pronged approach to the study of leisure forms and practices that recognizes the umbilical cord between action and representation. The encoding and decoding questions posed by the study of representation in turn raise questions of ideology, interpellation, economics and politics that clarify how leisure is framed, the leisure choices that we make and the leisure trajectories that we pursue.

MacCannell and Gottdiener: markers and theming

In the study of leisure, tourism and consumer culture there have been several attempts to develop a **semiotics** of free time behaviour. Two of the most useful are Dean MacCannell's (1999) theory of markers in tourist practice and Mark Gottdiener's (1997) work on the theming of consumer and leisure cultures.

Semiotics is the science of signs. It holds that the sign is a spoken or written marker (signifier) for a culturally prescribed concept (signified). The investigation between the signifier and the signified reveals how power functions in the articulation between cultural symbols and material objects.

MacCannell (1999: 109) follows the philosopher Charles Peirce (1992) in arguing that *a sign represents something to someone else.* His work differentiates between *a sight, a marker* and *a tourist.* The sight refers to the physical object (the Tower of London or the Lincoln Memorial); the marker is data that represent the sight (postcards, tourist brochures, guide books, stories told by visitors); and the tourist is the individual who culturally assimilates the marker and the sight. Sights, markers and processes of assimilation are culturally constructed. This entails a *condensation* of meaning in which various sorts of data are mixed and blended. For MacCannell, sights are not simply physical objects but symbolic *systems of signs.* He makes the important point that signs *narrate* just as people *narrate.* The task of the researcher is to unravel the interrelationships between signs within the sign system and the fusion of meanings in popular consciousness. The fusion of these interrelationships is culturally coded. For example, the Statue of Liberty symbolizes, *inter alia*, the goal of liberty for mankind, America, hope, freedom from want and the friendship between America and Europe.

But this is only expressly so from the standpoint of Christian white American citizens or tourists. Conversely, for a member of an Islamic fundamentalist or militant African American, the Statue of Liberty symbolizes colonial domination, white power, Christian supremacy and ethnocentricity.

In media-saturated societies markers frequently *condense* many meanings. For example, the representation of London as a physical sight consists of symbolic markers. Tourists do not *see* London. They see Big Ben, the Tate Gallery, the Globe Theatre, red telephone boxes, Hackney cabs, mounted Horse Guards, pubs or Tower Bridge. The condensation of these symbolic markers constitutes the sight. But this process is itself mediated through cultural constructions that influence the tourist's assimilation of the sight. For example, the London that emerges in Shakespeare's plays, the novels of Charles Dickens, the pop music of the Beatles, Coldplay or Dido, the paintings of David Hockney or Lucien Freud or Mike Myer's portrayals in the *Austin Powers* comedy series imprints symbolic layers on the psychology of the sight that influence assimilation and orientation.

MacCannell's work on markers suggests that tourist and leisure space should be analytically recast as a system of hieroglyphics in which complex strands of meaning are mixed and cross-blended. Analogously, it points to a hallucinatory quality in leisure and tourist space that derives from the assimilation of physical cultures through condensation and the restaging of physical cultures by the same means (see also Hannigan 1998; Frisby 2001). In MacCannell's sociology, sights are always partly apparitions. For the consumer, the physical space is always squared off against an information overload that lays down various ideologically produced prompts for the assimilation of the setting.

One weakness in MacCannell's approach is that it is skewed towards the analysis of the popular *consumption* of markers and sights. To some extent, this is welcome since it places due weight upon the active role of the consumer in interpreting and exchanging data. However, by the same token it neglects to explore the conjunction between *producers*, markers and consumer culture. While it is legitimate to explore the non-commercial roots of myths and stereotypes in relation to tourist and leisure space, the analysis must be built upon an understanding of the role of commerce in manufacturing leisure and tourist culture.

In as much as this is so, Gottdiener's (1997) approach provides a serviceable counterpoint. Alive to the complexity of encoding and decoding processes in the circuit between production and consumption, Gottdiener assigns importance to the commercial manipulation of leisure and consumer cultures. The concept of theming refers to the cultural production of commercially defined spaces designed to operate as containers for human interaction. Among the examples he examines are Disneyland, Las Vegas casinos, shopping malls, cafés and airports. Each of these 'containers' directs consumers to operate programmatically and engage in preferred systems of action that are usually plotted to involve monetary exchange. For example, entry into leisure settings, like the MGM Grand on the Las Vegas strip, involves confronting gaming tables and one-armed bandits positioned to seduce you into gambling. The provision of a complimentary or subsidized buffet is designed to increase your time in the casino and magnify your exposure to opportunities for gambling, drinking cocktails or buying souvenirs. Employing a combination of perspectives drawn from Urban Studies, semiotics and Marxism, Gottdiener shows how the theming of activities is progressively colonized by the commercial imperative. The allocation of shopping, working and play areas in the city produces a variety of commercial ancillary settings and codes in which corporations and state officialdom manipulate and control communication to exploit and develop consumer culture.

On this reading, themed environments in leisure and consumer culture are regulated, commercialized spaces designed to stimulate consumption for the realization of profits. Like MacCannell, Gottdiener (1997: 156) acknowledges the importance of markers and condensation in making voluntary behaviour programmatic. However, crucially he relates the production of markers to *mass marketing* and powerful commercial interests. This acknowledges layers in the sign system of leisure and culture, but reconciles the juxtaposition of these layers to the capitalist dynamic of profit maximization. As Gottdiener (1997: 156) elaborates:

> Themed environments display a surprisingly limited range of symbolic motifs because they need to appeal to the largest possible consumer markets. They have replaced the public space of daily life, characteristic of the early cities, with a regulated place of consumer communion that restricts access by privileging its availability to the more affluent members of society.

While this prioritizes the role of commercial producers in the construction of themed environments it does not necessarily reduce the role of consumers to mute dependence. On the contrary, Gottdiener (1997: 156–8) vigorously rejects the dominant ideology model of consumer and leisure behaviour that holds that conduct blindly fulfils the imperatives of capitalism. Instead, he insists on the role of consumers as active agents with the capacity to negotiate, resist and oppose dominant themed imperatives. However, modes of negotiation, resistance and opposition are conditioned by economic scarcity and cultural inequality. Our ability to wrest autonomy from the themed markets of modern consumer culture is socially patterned.

One weakness of Gottdiener's approach is that the emphasis upon corporate capitalism and the state produces a thin reading of subcultural theming. There is an obvious link between identity, practice and theming in gang and drug subcultures. These subcultures frequently define themselves in opposition to the values of corporate capital and the state. Studying them shows how theming in leisure and community settings operates to create alternative or oppositional forms of identity and action. Looked at in this way theming is a pivotal feature of human groups. While the forms adapted by multinationals and the state are harnessed to commercial goals and the project of social control, they draw on a repertoire of solidarity representation that is pre-capitalist. In particular, they frequently incorporate myth.

Mythogenesis and leisure

Mythogenesis refers to the development, reproduction and transformation of a narrative that dramatizes world vision and sense of community and reduces it to a series of compelling metaphors. The narrative form selectively, and, one might add, *seductively*, encapsulates human action upon nature and culture. Thus, it draws on people's relation to the land, the place of God (or gods) in the community and the marking and commemoration of decisive events such as battles, wars or heroic journeys. The celebration and reproduction of these symbolic materials are centrally concentrated in leisure forms and practice. Myth transforms these features into original and eternal markers of national or racial identity.

In capitalist culture theming often draws upon myth, but its imperative is to match continuity with consumption. In contrast, myth matches continuity with solidarity, in the sense of accentuating social inclusion and enlarging imaginary space beyond the mundane world of goods and services. Myths are non-rational and ultimately articulate relations of racial or religious faith. This is one reason why they are hard to dispel. At the levels of individual psychology and social consciousness they operate as mechanisms that delineate lines of social inclusion and exclusion. They may also be enlisted as resources for radical critical ideologies in which the excluded seek to redraw boundaries (Slotkin 1973: 6–24; 1985: 19).

Although both involve idealization and stereotypes, myth differs from ideology in important ways. Ideology is the self-image of a group or class within a race. While it is imposed upon others to legitimate domination, it derives from the consciousness of a group or class in relation to other men and women. Myth is a marker of race or religion that ultimately relies upon supernatural beliefs and convictions for its power. It invokes spiritual distinctions of destiny or fate. Typically, these are presented as timeless and unchangeable. Ideology is historically and spatially anchored and knows itself to be so. Myth is part of racial psyche and cosmos. Although it may be embodied in morphology it is as migrant as race. An example of myth is the belief of the Third Reich in Aryan supremacy. An example of ideology is the proposition that working-class heritage is not as worthy of preservation as elite culture.

Ideologies and myths leave inscriptions upon landscapes, cultures and leisure forms. But because they are disseminated throughout culture in art, literature, schooling, sport and leisure as eternal verities, myths are more difficult to isolate and uproot. Although they are usually most cogently expressed by dominant racial groups, they permeate the racial formation and operate as one of the central markers of social membership. Just as historians routinely question the idea of myth-proof history, geographers query the notion of myth-proof space. Even 'wild' places like deserts, jungles and mountains are etched by myth. They have been 'preserved' as symbols of unmediated Nature for the purposes of tourism, or 'protected' as markers of heritage (Urry 1995; Whatmore 2002). The implication is that they represent a timeless reality that precedes man. Yet at one important level the preservation and protection of Nature and culture produce and reproduce delusion.

Nature and heritage symbolize spaces that are, as it were, timeless, and through which successive individuals and generations can ritually acknowledge racial, national or human bonds of community. Yet preservation and protection are actions that change the character of 'natural' and 'cultural' space as decisively as acts of urban–industrial colonization. Preservation reveals the myth of permanence, since to preserve is to interpret and, by this means, to lay the foundations for reinterpretation (Lowenthal 1985: 410). What the study of heritage sites reveals is the values and interests of those who attribute to a sight the distinction of preservation.

The myth of the native as a 'leisure resource'

It seems extraordinary to us to think of American Indians and Africans as leisure *resources*. Yet this is how Cortez and his conquistadors saw them. Later stages in colonialism muddied the picture. Cortez regarded the native as a play resource for Europeans because he believed the West to be incontrovertibly superior. Natives could be abused sexually and butchered, their cultures and religions could be denounced and they and their children could be forced into slavery because they were believed to be intrinsically inferior to their Western masters.

Todorov's (1982) study of the conquistadors and America addresses the power of the myth of the 'New World' in Spanish history. Eventually, upon the 'untrodden' soil 'discovered' by Columbus, Cortez and Diaz, the Western heights of science, government and Christianity would be erected. But first, from this soil, the myths of cities of gold, bullion and the comely savage would be plundered by conquest. The New World heralded natural abundance and hope, but in every important particular of government, culture and religion the Spanish conquistadors believed it to be inferior to the Old World of Europe.

The natives were excluded from partnership in the European world of science and government because their assumed barbarism branded them as an inferior species. New World natives were mythologized as an awkward mix between innocence and barbarity. Worshippers of strange gods, cannibals, slaves of magic and superstition, apparently work-shy, indolent, above all *naifs*, the natives were cast as *permanent Others*, despite Christianity's rearguard efforts to 'redeem' the brightest and the best. Although these myths clustered around the incontrovertible fact of racial difference, they filtered through every institutional level including play and recreation.

Todorov's account assigns proper attention to the violence inherent in the European self-image of superiority. The myths of native innocence and barbarism launched a programme of near genocide against Mesoamerica's Indian population. But he also demonstrates the emergence of hybrid mythologies as the natives reacted to European condescension and physical aggression. Natives and native cultures were repositioned as more 'pure' than Western forms and the native body more innocent and sensual.

These myths did not die with Cortez and his conquistadors. The association of a new beginning and the mobilization of violent myths about the Native Indian were appropriated in the expansionist American attitude to the Western frontier. The West was explicitly regarded as the boundary of Eurocentric civilization and native Indian traditions were classified as dangerous, wild and intensely sexual. The landscape was believed to teem with life options unavailable in the East. Although much attention has been devoted to the economic careerism of nineteenth-century adventurers like Andrew Jackson and William Tecumeseh Sherman who headed West to make their fortunes, the promise of sexual licence, open spaces and clean air was also a powerful magnet for male migrants from the Eastern seaboard and Europe (Kennett 2001; Rimini 2001).

Western colonial thought developed a habit of categorizing 'native' bodies, landscapes and ethnicities as 'pre-civil'. Western myths of the 'New World' operated with the seductive notion of a cultural–geographic border beyond which sexual repression, inhibition and control are suspended. This is deeply engrained in Western ideology. For example, the Crusaders were attracted to the Orient as a means of not simply vindicating their faith but discovering the reality behind the stereotypes of the harem, Arab and African fornication, opulence and ease of living (Wheatcroft 2003: 195–7). This was frequently expressed in the West's *faux* concern to assimilate the Other. Generally speaking, this was no more than a pre-technological form of *sampling*, in which elements of Otherness were briefly absorbed only to be whimsically discarded.

For instance, when the first Ottoman embassies opened in France in the 1720s, it became fashionable for the French to dress in turbans, heavy silks, furs and flowing robes as a statement against Christian puritanism and prudence. In the 1840s Bohemian Paris and London were entranced by myths of Oriental libertinism. Flaubert (1983) and Nerval (1851) travelled to the Orient in search of colour, excitement, opium and courtesans schooled in the sexual arts of the *Kama Sutra*. Images of the Orient abounded in the poetry of Charles Baudelaire and later Arthur Rimbaud. The Orient combined dreams of escape and travel. This flirtation with the Islamic world may have left important traces in Western culture but, as Elizabeth Wilson (2002: 141) shrewdly notes, the Bohemian dream of escape probably had more to do with 'inverted imperialism' than a genuine attempt to defy and subvert bourgeois society.

Although the myth of the New World is regarded sceptically today and the Eurocentric, white myth of superiority is routinely scolded, both have left powerful marks on the human relation to landscape, culture and leisure. The American West continues to be regarded as more wild, untamed, primitive and exciting than the East or the European homelands (Slotkin 1973, 1985, 1998). Racist myths about Caucasians and non-Caucasians persist in leisure and society, even if it is much harder to proclaim them now without censure.

Deciphering myth

Myth problematizes the relationship between object and subject because it permeates both categories, often in ways that operate below the level of consciousness. Myth is embedded in complex ways in the morphology of the leisure landscapes and cultures we study, and the system of perception and analysis we deploy to further this end. However, we can take some steps to decipher and understand it through comparative and historical analysis.

For example, the late eighteenth-century and early nineteenth-century Romantic tradition bestowed on wild places, such as the English Lake District, the Scottish Highlands and the European Alps, natural, immemorial qualities. Poetry, fiction and travel literature acted as markers influencing the assimilation of these physical spaces. They eventually delineated new cultural categories of romanticized Nature. In constructing these categories the relationship between mankind and Nature was irrevocably changed. Nature became aestheticized.

The rational recreation movement in the late nineteenth century also contributed to coding and theming natural leisure space, but in different ways. In particular, the idealization of the countryside was partly achieved by the promotion of healthy exercise and the requirement to create beautiful, natural fresh-air settings (Bunce 1994). These settings were prized as aids in improving the balance between mind and body that was deemed essential for the health of mankind and which urban–industrial culture threatened.

Both the Romantic and rational recreation attitudes to Nature are constructed around disenchantment with the city and urban–industrial culture in general. They are attempts to re-enchant a world that has largely succumbed to urban–industrial colonization. Re-enchantment operated through practical measures to sequester Nature and countryside for leisure and, crucially, the mobilization of myth.

Actually, the Romantics *reinvented* the relationship between man and mountains, deserts, woodland, rivers and the sea by defining them as more authentic than the relationships between man, technology, industry and the city. This vision was wrapped up in representations of eternity but in fact was based on the historical realization of human control over Nature. After all, before the Romantic era, mountains, deserts, woodland, rivers and the sea were regarded to cloak many hazards as well as wonders. Only with the rise of science and technology did the notion of preserving wild natural space as heritage become culturally captivating. It did so because men knew they possessed the unequivocal power to tame Nature.

The rational recreation movement took this a stage further by relating to Nature as a resource in the wider task of self-improvement. By protecting the countryside and visiting it, we create, so to speak, a *medicinal* landscape that contributes to our health as a species. The **medicinal landscape** was overtly utilitarian.

Medicinal landscape of nature

- Provides balance for mind and body
- Restores energies dissipated in work and urban existence
- Renews relationship between man and the land
- Cleanses life options

Breathing clean air, rambling over unspoiled hills and dales and fording natural mountain streams were promoted as inherently therapeutic. The countryside was allocated the task of restoring the Cartesian balance between mind and body that the city violated by the requirements of the labour process. Rational recreation promoted the country and Nature as alienable from the urban–industrial world. This convention was again based on the presumption of superior human power – a presumption which was so authoritative that it was not until the end of the twentieth century that the effects of urban–industrial pollution on the natural environment became widely acknowledged and a cause célèbre for Green politics.

Nostalgia is a pronounced feature of urban–industrial cultures because they produce an atmosphere of change and uncertainty in the urban–industrial landscape that is associated with anxiety about the present. Where the environment is recognized to be at risk through pollution, roads and dwelling space expand remorselessly and economic conditions are volatile and unpredictable, the past presents a seductive image of refuge. The preservation of the countryside and Nature can certainly be viewed as the expression of nostalgia. But so is the incorporation of sites of historical importance into the landscape of heritage and leisure.

The theming of these sites is one of the most significant leisure developments of the last quarter of a century. Urry (2002) has written of the importance of heritage in the economic restructuring of declining industrial centres. The 1970s and 80s were a period of heritage boom in which the US National Register of Historic Places increased its listings from 1,200 in 1968 to 37,000 by 1985.

The rise of heritage centres in leisure has gone hand in glove with the exploitation and development of myth and its representation in leisure and tourism. Literary heritage landscapes like Hardy's Wessex, the London and Kent of Dickens, Steinbeck's Monterey Peninsula and Margaret Mitchell's *Gone with the Wind* country in Georgia are mobilized through advertising, theming and interactive events involving actors to recreate the (fictional) past to act as a substitute for reality (Rojek 1993: 152–61). Heritage educational centres, like the 'Way We Were Centre' on Wigan Pier which uses interactive technologies to recreate life in the North West of England at the turn of the twentieth century or the 'Plymouth Plantation' in New England where the life of settlers is recreated, employ stereotypes and myth as part of their narrative.

Heritage and multiculturalism

The emergence of multiculturalism has raised many questions about cultural relationships with natural space. These have crystallized around the problem of heritage. As Hall (1999: 14) puts it:

> Heritage is bound into the meaning of the nation through a double inscription. What the nation means is essentialized. It appears to have emerged at the very moment of its origin – a moment always lost in the myths, as well as the mists, of time – and successively embodied as a distilled essence in the various arts and artefacts of the nation for which the Heritage provides the archive.

The difficulty with the notion of an 'unfolding national story' is that it is necessarily *selective*. Heritage is imposed on culture as it is lived. This is a source of profound tension in the context of multicultural society because 'the unfolding national story' is partly experienced by some strata as a tale of dominance and oppression. It follows that leisure forms organized around processions or festivals that commemorate these forms of heritage may be alienating to many groups.

Public recognition of this had produced agonizing debates about appropriate symbols to draw the multicultural nation together. The controversial Millennium Dome, built in London to celebrate the millennium, may be an engineering triumph but it is a financial and cultural disaster. In part, the problem stems from a lack of cultural ownership. The design is culturally neutral in an effort to embrace all of the UK's multicultures, but it ends up belonging to no one. Multiculturalism presents formidable challenges for the public provision of leisure and heritage. How can you include everyone? Where are lines to be drawn when lines are recognized to be part of the problem?

Myth permeates the architecture, politics, economics, culture and leisure of society. It articulates relations of inclusion and exclusion and provides validation for this which is measured not in decades or centuries, but eternity. It is improbable that myth will ever be replaced by science. To date, science has been unable to generate the intensity of passion associated with myth. One task of Leisure Studies must be to elucidate the place of myth in representations and practices of leisure. Harmful myths of racial or sexual superiority should be ruthlessly exposed. But it will probably be impossible to uproot myths that inspire human energy and progress and in any case it would arguably be regressive to attempt to do so.

Key points

- Leisure must be understood as a system of representation as well as institutions and trajectories of practice.
- Leisure forms, practices and representations reflect power relations that involve processes of encoding and decoding.
- Markers and theming of leisure forms and practices proliferate in consumer culture.
- Mythogenesis is embedded in culture and society and influences the meaning and assimilation of leisure forms and practices.

5
The Life Course and Generations

In this chapter you will be:

- Invited to consider the relevance of the the 'life cycle' as a core concept in Action analysis.
- Guided through the distinctions between youth, middle age, old age and leisure.
- Asked to examine the validity of 'generations' in leisure forms and practice.

The life course

A long tradition in the study of leisure behaviour argues that our interests, dispositions, tastes and political attitudes change as we age. Although this tradition borrows metaphors from psychological and social analysis it is rooted in a biological perspective on leisure, especially in the notion of a regenerative cycle of birth, immaturity, maturity, reproduction, old age and death. For example, the Rapaports (1975: 14) argued that leisure behaviour is shaped by a 'psycho-biological–maturational process' underlying distinctions of class, gender, race and subculture. This posits a biological basis to leisure that exists in some tension with agency approaches that stress the role of conscious struggle over scarcity and ethical imperatives in the development of leisure.

Although contributions to the life course approach are varied, nearly all operate with a version of a threefold distinction in the life cycle between youth, adulthood and old age. The main characteristics of each stage are as follows.

Youth

This is typified by light social responsibilities and obligations, limited finance and general family dependency. It is an experimental period in identity formation and status acquisition as individuals absorb role models and stimuli from peer groups and the media that contrast with family and community values. Compared with the play experience of children, the leisure of youth is dominated by the process of individualization and developing sexualized identities.

By the age of 16 the majority have adopted adult leisure pastimes, although their ability to engage in them fully is constrained by financial restrictions. Important differences in time budgets exist within the youth category. For example, Robinson and Godbey (1999: 208) report that adolescents (aged 12–17) do less housework, childcare and shopping than young adults (18–24 year olds) and in general obtain four to six hours more sleep. The same study reported that adolescents average less than three hours a week in work-related activity compared with young adults who typically work 23 hours a week. Adolescents spend 24 hours per week on school-related activity compared with an average of nine hours for young adults. Adolescents spend four to six hours longer sleeping and napping than 18–24 year olds. Sports, board games and cards loom large in the leisure time of adolescents; while 18–24 year olds spend more time hanging out with friends, going to parties, visiting bars and talking on the phone (Robinson and Godbey 1999: 209).

There is evidence that the youth stage in the life cycle is expanding. Research by Hollands (1995) suggests that it now lasts until one's early thirties. This reflects a combination of factors, the most important of which are increasing participation rates in higher education and the casualization of employment. One result of this is that financial and emotional dependence on the family has been prolonged.

Research indicates that since the 1970s, gender and class divisions between youth subcultures have become less significant. Club cultures, raves and house communities have fluid boundaries which may be ad hoc or persist for a number of years (Thornton 1995). Changes in the labour market have altered the relation of young people to this stage in the life cycle. In particular, the trend towards greater flexibility in work patterns, the casualization of labour and the expansion of part-time work have complicated the transition between youth and adult stages. Until the late 1970s university-level credentialism correlated strongly with well-remunerated, secure employment. While credentialism is still significant in youth identity formation, the correlation with well-remunerated, secure employment has weakened. The relationship between young people and the labour market is overshadowed by multiple uncertainties. The relevance of their degree to their employment role is one issue; the instability of work roles is also significant. Drawing on Beck's (1992) work on 'risk society', Roberts (1999: 115–16) points to the pronounced importance of risk and uncertainty in the youth stage, a point that is illustrated not simply by the complexity of achieving security in the labour market but also by the threat of HIV and Aids in sexual relations.

Middle age

Cohabitation, marriage and parenthood are associated with a 'life-cycle squeeze' (Estes and Wilensky 1978). This refers to new financial restraints caused by mortgage or rental payments, spending more on household expenditure and supporting dependants. By the same token, freedom and choice in leisure are inhibited by the decline of spare time. The extension of the youth stage means that adult leisure is constrained by financial and time-budget restrictions for longer periods.

The result of this condition is that leisure generally becomes more privatized in the adult stage. Privatization should not necessarily be regarded as a retreat from life. On the contrary, the move to home-centred leisure in the adult stage involves significant participation in popular culture, particularly music, reading and television (Horna 1994: 207).

Research by Sullivan (1996) and Gershuny (2000) indicates a tendency for couples to aim for joint conjugal leisure patterns. Socializing together or with other couples is positively valued. However, the same researchers found that work and family obligations often make it difficult to achieve the joint coordination of leisure. This usually changes with late middle age when children become less dependent. In this phase of the adult stage individuals engage more seriously in planning life options for retirement. This may result in the diversification of leisure activities as individuals relinquish some restraints involved in the parental role and prepare for life without children. This contrasts with the work of the feminist sociologist Arlie Hochschild (1989) who contends that there is a 'leisure gap', to the disadvantage of women, at all stages in the life cycle.

The findings of Robinson and Godbey (1999: 53–4) and Gershuny (2000: 73–4) take issue with Hochschild's position. They accept that gender inequality in the distribution of paid labour, unpaid labour and leisure has not been achieved, although they note considerable variations between the manual and non-manual classes. According to Robinson and Godbey (1999: 100), women spend 19 hours on household work per week and men ten hours. If family care responsibilities are included women put in twice as many hours per week as men, and non-employed men and women devote approximately 50 per cent more hours to family care than the employed. Taking a long-term historical perspective, the research of both Robinson and Godbey (1999) and Gershuny (2000) suggests a gradual gender convergence in respect of unpaid domestic labour and leisure.

Schor's (1992: 11–12) work warns against presenting an oversanguine picture of gender convergence. Their analysis points to a general intensification of work hours and the development of multiple jobs per individual. This points to a chronic time-famine, an argument also made by Linder (1970). However, because women are under strong pressures of location and context to give more time to childcare, their experience of stress is especially severe.

Interestingly, Gershuny's (2000) time-budget analysis also concludes that the highest-paid groups now work the longest hours. They also have the highest participation in out-of-home leisure activities. To explain this he enlists the work of Gary Becker (1965, 1979) who argues that those engaged in high-paid work that involves long hours select intense, expensive bursts of leisure activity. Among the high-paid, domestic labour and childcare responsibilities may be offloaded to service workers. Nannies and home helps free up time for work. Higher disposable income also supports the acquisition of labour-saving devices. However, in an earlier book Gershuny (1978) argues that domestic labour-saving technologies may actually increase the domestic workload in that they require more regular work to maintain higher standards.

Old age

Old age correlates with the decline of leisure activities, especially out-of-home forms of leisure. By this stage in the life cycle leisure patterns have solidified and are unlikely to change. Lower incomes and the loss of work-based networks are the main causes for the decline in leisure activity. In some cases deteriorating health and increasing infirmity are also significant.

What increases dramatically is non-allocated time. Robinson and Godbey (1999: 213) report that even for those seniors who remain in part-time employment, work time is less than 25 per cent of what it is for those aged between 18 and 64. They calculate that retirement liberates up to 25 hours per week for men and 18 hours for women. Some of this time is assigned to increased housework. For example, older men carry almost double the housework load of men in their thirties and forties. In contrast, older women spend only one third more time doing housework than younger women. For both men and women the leisure time dividend tends to be allocated to television, radio and newspapers. Typically, older men spend 25 hours per week watching TV and older women 22 hours. Men aged 75 and over work only five hours per week and women less than three hours. Eating out declines, while time spent on grooming increases. The consumption of leisure time spent on TV, radio and newspapers is greater compared with the 65–74 age group. Robinson and Godbey (1999: 215) conclude that employment, not age, is the major influence on the distribution of leisure time among the elderly.

However, the trend towards increasing longevity and improvements in personal health management mean that the old-age stage may be undergoing a transformation. The US Census Bureau report in 2004 on global demographic trends anticipates that the world's population will grow from 6.2 billion today to about 9.2 billion in 2050. While the number of children is expected to stay roughly the same, there could be three times as many old people as today (www.census.gov).

As we live longer in the old-age stage of the life cycle and as our chances of retaining good health for longer periods generally increase, greater diversity in leisure forms may result. One threatening factor here is inadequate pension provision to cover the old-age stage. As the 65-plus generation becomes a bigger part of the population, public pension provision will be increasingly stressed. Already in the USA, Robinson and Godbey (1999: 310) report that one out of five of the 52 million Americans aged 55 and over is in the employment force. The greying of the leisure market may not translate into higher rates of participation in the final years of the life cycle. Private pension schemes which are tied to the stock market are also vulnerable to fluctuations in value during a bear market. In these conditions there is likely to be considerable pressure to abandon the fixed retirement age and move towards flexible patterns of ending work careers.

The longer life/fuller leisure equation is an attractive one, but it depends upon the consolidation of trends in health policy and medical science. Genetic engineering promises huge health dividends with a substantial increase in life expectancy. One result of this is that the periods of youth, middle age and old age may lengthen, producing new adaptations in leisure forms and practices. Conversely, if the claims of genetic engineering are not fully realized, the prolongation of life may result in longer periods of chronic, degenerative disease in the old-age stage which in turn suggests the impoverishment of leisure experience and the extension of dependency upon family and kin networks and state remedial care services.[1]

Life course analysis proposes a strong correlation between age, life options and identity formation. For youth, the range of available life options are subject to a different biological regime than in the adult and old-age stages. Because we generally have more energy in the youth stage of the life cycle than in the adult or old-age stages, we are predisposed to make leisure choices that involve more physical exercise and less home-based activity.

Life course analysis seems to offer a strong, quantifiable set of propositions about the relationships between age, choice and leisure practice. The quantifiable element is especially significant since it seems to posit the foundation for a *science* of leisure based an objective data and propositions as opposed to qualitative interpretation.

However, Featherstone (1987: 117–18) urges caution about proposing a universal life cycle involving psychological development based on stage theory. The position of the individual in the life cycle is *relational* and considerable variation is associated with factors like class, gender, ethnicity, subculture and religion. He argues that researchers should balance a psycho-biological model to investigate identity formation and the life cycle with a *social institutional* model which explores discrimination against individuals on the grounds of age and is sensitive to historical transformations in the life course.

Similarly, Freysinger (1999) distinguishes between a 'core' and 'balance' of activities through the life cycle. Core leisure activities and the balance between them and other activities are a function of taste cultures and marks of distinction as well as class, gender, ethnicity and religion. They cannot be read off a life course model of personal development. Instead they point to power relations and ethical imperatives in identity formation.

The emphasis upon the relational situation of the individual is welcome. Evidently the life course is mediated through many social variables, of which the most important are, arguably, class, gender, ethnicity, generation, levels of education and religion. The individual's relation to these variables influences the distribution of leisure time and space at each stage in the life cycle and the pattern changes in leisure practice as one ages. A comparative and historical perspective quickly reveals significant variation in the life course. For example, rising life expectancy has been a general characteristic of Western patterns of social and economic development. Average life expectancy in the UK is now 78.2 years, over twice the figure that applied in the 1830s. This has been achieved by improvements in public health, diet and medical knowledge. In contrast, average life expectancy in Zimbabwe which had been rising over the past one hundred years is today 33.1 years: a result of civil unrest, agriculture failure, the spread of HIV/Aids and inadequate public health services.

The length of life expectancy obviously affects the stages in the life cycle. Throughout the West over the past century, the dependency stage of youth has increased and the probability of living for more years in the old-age stage has increased.

One issue that will complicate the life cycle approach is bio-engineering. Mapping the gene code system offers enormous long-term advantages in the treatment of illness, disease and ageing. A relational perspective on ageing demonstrates that our 'traditional' concept of the life cycle is historically and culturally conditioned. Bio-engineering may eventually have far-reaching consequences on the conventional understanding of youth, middle age and old age. Already cosmetic surgery and dietary change are blurring the divisions. The middle-aged and elderly who have the financial resources are resorting to nip and tuck surgery and hair-weaving and transplants to make themselves look younger. Bio-engineering has the potential to delay the onset of ageing in various far-reaching ways that will gradually become clearer in the next twenty-five years. This carries the potential to alter the relationship between the individual and society as well as eroding the divisions between youth, middle age and old age. Students of leisure should develop an awareness of the implications of these issues both for the nature of physical embodiment and for the cultures of leisure associated with it.

Generations

One aspect of the life course that has not received much attention from researchers in Leisure Studies is the question of generations. Karl Mannheim's (1952) classic statement distinguished between three elements in the formation of generation:

1. *Location* – the emplacement of individuals in time and space circumscribes their life chances with respect to wealth, power, social values and political beliefs.
2. *Actuality* – the material and social facts of generational location orientate individuals towards one another and contribute to a sense of collectivity and the unfolding of a common destiny.
3. *Unity* – the recognition of common attitudes and principles of interpretation and action with regard to socio-cultural conditions.

Mannheim argued that the potential of generational solidarity is only fully realized during moments of accelerated social, political and economic change. For example, war, economic and political turmoil or a natural catastrophe such as a drought or earthquake enhances the consciousness of generational actuality and unity. Underlying this concept of generation is a neo-Hobbesian principle of competition. According to Mannheim generations want to make their interpretation of the world universal. This involves conflict since it is based on a war of ideas between generations and the struggle to obtain positions of influence.

Within Leisure Studies the question of generations is usually dissolved in the question of youth subcultures. Cyclical movements in the economy and politics are recognized as producing general characteristics of identity formation among youth (Roberts 1999; Olszewska and Roberts 1989). Beats, hippies, punks, new romantics and goths are presented as successive instalments of subcultural formations that are doomed to be replaced as their representatives enter the greying stages of the life course. Yet the marks of these formations are evident in the attitudes and life chances of different age groups. Generations are important, and undertheorized in studying leisure forms and practice. For example, generally speaking, the 60s generation had wider life chances than succeeding generations. They arrived on the employment market at a juncture when construction of the welfare state and economic expansion combined to produce both more jobs and greater job security. Society, culture and economy were shaped by *corporatist* management strategies in which the state, business and trade unions formed a partnership to govern affairs. The 80s generation arrived on the market at a moment of straitened circumstances in which unemployment, inflation and monetarism combined to reverse the expansion of the welfare state and renew the centrality of the market. The New Right advocated market solutions to economic and social problems and rejected corporatism by unravelling the partnership with trade unions.

These formations resulted in contrasting generational views of the importance of work, the meaning of leisure, the role of the state, the functions of business and trade unions, and many other issues besides. These views are aestheticized in leisure forms like film, television drama, theatre and popular music that symbolize popular attitudes and generational differences. Students of leisure may read these forms as types of *coding* which differentiate generational attitudes and perspectives. This whole area is under-researched in leisure studies and is a major gap in our knowledge of how leisure forms and practice develop. In particular, questions of how aesthetic forms code generations and the ways in which forms are transferred and negotiated *intergenerationally* are relevant and require study.

Key points

- The Action approach to leisure seeks to go beyond the structure–agency division of the systems and interactionist approaches. It explores the trajectory of leisure in terms of the nexus between subjective choice, location and context.
- The emphasis on the political dimension of leisure and the influence of ideology and interpellation is stressed.
- The biological model of the life course is challenged by an approach which pursues a relational approach to leisure based on the power relations between social institutions.

6
Power and Leisure

In this chapter you will:

- Address the twin axial circuits of production/consumption and the regulation of aggression and sexuality as the foundational principles of society.
- Understand the relationship between leisure and surplus wealth.
- Examine the proposition that leisure forms and and practice revolve around the dual principles of the allocation of scarce economic resources and distribution of prestige.
- Understand the power hierarchy that governs society and be introduced to the concepts of *predatory strata*, *regulative mechanisms* and *oppositional blocs*.
- Differentiate between institutions of normative coercion and regulative mechanisms.
- Understand the significance of regimes of power for leisure forms and practice.

The **axial** circuits underpinning every society are the relationship between production and consumption and the management of aggression and sexuality. All societies need to produce goods and services to survive and grow. All must develop an economy of drives that allow aggressive and sexual desires to be expressed without threatening social order. Since societies operate in some version of the condition of scarcity, all must devise a stable means of resource allocation and prestige distribution. This is fundamental for the organization of purposeful activity, whether it be the pursuit of work, leisure, policing or marshalling society as an

Axial means pertaining to the axis of society. The term 'axis' rather than 'foundation' is preferred because it better conveys process and movement, whereas foundation has a more static connotation. Axial circuits are central to the selective capacities of society, that is, the capacities to survive, maintain order, compete and expand. They therefore influence all social, economic, political and cultural relations.

effective attack and defence unit. Axial circuits are the bedrock of society. But their salience in everyday life is *positioned* through the actions of *predatory strata* and the unintended consequences of these actions. *Positioning* is the process of coding and theming through ideology and interpellation that elicits a *natural* or *common-sense* response to the allocation of economic resources, the economy of drives and the distribution of prestige. Through it individuals are encouraged to regard the condition of economic, cultural and political inequality as a *state of nature*.

Predatory strata are social formations that seek to control the operation of the circuits in order to advance their interests. The term 'predatory' is used in relation to them, because their purpose is to maximize the share of resources that are left over after the needs of subsistence have been satisfied, in ways that are consistent with maintaining the legitimacy and stability of the general system.[1] They are the denizens of the power bloc that dominates social order and their membership is chiefly composed of representatives of the political directorate and the decisive owners–managers of private economic capital.

Predatory strata position axial circuits in everyday life through a range of **regulative mechanisms** that allocate economic resources, distribute

Regulative mechanisms develop in response to the problems of scarcity, the requirement to construct solidarity and the need to legitimate the power structure. They generate economic and social hierarchies of power. As societies develop and produce more surplus, individuals and groups prosper and find the hierarchies of power to be impediments to progress. When this happens new types of solidarity emerge which challenge the legitimacy of the regulative order. Regulative mechanisms then have two principal social characteristics: they distribute economic surplus, prestige and other resources, and they are the basis for challenging social hierarchy and order.

prestige and manage the economy of instincts. Think of a dynastic tribal society ruled by one chief. The society produces more than enough to satisfy the tribe's basic needs for food, drink, clothing and shelter. What is left over is known as the *surplus*.

The surplus must be managed in various ways. The tribal chief may use a portion of it to support celebratory events that ritually give collective thanks for the production of more than the tribe needs to survive. Other parts of the surplus may be reinvested in improving the productive capacity of the tribe or developing its capacity for attack and defence.

Since the chief is unable to manage all aspects of this process because his tribe is composed of too many individuals, he faces the problem of delegating power to others. This is done by rewarding favoured others, usually family members or trusted tribal members, with economic resources, prestige or sexual and aggressive rights that underpin their superior position in the tribe's social hierarchy. These produce additional social and economic divisions in the tribal structure and give birth to the problem of *legitimating* these divisions, which tribal societies typically do by means of a mixture of myth, magic, religion and force. The example shows that regulative mechanisms are not static or universal. In contemporary Western society warrior classes and religion have experienced a decline in power (Turner 2003). As we shall see in the next chapter they have been displaced by secular regulative mechanisms.

If regulative mechanisms perform adequately, the axial circuits should eventually produce more wealth which, in turn, requires longer chains in the distribution of prestige, since there will be more surplus to delegate. At this point, there is a strong likelihood that **oppositional blocs** will emerge in the power hierarchy who make it their purpose to challenge the position of predatory strata and the regulative mechanisms they support.

Oppositional blocs are common when the surplus is too great for the regulative mechanisms to manage without creating unacceptable disparities in resource allocation and the distribution of prestige. Typically, they attack the power hierarchy by questioning the legitimacy of the regulative mechanisms to allocate resources and distribute prestige in their habitual patterns of practice. When this happens the composition of the regulative mechanism may change. Those who were in charge of the management of economic resources and prestige may be replaced by representatives of the oppositional bloc who seek to redefine the legitimacy of governance. Alternatively, oppositional blocs may organize and act to overturn the entire system of regulative mechanisms and introduce their own blueprint for managing the axial circuits upon which all wealth ultimately depends.

They do so by exposing the contradictions between predatory strata, regulative mechanisms and the positioning of axial circuits. If positioning can be demonstrated to be detrimental to the interests of all, or even a clear majority, oppositional blocs possess leverage to change the balance of power between predatory strata and regulative mechanisms.

The example is offered as a *heuristic* device to illustrate how, in a basic society, regulative mechanisms relate to axial circuits in order to achieve solidarity. By the term 'basic' I do not mean 'simple'. Tribal societies are complex social formations that use sophisticated methods of coding and theming to position axial circuits in everyday life. However, they are more basic than modern, democratic, industrial society since in the latter the population is incomparably bigger and more differentiated and the surplus is very much greater. Consequently, the allocation of wealth, the distribution of prestige and the governance of the aggressive and sexual economy are much more complex, involving multiple layers and combinations of diverse strata and various types of solidarity. In particular, these societies have evolved a type of civil society in which individuals possess formal equality and, outwardly at least, impartial laws that justify the system of governance.

Formal equality is not equivalent to *real* equality. In a society that allows people the equal right to hold vastly unequal resources of economic wealth and prestige, informal systems of power exist which mean that the formal system of equality is vulnerable to manipulation by the powerful so that their interests prevail. As Veblen (1899, 1904) observed long ago, urban–industrial societies maintain predatory strata and they function to position axial circuits and regulative mechanisms to confirm their stamp of authority and economic and political interests over the entire system.

Notwithstanding this, the creation of civil society in which formal equality and impartial law are publicly affirmed is a huge advance over tribal dynastic rule. It means that predatory strata have to be *accountable*.

For example, if their actions are judged to be so disadvantageous to civil society that they imperil the legitimacy of the formal order, they can be forced to correct their heinous behaviour. The positioning of axial circuits and the organization of regulative mechanisms is much more intricate and contestable in societies of this type. The regulative mechanisms that allocate economic resources and distribute prestige have to operate in more subtle ways than by the whim of the chief. They have to interpellate subjects (citizens) and situate them in respect of ideology so that the whole system of informal equality is portrayed as natural and preferential. Since it is inherently difficult to present a condition of economic, cultural and economic inequality as a state of nature, these societies generate many different types and levels of oppositional bloc. Moreover, because civil society makes a virtue of formal equality and impartiality it invests significant power in a nominally free mass media to represent the management of the system and issues arising therefrom. What part do leisure forms and practices play in this type of society?

Leisure and the structural hierarchy of power

Before coming to this question, we should summarize the substance and illustrate the import of the chief points in the discussion. So far we have identified three basic structural levels in social order. We may call this the **structural hierarchy of power**. Versions of it are common to all societies.

The structural hierarchy of power

1. *Predatory strata*, which dominate the axial circuits and support regulative mechanisms designed to enhance their power.
2. *Regulative mechanisms*, that are based on management of economic surplus, the distribution of prestige and the governance of solidarity.
3. *Oppositional blocs*, that develop through the social and cultural differentiation enabled by surplus, and who challenge regulative mechanisms and the governance of solidarity that they support.

Leisure is codependent with this hierarchy in various ways. Three relationships between leisure and the power hierarchy are particularly significant:

1. *Ceremonial* – in which leisure forms and practice renew collective solidarity by celebrating the power hierarchy. Examples in monarchies are investitures and jubilees, and in democracies patriotic national holidays and sporting events.
2. *Social distinction* – the application of leisure forms and practice to represent positional advantage in relation to scarcity. Examples include society balls and parties, and the consumption and display of luxury goods.
3. *Social division* – the use of leisure forms and practice to signify dissent or opposition to the system. Examples include festivals, musical events and drama designed to symbolize social exclusion.

Each of these relationships suggests that the characteristic forms and practice of leisure are bound up with the production and distribution of surplus wealth. It is only when the axial circuits produce surplus wealth that a consistent resource base is in place to generate a power hierarchy and to engender leisure as a social institution that codes and themes the presence of this hierarchy in society.

There have been significant changes in the twin circuits and attached regulative mechanisms in history with corresponding implications for the meaning of play and leisure in everyday life. We might think of primitive consumption as the original state of mankind in which the need to achieve subsistence is paramount. Nature is the original and primary source of subsistence. The roots of culture, one might venture, lie in the attempt to construct institutions and practices that maintain subsistence and defend the tribe against internal conflict and external attack. The hunting and gathering cultures of the first human tribes are an example of this. It is a state of primitive consumption because it is a regime that involves no cultivation and minimal technology. Of course, the latter is a means of competitive advancement in the sense that the human group that develops superior technology (clubs, spears, bows and arrows) will be ahead in the race to maintain subsistence.

The stage of primitive consumption is superseded when a human group achieves the wherewithal to produce a *surplus*. For example, a surplus may be the result of victory over another tribe and seizing the possessions of the vanquished; it may follow a technical innovation in hunting or agriculture which creates a bigger reserve of food; it may follow changes in tribal leadership which produce a more efficient type of administration; it may even develop by chance as when climatic conditions allow for the greater production of food. What is of absorbing interest for our purposes is the relationship between surplus and luxury.

Surplus provides the means for developing social and cultural distinction and advancing control. This is reflected variously through, for example, the development of bodily ornamentation, the institutionalization of play forms, the development of rituals of sacrifice and waste that celebrate excess and the emergence of strata in the human group who earn their keep not by generating production or engaging in warfare, but through non-work or play activity such as magic, religion, music and story-telling (Briffault 1965).

For a long time writers portrayed the rise of capitalism in terms of the steady expansion of *productive forces* and *warfare*. Empire subdued spontaneity and consolidated populations under a centralized power regime that upheld standardization and uniformity. The consequence of this was a distorted reading of how capitalism operated because it left consumption out of the picture. We now know more about how the emergence of surplus and contact with other cultures stimulated the acquisitive desire for perfumes, silks, spices, tobacco, music and so on. To be sure, we know enough to hypothesize that surplus was the *precondition* for the emergence of leisure.

The distribution of surplus and the function of distinction in leisure demonstrate considerable historical and cultural variation. However, their basic functional features are common:

1. Surplus and distinction serve as the basis for recognizing social inclusion and exclusion. Individuals and strata use excess and luxury as status-placing activity.
2. Surplus and distinction operate as a basis of social control. In tribal society feasts and sacrifice enhance social integration by acting as the reward for periods of mundane labour. In feudal Europe, carnival performed a similar function (Bakhtin 1968; Rojek 1985: 26–9).
3. The formation of luxury and the development of status-placing activity around cultures of luxury provide an important symbolic means for political solidarity and struggle.

Leisure is then born, not through industrial production, as some theorists have asserted (De Grazia 1964; Bailey 1978; Cunningham 1980), but through *luxury* which is itself the result of *surplus*.

Now to come back to the question posed in the last section: if leisure is integrally related to the production and distribution of surplus, how do regulative mechanisms and oppositional blocs interact in our own society? The first thing to note, and to paraphrase the historian Edward Thompson (1978: 298), is that regulative mechanisms are not *things*, they are *happenings*. They do not merely refer to social classifications of people, but to the whole range of interests, frictions, tensions and movement that position people in relation to economic resources and prestige, that is, in relation to the ultimate problem of *scarcity*. To refer to Thompson (1978: 298) again, regulative mechanisms are not references to this or that part of the machine, *but the way the entire machine works*. At the level of logic, regulative mechanisms have the following consequences for leisure practice:

1. They *shape* the multitude of individual leisure choices and actions by allocating cultural and economic capital.
2. They *establish* the context and location for leisure interaction which bestows regularity and predictability upon leisure conduct.
3. They *assign* distinction and solidarity to leisure forms and practice.

The balance of power between regulative mechanisms is best understood in terms of motion. If the influence of one regulative mechanism becomes more pronounced at one moment it produces a reaction in the motion of the others which results in a new balance in the positioning of axial circuits in everyday life and the situation of predatory strata in relation to these circuits. The balance of power must be understood as a moving equilibrium, the shape of which is not guaranteed by historical necessity, that is, it is subject to change.

Each society can be shown through study to develop and perpetuate distinctive ideologies that justify the balance between surplus and scarcity. The relationship between primary functions in leisure, ideology and human practice may be described as a **regime** of power. Regulative

---

Regime derives from the work of Michel Foucault (1975, 1981) and refers to a system of habit, rules and incentives that pattern human behaviour. Foucault regards the concept to be the expression of power and, as such, he attributes a shaping or disposing capacity to it which may be against the will of the individual. Because it is the expression of power it is subject to historical change.

mechanisms are integral in producing and reproducing ideology as well as servicing the twin axial circuits. They set boundaries, establish the principles of social inclusion and exclusion and influence the disposition of oppositional blocs. However, their function is not solely reproductive. Through their articulation in everyday life, they are also the basis for disputes about the meaning and boundaries of these terms.

We can express this slightly differently in order to come back to the theme of scarcity. Individuals are the bearers of location and context since all of us are embodied and emplaced beings whose beliefs and values are drawn from a variety of institutions and traditions that precede our individual existence. Location and context place individuals in different positional situations with respect to scarcity. They come with certain kinds of social solidarity built into them. The relation of individuals to scarcity is ultimately the result of how regulative mechanisms allocate economic resources and distribute prestige. So location and context might be said to bear the fingerprints of the regulative mechanisms that manage, code and theme axial circuits and also the responses to this condition that have resulted in social solidarities. As agents we both reproduce regime conditions and innovate. Through agency the power regime is maintained, challenged and transformed. This brings us to the question of the type of regulative mechanisms abroad in our society. However, before coming to it an additional conceptual clarification has to be introduced, having to do with what might be termed *the institutions of normative coercion*.

Institutions of normative coercion

In civil societies based on formal equality and impartiality, regulative systems cannot engage in the *naked* allocation of unequal economic resources and prestige. To do so would be to invite oppositional blocs to amalgamate and challenge the legitimacy of the entire system. So they are forced to present the condition of economic, cultural and social inequality as the state of nature in very subtle ways. Regulative mechanisms have developed **institutions of normative coercion**. Examples

---

Institutions of normative coercion are the localized means in everyday life through which regulative mechanisms seek to make the condition of economic, cultural and political inequality appear as the state of nature.

in democratic urban–industrial societies include schools, the universities, the police, the armed forces, the judiciary and the various departments of the political directorate. Through a combination of ideological and repressive devices they seek to naturalize the concept of normal behaviour in a condition of economic, political and cultural inequality. Mechanically speaking, they are the switch-points that translate the power regime sustained by regulative mechanisms into a form of *common sense* that is so powerful that it persuades most people, most of the time, that either the system is the best of all possible worlds or that the disadvantages that are likely to accrue from trying to change it are greater than the advantages that it delivers.

At least one position in the study of leisure and culture has identified the state apparatus as a key institution of normative coercion. The Birmingham School analysis of the regulation of aggression and civil society maintains that the state in Britain has operated to organize conformity by a complex war of manoeuvre. The political directorate has engineered a series of concessions and coalitions, notably in the areas of redistributive taxation, welfare reform and trade union rights. Through a *complex unity* of social, political and ideological interventions they have engineered social and economic improvement without breaking the fundamental dependency relation of the working class in relation to the power bloc. Most notoriously, the drift to the right, involving intensified policing, the reduction of welfare spending and deregulation of the employment market, were presented as being *in the best interests* of 'the people', who were redefined as *victims* of the high-crime, high-tax economy of the permissive society. The Birmingham approach may be criticized for exaggerating the power of the state and neglecting the business corporation as an institution of normative coercion. Nonetheless, its analysis of the state is a very good example of how normative institutions of coercion naturalize the motion of regulative mechanisms to render them as 'common sense'.

However, we should be sceptical of one-sided approaches to the question of the operation of the institutions of normative coercion. Institutions of normative coercion have a signal quality that frequently places them in critical tension with regulative mechanisms. As part of their ordinary practice they take regulatory mechanisms and the power bloc that they represent as objects, the validity and functions of which are subject to scrutiny and critical debate. In other words, institutions of normative coercion have the capacity for reflexive analysis, and as such possess a degree of autonomy from central regulative mechanisms.

We may think of Leisure Studies as an example of this in universities. Questions of inequality and the justification of authority are properly debated in Leisure Studies. Propositions and hypotheses are advanced about their formation, interrelationships and consequences. Their action in regulating leisure trajectories and practices is investigated. Finally, a critical dimension is introduced which fastens upon the ways in which these institutions coerce behaviour and, by extension, develops proposals for empowerment, distributive justice and social inclusion. The critical study of leisure possesses the capability of feeding back into regulative mechanisms and predatory strata in ways that render their power *visible*. Of course, universities are not alone in doing this. The courts perform a similar function in making judgements about validity and responsibility. The caring and helping professions continuously raise questions of empowerment, distributive justice and inclusion. Be that as it may, universities occupy an unusual position in that they have the recognized duty of pursuing the task of unmasking power *systematically*. Perhaps only the arts and politics occupy an equivalent position. This is why both universities and the arts tend to be subject to censure and curtailment under repressive regimes of power.

Students often find it difficult to grasp the meaning of regulative mechanisms. After all, in leisure practice we do not meet *allocative systems* or *distributive processes*. Rather we meet flesh-and-blood men and women, like ourselves. How can we postulate regulative mechanisms and examine their operation in everyday life? The answer, of course, is by studying the leisure conduct of flesh-and-blood men and women to investigate if it bears tangible inscriptions or traces of power structures that precede the existence of the individuals who are shaped by them and to do this through a comparative and historical approach. To some extent, these questions can be probed by using the self as the methodological unit of enquiry. Some of the pertinent questions are: why do women hold opinions and taken-for-granted assumptions about leisure practice that are not shared by men? How does an African American or black Briton come to view issues of justice and equality in work and leisure differently from American or British Caucasians? Why are the employment opportunities and leisure pursuits of a judge's daughter superior to those of the daughter of a janitor? The effects of regulative mechanisms are as real as the effect of the heart in pumping blood around the body. But we often have to penetrate through a thick veil of ideological illusions and myths before we can examine them accurately.

Key points

- Leisure forms and practice are situated in relation to axial circuits and regulative mechanisms that position individuals and groups in relation to scarce economic resources and the distribution of social prestige.
- Axial circuits and regulative mechanisms constitute regimes of power in which predatory strata are positioned in conditions of advantage with respect to access to scarce economic resources and the distribution of social prestige.
- Leisure forms and practice originate in the creation of surplus and the notion of luxury.
- Institutions of normative coercion operate to normalize leisure conduct.

7
Regulative Mechanisms

In this chapter you will:

- See how leisure forms and practice are related to cultural reproduction.
- Identify class, gender, race and occupation as the central regulative mechanisms of leisure in contemporary society.
- Be introduced to the concept of 'life chances' and shown its relation to leisure forms and practice.
- Understand how regulative mechanisms are unplanned, unintentional structures for the allocation of economic resources and the distribution of prestige.

To begin by way of a short reprise, *regulative mechanisms* operate to allocate economic resources and distribute prestige in specific *regimes of power*. They position actors in relation to the balance between scarcity and surplus. Through socialization, individuals acquire access to unequal economic and cultural capital. The term 'cultural capital' comes from the sociology of Pierre Bourdieu (1984). It refers to knowledge, linguistic codes, values, beliefs, leisure interests and social networks that orientate the individual to society and form the basis for solidarity. We all need to feel belonging, whether it be expressed with respect to our family, our community, our country, our ethnic group and so on. You can think of cultural capital as a representation of belonging. It also possesses *value* in society.

Distribution of prestige

	Class	Gender
Allocation of economic resources		
	Race	Occupation

Figure 7.1   Central regulative mechanisms of leisure

Bourdieu was concerned to examine how *cultural reproduction* operates in society. He regarded cultural reproduction to be the transmission of cultural capital through inheritance. As such it is an accessory of the concept of the twin axial circuits governing the link between production and consumption and the economy of aggressive and sexual emotions, since it is the means through which normative coercion is cultivated. In Bourdieu's view, through socialization every individual internalizes symbolic master patterns of thought and value that facilitate social orientation and act as markers of belonging. Markers may be thought of as the articulation of cultural capital and the basis for ties of social inclusion and exclusion. Each master pattern is reinforced through interaction with others. Each carries distinctive value in the power hierarchy. Cultural reproduction conditions the **life chances** of individuals.

Life chances mean the probabilistic material advantages and disadvantages and social, cultural and economic opportunities that will accrue to a typical member of a social class in a particular society. The concept was developed by Max Weber to clarify how class influences the individual's choice of mates, career choices, leisure interests and life expectancy.

In pre-industrial societies warrior rule and religion played a prominent role as regulative mechanisms. Play and religions were heavily ritualized to emphasize the subordination of the individual to the group. Arguably, sacrifice was the foremost manifestation of this since it was a collective symbol of the continuity between tribal life and the sacred. The sanctioned obliteration of an individual broke the taboo against murder and was frequently accompanied by various ecstatic play forms in which transgression was symbolically celebrated (Girard 1988). Variations of these forms persist in contemporary society in some types of cultic activity and the equation of deviant leisure with adventurous transgression (Rojek 2000). However, in societies that have become generally secularized the significance of the regulative mechanisms of religion and sacrifice is greatly diminished.

The central regulative mechanisms of leisure in Western society are class, gender, race and occupation. They have developed, largely in unplanned, unintended ways, to allocate economic resources and distribute prestige. They operate to legitimate the unequal relation of individuals to scarcity. They are the basis of social solidarity and also social conflict. Let us examine each of them in greater detail.

Class

In the study of leisure, class is understood to be a relation of social groups to ownership and control of property. The most basic level at which class intervenes in leisure practice is through the distribution of leisure time, leisure space and life chances. Roberts (1999), who is critical of many aspects of class analysis in leisure, especially the Marxist version, nevertheless recognizes that the higher strata enjoy more leisure time and greater opportunities to participate in consumer culture. To be sure, he (1999: 85) refers to them somewhat caustically as 'privileged omnivores', by which he means that they enjoy superior access to economic and cultural capital that translates into the elaboration of exclusive leisure tastes and practices organized around an abundance of money and time. There is a moralistic as well as a descriptive overtone here which parallels Veblen's (1899) thesis that the richest echelon in society constitutes a leisure class that makes a virtue out of conspicuous consumption and utilizes leisure as a insignia of distinction, displaying freedom from the need to engage in paid employment.

Economic inequalities of class are undeniable facts of life. For example, the Institute for Fiscal Studies (2002) in the UK found that income in the top 20 per cent is 18 times that of the bottom 20 per cent. Despite social and economic policies of redistributive justice, the gap has grown in the last four decades. Median equivalent incomes have doubled in real terms since 1961. However, the income of the richest tenth has risen almost twice (137 per cent) as much as that of the poorest tenth (74 per cent). Economic inequalities translate into stark differences in life chances and experience. For example, the UK Department of Health (2002) reported that life expectancy for males in social class V is over seven years less than for professional social classes: 71.1 years compared with 78.5 years. For women the gap is over 5.5 years. Babies with fathers in social classes IV and V have a birth-weight that is on average 130 grams lower than that of babies with fathers in classes I and II. Low birth-weight is linked with death in infancy, as well as being associated with coronary heart disease, diabetes and hypertension in later life.

In the USA the wealth gap is equally disturbing. The top 1 per cent of the population holds 40.1 per cent of total household wealth. As with the UK, the gap has grown in the last fifteen years. The pay ratio of top corporate chief executives to the hourly wages of production workers increased from 93 times that of workers in 1988 to 419 in 1999. By the mid-1990s the percentage of employees in the bottom 10 per cent with health insurance provided by their companies *declined* from 49 per cent in 1982 to 26 per cent in the mid-1990s (Phillips 2002).

Inequalities in access to economic resources and differences in prestige directly influence leisure forms and practice. Thus, the masculine leisure repertoire in working-class youth culture of excessive drinking, having a laugh, occasional outbursts of violence and generally denigrating the system is an on-location response to formidable cultural and economic inequalities of class. Working-class men and women are positioned to follow these scripts of leisure behaviour that derive from their relative powerlessness. Although they involve rich forms of creativity and resistance, and constitute important types of social solidarity, essentially they are fatalistic responses to their class's isolation from decisive control and influence over property and knowledge. It is not a matter of the working class being without property or knowledge. Rather it is a question of this property and knowledge being positioned in relations of fateful dependency and intrinsic resistance to the power bloc.

Willis's (1977) study of working-class boys in school famously demonstrated how schools teach children to go into working-class jobs. Similarly, studies of masculine and feminine leisure forms show how working-class leisure achieves the same end in the sphere of voluntary behaviour (McRobbie 1978, 1993; Blackshaw 2003).

Working-class leisure forms ritualize freedom from the necessity to labour by employing a version of conspicuous consumption. The blue collar weekend break or vacation involves the celebration of autonomy, control and resistance by various ceremonies of excess including the consumption of alcohol and narcotics, unbuttoned language, gestures and acts of aggression and uninhibited sexuality and the cultivation of bonds of intense camaraderie and frivolity. They invest the world of work and class dependency with a carnivalesque quality and reinforce ties of solidarity. They make a totem out of leisure as a social form that permits breaking the rules of dependency and subordination. However, the sense of freedom that they generate carries an undertow of desperation, since it is predicated in subordination to the latent (during leisure time), but irresistible, principle of having to earn a living. It does not break the mould of wage labour with all of the limiting dependencies on personal aspirations, the use of free time and mobility that go with it. Working-class leisure forms ritualize excess and conspicuous consumption not to display freedom from the need to labour (as is the case with the leisure class), but to ritually articulate and impugn their latent subordination to the treadmill of paid employment.

Of course, there are exceptions to the rule. Just as Bourdieu (1984) argued that education is a route out of the culture of dependency and resistance for *some* working-class children, working-class leisure forms *can* provide opportunities for the generation of critical consciousness and upward social mobility. Reading groups, discussion groups, sports teams and physical exercise groups have a long history in working-class cultures. Authors like Richard Hoggart (1957) and Raymond Williams (1961) produced rather sentimental accounts of 'respectable' working-class life and self-help. Yet, even for writers who properly emphasize the creativity of working-class leisure practice and the capacity of the working class to lever the redistribution of cultural and economic capital in their favour, the *cultural reproduction* of class inequality is an inescapable feature of society. Indeed, Blackshaw's (2003: 6) account of the prominence of the pub, brawling, sexual stereotyping and scapegoating authority in male working-class youth culture proposes that these leisure forms have an 'immutable' quality in working-class culture. Later in life, they recall a sense of nostalgic solidarity in the midst of a world that is still controlled by remote and, to a large extent, invisible elements in the political directorate, decisive business interests and the media. The regulative mechanism of class stacks resource allocation and the distribution of prestige in favour of the highest class echelons.

Class solidarity in leisure settings such as the pub or the football ground is an important way of acknowledging belonging in a world where inequalities in resource allocation and prestige distinctions engender division, tension and friction. Attempts to correct this by enlisting leisure provision as a central feature in welfare policy have been strongly resisted. The attack on hedonism and self-indulgence launched by the New Right after the 1980s reasserted the traditional capitalist principle that the entitlement to leisure must be earned through paid employment. It triumphantly reaffirmed the fundamental values and moral obligations of family and community (Aronowitz and Di Fazio 1994).

The intensification of the *moral regulation* of the working class went hand in hand with the amplification of the drive to commercialize working-class leisure forms. The pub, many sports, notably football, darts and snooker, and music, were redefined as *leisure capital*. The introduction of theming, foreign cuisine and karaoke on the time-hallowed floors of the British working-class pub was designed to attract a younger clientele with more disposable income. Studies by Gruneau (1983) in Canada and King (1998) in the UK present a parallel analysis of the same process in the field of sport. Gruneau presents a narrative of the class control and commodification of Canadian sports, while King shows how corporations, especially Sky TV, redefined the traditional working-class game of football into leisure capital that could be commercially exploited.

The influence of class in the twin circuits is apparent in a number of ways. Taking the circuit of production and consumption first, sociologists of labour have posited a deep-seated *deskilling* of the labour process especially in the era of Keynesian-Fordism (Braverman 1974). As craft skills were replaced by machinery and the reduction of assembly and manufacture relegated workers to the performance of simplified tasks, labour's stock of skills dwindled. More recently, Castells (1996, 1997, 1998) has revived the Marxian concept of general replaceable labour to highlight the tendency of capital to automate craft and make workers redundant. The rise of shopping malls and themed consumption environments was concomitant with this process (Gottdiener 2000; Ritzer 2000). The reduction of labour skills from paid employment was accompanied by the gradual segregation of shopping from the community. At the same time the home emerged as the primary leisure setting, with television as the premier leisure form, taking up over 50 per cent of leisure time in the USA by the 1990s (Kubey and Csikszentmihalyi 1990).

Heavier reliance in working-class households upon public transport, combined with lower levels of disposable income and the expenditure of greater physical energy in the workplace, translates into a higher propensity to engage in home-based activities. The pub or sporting fixture constitutes a regular part of leisure behaviour where social solidarity is articulated. But participation in it is heavily constrained by income. The *sedentary* nature of home-based activities is associated with a variety of medical problems, including obesity. The National Center for Chronic Disease Prevention and Health Promotion in the USA has used the term 'obesity epidemic' to describe current conditions regarding weight distribution in the US population. Being overweight hinders many forms of leisure activity, especially those requiring physical mobility. It is also associated with a wide range of health risks such as colon cancer, diabetes, coronary failure and arthritis. Obesity is technically defined as an energy imbalance caused by the retention of too many calories. It is the result of the interaction between genes, metabolism, behaviour, environment, culture and socio-economic status. Some disorders of obesity such as Bardet-Biedl and Prader-Willi syndromes are primarily caused by genetic imbalances. However, Hill and Trowbridge (1998) propose that since the genetic composition of the general population does not change rapidly, the current obesity epidemic in the USA must be the result of non-genetic factors. One major factor is lifestyle changes. In particular, the increased accessibility of pre-packaged convenience foods and fast-food outlets is significant since convenience foods are usually high in fat, sugar and calories. Another important factor is the rise of ownership in labour-saving technologies in transport and housework, such as cars, lifts, computers, televisions, dishwashers, washing machines and lawnmowers, which have made Americans more sedentary. In 2000, the Behavioural Risk Factor Surveillance System estimated that as many as 26 per cent of adults reported no leisure-time physical activity.

For reasons given above, notably lower levels of disposable income, heavier reliance on public transport and higher levels of exhaustion caused by the physical nature of paid employment, it is probable that obesity risk is concentrated in working-class households. Certainly, fast-food companies use low pricing strategies and convenience as prominent factors in their marketing and product strategy.

Turning now to the question of how class influences the management of aggression and sexuality, Dunning *et al.* (1988: 208–9) argue that masculine members of the lower working class develop close bonds of allegiance to community and kin. These 'territorial identifications', together with 'segmentation' from the decision-making centres in society, result in the tolerance of higher levels of aggressiveness in social relations. Working-class life carries greater propensity to the use of physical violence in leisure. Other classes have certainly not succeeded in neutralizing aggression in leisure forms or the family. Katz's (1988) work on crime demonstrates the vitality of aggressive and criminal play forms in white-collar backgrounds. However, aggression here is typically more privatized and sequestered than in working-class life.

Gang structures, pub sparring, club brawling and hooliganism are mechanisms for relaxing the inhibitions of the work regime. This is not to say that leisure is the arena for working-class articulations of aggression, while work is a temple of self-control. We know from the work of Moorhouse (1983, 1989) that aggression and play also occur in work. However, the balance of expressing these emotions weighs in favour of the spectrum of leisure activities, because it is here that the external restraints and regime of internal discipline attached to wage labour are relaxed.

Class operates in the management of sexuality by screening leisure venues where members of the opposite sex meet. By definition, pubs, clubs, gyms and recreation centres located in working-class areas are frequented predominantly by members of the working class. Other classes are not *excluded* from these venues. But many social, cultural and economic factors combine to make them feel incongruous in these venues. As Murdock (1989: 93), drawing on the work of Bourdieu, notes, participation in leisure mobilizes cultural capital that presupposes *cultural competence*. Bona fide participation and acceptance in leisure forms like being a football fan, an opera enthusiast, a gardener or a connoisseur of illegal drugs are structured by class location. As Murdock (1989: 93) puts it:

> The specialized knowledge and skills involved in competences are part of wider patterns of collective meaning and response developed by particular class segments – they are embedded in specific class cultures. Differential patterns of cultural consumption and leisure participation are therefore rooted in the differential distribution of cultural competences and class-based meaning systems. This distribution, in turn, is anchored and reproduced through class-based differentials in family socialization.

Access to leisure venues where you are likely to meet people of the opposite sex is shaped by factors like where you live, income, free time and transport. All of these factors are strongly correlated with class structure.

Gender

The question of gender inequality and leisure forms and practice is complex and many-sided. It is best examined under four subheadings relating to the central dimensions of female inequality and dependence covering paid employment, housework, sexuality and violence.

Paid employment

In the UK since the Equal Pay Act of the 1970s the earnings gap between the sexes has decreased from 31 to 18 per cent. There are 12 million female workers in the UK economy. Women working full-time earn 82.1 per cent of the average hourly earnings of men. The earnings gap is wider because women generally work fewer hours per week and are less likely to do overtime owing to family responsibilities. Women's full-time weekly earnings are 74.8 per cent of those of men (Kingsmill Review 2003). The Cabinet Office (2002) estimates that the difference in lifetime earnings between men and women is £197,000 for low-skilled workers, £241,000 for medium-skilled workers and £142,000 for highly skilled workers. Women predominate overwhelmingly in part-time work and the low-paid sector. Robinson and Godbey (1999) report similar trends in the USA, especially in respect of marked and persistent inequalities in the pay gap between men and women, the tendency of women to work fewer hours in paid employment per week and the concentration of women in part-time work and the low-paid sector.

Lower weekly pay and lifetime earnings have obvious implications for participation in leisure cultures. Women have less disposable income to spend on leisure activities and consumer culture. They are more likely to be financially dependent upon their male partners to pay for holidays, meals, the cinema and the pub. Financial dependency brings with it emotional indebtedness, complicating women's relationship with men by introducing a financial underside to emotional relationships.

The reasons for the earnings gap are complicated, but most commentators agree that three factors are central. First, women's work has historically been undervalued. Second, there is marked gender segregation in the employment market. For example, few female employees enter jobs in engineering and the construction industry, while at the same time females predominate in hairdressing and clerical and secretarial work. Third, the identification of women's role with domestic labour and child and adult care means that women are under greater pressures to enter part-time employment. In the UK, 80 per cent of all part-time workers are women and only 17 per cent of them are in professional occupations (Low Pay Unit website 2004).

Housework

The Office for National Statistics *UK 2000 Time Use Survey* reported that women do twice as much housework as men. Housework is defined as work relating to housing, transport, nutrition, clothing, laundry and unpaid care. Twenty-seven per cent of women's weekly time is devoted to housework, compared with 7 per cent in paid employment. For men, the respective figures are 20 per cent and 12 per cent.

There has been significant variation in the division of domestic labour over the past thirty years. Gershuny (2000: 128–9, 198–9) provides quantitative evidence to suggest that there has been significant gender convergence in household work, with men taking on more domestic labour. However, his research confirms the general finding that there is still a strong tendency for women to take responsibility for a larger proportion of housework and, arguably, to *feel* that it is their responsibility and hence spend more time worrying about it than men.

Research in the USA confirms that women shoulder most of the workload at home. Schor (1992: 20–1) estimated that the total unpaid working time of employed mothers averages about 65 hours a week. As in the UK women do twice as much unpaid domestic work as men: 30.9 hours for women as against 15.9 hours for men. Although there is some evidence of growing teamwork or gender convergence, the differences between labour tasks remain remarkably stereotypical. The main tasks of women are cooking, cleaning, childcare, shopping and laundry work; the equivalent distribution of male unpaid domestic tasks are repairs, childcare, gardening and financial management (Robinson and Godbey 1999: 100–1).

The quantitative and qualitative segregation of household work between the sexes means less free time for women. Women are more likely than men to feel guilty about enjoying leisure outside the home since it takes them away from childcaring responsibilities. By the same token, they are more likely to volunteer for this work as part of their gender duty. These responses are the automatic, unreflective articulation of the master patterns of thought and value internalized through the gendered socialization of the sexes. Even if home helps or babysitters are employed, women are more likely to organize and manage substitute domestic labour. The identification of the woman's ultimate role with the family and housework means that they are more likely to be anxious about fully pursuing a career in paid employment. Women's participation in paid employment is a crucial source of increasing relative independence and building self-esteem. 'The difficulty is', writes Hochschild (1997: 247), 'not that women have entered the workplace but they have done so "on male terms". It would be fine for women to adopt the male model of work, to enjoy privileges formerly reserved for men, if this model were one of balance. But it is not.'

Sexuality

The feminist pairing of embodiment with property raises the question of who 'owns' the female body. In Leisure Studies this has been most interestingly explored along two main fronts: (1) pornography and (2) women and leisure space.

Men are the main consumers of pornography, a sector in the US leisure market with an annual multibillion-dollar revenue that rivals the three major US TV networks combined (Kipnis 1999: ix). One reason why pornography is obviously objectionable is its rank dishonesty.

Pornography systematically erases the relationships between women, family and work. Women are abstracted from community and family and portrayed as autonomous actors intent on gratifying male entitlements to carnal gratification and subservient emotional support.

The orthodox feminist interpretation of pornography decrees that it degrades, demeans and exploits women. The feminist anti-porn lobby in the USA holds that pornography is the core of female oppression (see in particular Dworkin 1978; MacKinnon 1993). There has been surprisingly little empirical work into the question of women's attitudes to pornography as a leisure resource.

One notable exception is Shaw's (1999) study of Canadian women. She found that her sample of women was generally resentful of narrow, stereotyped, passive heterosexist views of female sex. Some of them engaged in strategic collusion with their husbands and partners in the consumption of pornography. They were strongly dismissive of the masculine, idealized version of the female body that dominated pornographic narratives. Shaw found that the women in her sample strongly disapproved of violent images of women in pornography. Conversely, without being positive, they were less antagonistic to non-violent sexual images and narratives of consenting or same-sex couples. This finding exists in some tension with the anti-porn argument and suggests that women's responses to pornography may be more variable and nuanced in relation to content. Shaw's respondents excluded men, but it would be interesting to find out what male respondents feel about the idealized masculine bodies portrayed in pornographic narratives and also if men generally believe that the stock-in-trade of pornography is female subordination or male gullibility.

By way of a contrasting voice, Kipnis's (1999) non-empirical study suggests that the situation is more complex. She maintains that pornography frequently represents male authority as absurd and perverse and male vanity as pitiful. She does not discount that degrading, demeaning and exploitative images of women abound in pornographic genres. At the same time she submits that the same adjectives apply to pornographic representations of men. Her work stands the male/female binary opposition of the anti-porn lobby on its head. Echoing the themes of the transgressive body and unruly sexualities found in the work of Bakhtin (1968), she argues that another way to read pornography is as an affront to the flimsy, tenuous constructions of the idealized sexual body whether it be located in masculine or feminine repertoires of representation. As evidence, she cites the emergence of specialist sub-genres in pornography during the 1990s, devoted to sex between the over-50s, obese couples and transsexuals. She interprets this as a reaction *against* essentialist constructions of the female/male body and evidence of a new interest in pornography with bodily *transgression*. Together with the renewal of fashions of piercing, tattooing and other forms of bodily decoration, this trend supports the view that anti-essentialism, or the repudiation of binary boundaries, is at the forefront of practice in the field of leisure and sexuality.

Turning now to the question of women and leisure space, male fantasies about the female body associate it overwhelmingly with fecundity and play. This projects women as central elements in the landscape of the home and the holiday. Skeggs (1999: 228) maintains that the spatial representation and positioning of the female body is constructed around a powerful 'discourse of respectability'. State agencies (education, health, welfare and the media) continually misrepresent women by making them justify their 'negligence' and 'irresponsibility' in straying out of 'safe space'. The beach and the holiday resort may be the exception to this, since these **sexogenic** spaces are encoded for casual sexual relationships (Wyllie 2000: Ryan and Hall 2001). However, even here, women are more likely to be subject to censure if the relationships 'go too far' or 'get out of hand'. Women have to defend themselves for 'leading men on' in sexogenic space, when the real question is masculine collusion in the construction of these settings in the leisure landscape.

Sexogenic space refers to physical and cultural settings in which sexual arousal is a preeminent feature of locale. Examples include red-light districts and lap-dancing clubs.

Skeggs (1999: 227) refers to the 'normalization' of gay spaces and leisure events in cities, such as Old Compton Street in London's Soho and the Castro district of San Francisco, Gay Pride parades such as the Sydney Mardi Gras, the Manchester Mardi Gras and the Pride Festival in London. These phenomena provide important data about how sexuality and space is changing. Skeggs (1997: 227) also suggests that it is producing new 'safe sex' spaces for women, in which the risk of male violence and 'straight gawking' is reduced. However, this is in the context of sexual inequality in which many public spaces are colloquially understood to be 'risky'. Scraton and Watson (1998: 135) counsel against notions of 'shared oppressions' or 'shared resistance' in the structure of public space. Nonetheless, even in the setting of what they call 'the postmodern city', they insist on the continuation of gender-based spatial inequality and injustice.

Violence

Violence against women is concentrated in leisure. This is because leisure generally involves the relaxation of general emotional and physical inhibitions that apply elsewhere in social life. Elias and Dunning's (1986) work on leisure and the civilizing process argues that inhibitions and controls do not vanish in leisure practice. Rather they enter a different key or 'tension-balance' in which the balance of inhibitions against aggression and sexuality are reconfigured. This process of shifting the tension-balance into a new key is symbolized ritualistically. For example, at the level of dress most of us swap work clothes for leisure wear when we come home from the office or factory. Similarly, at the level of intimacy in bars and pubs alcohol is used to reduce social controls and sponsor intimacy. Likewise, in sports grounds levels of swearing and aggressive gestures are tolerated which would invite censure in other areas of social life.

The question of violence in women's leisure can be explored briefly by examining the topic of rape. The Rape Crisis Federation of England and Wales reports that between 1976 and 1997 the number of women alleging rape increased by 500 per cent. At the same time the number of convictions fell. In 1977 one in three women reporting rape saw their assailants convicted, in 1996 less than one in ten did. There are two explanations for this. Either society is becoming more lenient in dealing with cases of rape, or rape allegations have been exaggerated.

Data from the USA suggest that the incidence of rape has fallen every year since 1992. The US Centers for Disease Control and Prevention and the National Institute for Justice interviewed 8,000 men and 8,000 women, and estimated that more than 876,000 rapes are committed in a typical year. One in seven American women have been raped and the typical rape victim is raped nearly three times a year, usually by her husband or domestic partner (Johnson 1998). The British Crime Survey for 2000 estimated that 61,000 women were victims of rape (Bindel 2003). Although cases of male rape are reported, they are statistically insignificant in comparison with the incidence of female rape. The crime is a major component of violence against women and it is concentrated in the leisure sphere.

Cases of rape involve a range of sexual prohibitions that operate against disclosure. Victims suffer from feelings of shame and anxieties that they will not be believed. The adversarial system of court investigations mean that a woman's character and credibility will be questioned by defence lawyers and in some cases malice will be attributed to her. Women may be accused of 'leading a man on' by sexually provocative dress or flirting. As a result, just as with the question of domestic violence, many cases of rape never come to trial.

On the other hand, one effect of the permissive society of the 1960s is the casualization of sexual relationships. In such a climate intent on the part of the alleged rape victim or the perpetrator is often very difficult to establish. The rise in allegations of rape against male celebrities suggests either the growth of omnipotence in male celebrity culture or the growth of a culture of sexual incitement among female fans. Representations of sexuality in celebrity culture and the response of the fan base to them constitute a hugely under-researched area in Leisure Studies.

The examples of work, domestic labour, pornography and rape demonstrate how the regulative mechanism of gender positions women unequally in relation to scarce resources. At its most effective, it *naturalizes* sexual inequality, so that women, especially married women, automatically feel disentitled to leisure and connive to assign greater leisure life chances to males.

Race

Genetic approaches attempt to explain inequality in leisure and society by proposing that it faithfully expresses differences in genetic endowments between individuals and the groups to which they are attached. Arthur Jensen (1969) and Hans Eysenck (1971), two major twentieth-century psychologists, maintained that genetic composition determines the intelligence quotient (IQ). They argued that class and race differences in achievement at school reflect unalterable differences in the genetic endowment of classes and races. The social policy implications of this argument are controversial. Most notably, it proposes that assigning increased funds for schooling, health and welfare to socially disadvantaged groups will have little effect since the genetic endowment of these groups prohibits them from making significant progress.

The argument has been roundly attacked for being unduly pessimistic about the achievements of social and economic reform in widening life options and engineering upward mobility for disadvantaged groups (White 2001: 160–5). However, it remains a powerful approach, especially in the hands of Conservative and right-wing groups who wish to drive levels of personal taxation down and roll back the state (Hernstein and Murray 1994).

A genetic explanation of leisure behaviour:

- Focuses on human behaviour rather than the social, economic and cultural location and context of action.
- Posits biochemical dispositions in conduct which are not remedial through social policy.
- Reduces human behaviour to the biochemical properties which compose it.
- Legitimates unequal economic resource allocation and the distribution of prestige by holding that it is the *natural* articulation of racial difference.

Genetic approaches are a version of essentialism and as such are vulnerable to the criticisms made in Chapter 1. In particular, they are unable to marshal a satisfactory explanation of comparative and historical variation in behaviour.

Empirical work into the relationship between genetic endowment and leisure conduct is scarce, although the recent Parekh Report (2000) in the UK made some noteworthy observations on racial inequality in respect of the arts, media and sport, which we will consider at the end of this section. Conversely in Sports Studies there is a strong tradition of research, especially into the question of football hooliganism, which exposes profound limitations in the genetic approach. For example, a strong tradition in the study of sport attributes the superior performance of black male athletes over their white counterparts to heredity. It is proposed that the genetic endowment of male blacks has produced a distinctive skeletal system, musculature and metabolic structure that confer competitive advantage in athletics (Bouchard 1988; Malina 1988; Burfoot 1992; Entine 2000). In a compelling critique of the argument, St Louis (2003) demonstrates how stereotypical racial taxonomies have been conflated with tendentious genetic analysis to create a false set of conclusions. He uses cross-cultural and historical methods to prove that the performance of black athletes is variable. Citing the work of Edwards (1973) and Cashmore (1982), he (2003: 87) attributes conscious motivational causes behind the success of black athletes. Their desire to emulate successful role models is intensified in a generalized socio-economic context of racial inequality and institutionalized racism. Ideology and the interpellation of racial stereotypes are therefore prioritized in this explanation.

Genetic accounts provide an insufficient explanation of leisure behaviour. Abstracted from history and cross-cultural conditions, they are of limited value, while inserting them in these conditions often reveals ideological undertones that diminish their force. Obviously, genetics is an axial principle in human behaviour but its instrumental effect in shaping behaviour is a question of balance with many other factors including metabolism, environment, culture and socio-economic status.

Post-colonial and cultural accounts of racial inequality have focused on the role of economic, political and cultural power. They treat race as a socio-historical concept and reject transhistorical approaches founded in biology. Stuart Hall (1991, 1992) argues that racial identity and indeed *all* forms of identity are constructed through splitting. Colonialism, he argues, was a socio-historical formation constructed around splitting between the European colonial power and the non-European, non-white native 'Other'. The 'Other' was systematically alienated from history and culture. *Their* history and culture were erased and they were inserted into white narratives by a variety of *discursive strategies*. Hall (1992: 308) identifies four strategies as having decisive importance:

1. *Idealization* – the notions of 'the noble savage' or the 'barbarian' which are culturally coded as separate categories in Western civilization.
2. *Fantasies* – of desire and degradation centring upon the 'raw' sexuality of natives.
3. *Erasure* – of recognition or respect for cultural difference.
4. *Imprinting* – of Western categories and norms on to all colonized forms of life.

These colonial strategies have exerted an influence over the construction of race that has lasted long after the formal dissolution of empire. Post-colonial and cultural accounts of race address how racial Otherness is constructed and reproduced in culture and history. The aim is to expose discursive strategies of idealization, fantasy, erasure and imprinting and foster *a politics of difference*. The latter is more complex than it looks. It incorporates the determination to acknowledge and respect racial difference but is also committed to responding to newly exposed forms of positional domination. In Hall's (1991: 57) words:

> We are all complexly constructed, through different categories, of different antagonisms, and these may have the effect of locating us socially in multiple positions of marginality and subordination, but which do not yet operate on us in exactly the same way ... any counter-politics of the local which attempts to organize people

through their diversity of identifications has to be a struggle which is conducted positionally. It is the beginning of anti-racism, anti-sexism and anti-classicism.

Hall's work, post-colonialism and post-feminism can be best understood as exercises in anti-essentialism (Rojek 2003). That is, they reject foundational categories of culture, race and gender in favour of an approach that recognizes multiple difference and plural desire. Ultimately, the politics of difference poses the question of 'post-identity' thinking, which brings with it distinctive analytical benefits but also serious problems. However, because they relate to issues well beyond race and gender it is best to postpone addressing these until later in the chapter on 'Central Problems' for leisure theory.

Although Hall's work and post-colonialism have primarily addressed *theoretical* issues, most notably at the level of discursive strategies and constructions of identity, it has generated policies. The recommendations of the Parekh Report (2000) on multicultural Britain are important in this regard. The Parekh Report (2000: 161) noted entrenched racial inequalities in the arts, media and sport. For example, of the first £2 billion spent on the arts from the National Lottery, a derisory 0.02 per cent was assigned to organizations representing black and Asian artists. Media coverage of African, Caribbean and Asian communities is often condescending and distorted. Non-whites are vastly under-represented in central and local government. Among executive managers in the UK's main television companies, the BBC, ITV and Channel 4, there were fewer black and Asian people in 2000 than there had been a decade before. Parekh's recommendations centre on racial inclusion. With respect to the arts and the media, the national canon and the core institutions of cultural transmission need to be reconstituted to overcome Britain's 'selective amnesia' about its former empire and ethnic diversity. The catalyst for this is supporting new ethnic work, via central funding, on migrant experience through drama, photography, heritage and film. A more far-reaching recommendation is that every major arts and media organization should be required to commission an independent audit of its programmes, output and employment profile, representation of cultural diversity and financial investment to ensure wider racial inclusion. Media bias should be subject to independent monitoring and newspapers and television companies should be 'named and shamed in high profile ways' (Parekh 2000: 171). Turning to sport, Parekh commended the 'Kick Racism out of Football' campaign set up by the Commission for Racial Equality and the Professional Footballers

Association as a model for anti-racist programmes in other sports. The report (2000: 175) recommended that all sports organizations be required to determine and publish equal opportunity policies to show how they intend to increase numbers of black and Asian people involved as managers, administrators, coaches and officials. In addition, sports organizations should be required to publish anti-racist statements and monitor their effectiveness.

In a series of works the black British sociologist Paul Gilroy (1993, 2000, 2004) has warned of the dangers of racial stereotyping through *raciology*. His work confirms the proposition that race is a central regulative mechanism in contemporary society, but seeks to clarify the complexity of racial categories by emphasizing the place of **hybridity** in racial categories. By doing so he seeks to destabilize the category of racial purity,

---

Hybridity means mixed ancestry or a subject derived from heterogeneous or incongruous elements. In post-colonial theory the concept is deployed to attack the notion of racial purity and the concomitant propositions of racial superiority and inferiority.

---

since by demonstrating that each race is a mixture of heterogeneous, incongruous elements the pretext for the claim of racial superiority crumbles. Gilroy argues in favour of a form of race relations in which each member of each race cultivates a *double consciousness* under which racial solidarity and hybridity are simultaneously acknowledged. The question of what institutional forms are going to make this happen is opaque.

Gilroy tends to fall back on a faith in education and support for *planetary humanism*, by which he means the recognition of the common predicament of hybridity and dependence on a stable physical environment. What this ignores is the sheer weight of vested interests in race as a regulative mechanism that allocates economic resources and distributes prestige unequally. The roots of racism are very deep in Western culture. The uprooting of them is an intergenerational task which, as the Parekh Report (2000) recommends, requires coordinated positive discrimination. There has been enormous progress in this area since the days of Martin Luther King and the civil rights movement. This has led to the formal recognition of racial equality. However, there is a long way to go before this is consistently recognized in informal relations between the races.

Occupation

Within Leisure Studies a long tradition exists that recognizes constraints on freedom of choice. Because, in our type of society, paid employment is regarded as the prerequisite for exercising leisure choice and life options, the main constraint on leisure practice is often attributed to occupation. It is easy to see why this should be so. The type of job one has is the primary influence on income, free time and the quality of surplus mental and physical energy that can be exercised in leisure practice. It is also a major source of status. Non-manual, professional workers are positioned in a different relation of access to resource allocation and the distribution of prestige than manual, unskilled personnel. The type of work that you do is related to the leisure trajectories that you are likely to develop.

A variety of models for exploring the subject have emerged. For example, Wilensky (1960) distinguished between 'spillover' and 'compensatory' patterns of work and leisure. A spillover pattern is one in which work and leisure experience converge. This is most likely to occur when workers have high levels of job satisfaction. For example, workers who are involved in highly skilled design tasks may take up model-building or woodwork as hobbies. Similarly, workers involved in the information, knowledge and communication sectors may devote their leisure time to reading, surfing the internet or researching a topic for pleasure.

In contrast, a compensatory pattern takes the form of activities designed to compensate for the deprivations of work. For example, active, manual forms of work may elicit passive forms of leisure such as watching TV or getting stoned. Similarly, sedentary, unchallenging desk-work may produce the desire for active leisure forms such as the gym, sport or walking.

Building on Wilensky's model, Parker (1983) devised a threefold classification of work–leisure patterns:

- *Extension pattern* – similar to Wilensky's 'spillover' model in which work routines carry over into leisure practice. Work satisfaction is valued highly and the same forms of behaviour are cultivated and refined in leisure practice.
- *Opposition pattern* – leisure forms are exploited and developed which compensate for work experience. Work is experienced as a source of imposition or deprivation. Leisure practice is selected to contrast with work experience.

- *Neutrality pattern* – where work is not intrinsically satisfying but also not experienced as a source of imposition or deprivation, leisure is embraced as a variation from work experience. Leisure practice is not valued as a means of compensation or opposition to work experience. Rather it is embraced as having a complementary status.

Today the work of Wilensky (1960) and Parker (1983) is regarded as somewhat old-fashioned in as much as it assumes that work is the central life interest. This reduces leisure to a dependent variable of paid employment. Thus, the exertions of paid employment determine leisure choices either by predisposing individuals to engage in leisure practice that confirms work experience or attempts to compensate for it by exploiting and developing contrasting forms of experience. Against this, a powerful position in Leisure Studies today holds that it is no longer satisfactory to assume that work is pivotal. According to this view, status is no longer tied so closely to work. Instead, it reflects choices in the area of consumption and politics. The proposition of the shift from a production-centred to a consumer-centred culture needs to be handled with caution. After all, participation in consumer culture presupposes an income. As we have already noted, the main source of income for the majority is paid employment.

Nonetheless, bearing this important caveat in mind, Gorz (1978, 1983) contends that paid employment has declined in salience as the central life interest. Indeed, he claims that most workers are now only interested in work as a means of financing their involvement in leisure practice. The casualization of the employment market has made the experience of a job for life less common. Workers now experience a variety of jobs, frequently of a part-time nature. They are often required to be geographically mobile, taking them away from the communities that formerly supplied them with a sense of community and status.

Roberts (1999: 62–3) broadly concurs. He argues that the destandard-ization of working time, the increased variation in total hours of work and the widespread use of flexi-time work schedules sponsor the emergence of *the portfolio worker* in the employment market. Under Keynesianism–Fordism work identity was characterized by the security of holding a job for life. With the collapse of Keynesianism–Fordism, work experience has become more discontinuous. Workers have adopted flexible patterns of employment that mean they will be employed in either multi-work where they have several simultaneous work contracts, or fixed-term contracts, in which they are employed by consecutive employers for finite periods of time. Portfolio workers are likely to have reduced work benefits. Simultaneous multitasking is usually only possible on the basis of part-time employment contracts which limit pension and national insurance contributions. Conversely, while consecutive portfolio work may be full-time it is often punctuated with non-work periods in which workers may be forced to draw on savings rather than invest them in pension and insurance contributions. The rolling back of the welfare state has removed the safety net that afforded workers extensive and, by today's standards, generous guaranteed income support for illness, unemployment and old age. This has direct implications for leisure practice and old age.

Portfolio work patterns transfer the burden of subsistence back on to the worker. They also influence leisure practice in obvious ways. Multi-work may increase living standards by producing a higher income, but it leaves workers with a time deficit which means that they have time restrictions on leisure. By the same token, interrupted work patterns may curtail leisure activities by alternating between cash-rich and cash-poor leisure moments.

Pahl's (1995) work on the effect of upward mobility on workers' attitudes reveals a set of status tensions that are concomitant with the transition to higher-status work. Individuals who experience high occupational mobility may improve access to resource allocation and product distribution, but they frequently suffer from anxieties about losing contact with their roots. Feelings of guilt and unworthiness are not uncommon responses to success. Upwardly mobile working-class and underprivileged ethnic individuals are often compelled to exchange collectivist orientations and leisure forms for more individualistic alternatives.

Beck (2000) and Schor (1992) argue that casualization and multitasking have transformed work experience, rendering many of the propositions about work–leisure patterns in the postwar period obsolete. Ulrich Beck (1999) has coined the term 'the Brazilianization of the West' to characterize the emerging labour pattern. He notes that in Brazil, the *casualization* of paid employment is pronounced. By this term is meant the tendency for companies to outsource as much work as possible, thereby minimizing their responsibility to provide work entitlements. The result is a substantial rise in the number of workers employed in fixed-term or part-time contracts. Traditionally, paid employment for life was presented as character-forming. However, its discontinuous character now militates against this. Workers in Brazil have to be mobile between both jobs and geographical regions. This has deep implications for leisure. Most importantly, leisure practice is more likely to be the source of

continuous status rewards, especially if it does not require deep participation in consumer culture, for example walking, running, sport, reading
(public libraries). This is because while portfolio work does not elicit
a strong sense of identity or work community, leisure forms can be a
source of personal validation through the development of a career and
ties of collective recognition. The proviso to this is that individuals
must earn enough money to be able to persist with their leisure prefer-
ences. Thus, forms of leisure that do not require high expenditure, such
as walking, running, sport and reading, have a higher propensity to
achieve the continuous experience of validation and recognition.

Another important implication is that dislocated work patterns
disjoin leisure networks. The capacity to build serious leisure careers is
obviously impeded by the need to be geographically mobile in work.
Family and friendship leisure patterns become discontinuous. This has
implications for the formulation of ties of belonging between children
and parents and also identification with communities and groups.

Schor's (1992) work develops the theme of disjoined leisure patterns
and social corrosion. She argues that multi-work is producing generations
of *overworked* workers. The rise of part-time work and the incessant
pressure to participate in consumer society combine to produce a
condition of serious time deficit. Overworked workers do not have the
time to develop continuous leisure 'careers'. Their leisure is often experienced as a time of non-intrinsic reward since they are too exhausted to
enjoy it. In addition, Schor (1992) maintains that overworked workers
are prey to a series of physical and emotional risks. They are more likely
to develop life-changing or life-threatening illnesses and they are less
able to build stable enriching relationships with their children. Overwork
decreases the quality of leisure and the quality of life. In Schor's (1992:
161–2) words:

> The ability to use leisure is not a 'natural' talent, but one that must
> be cultivated. If we veer too much towards work, our 'leisure skills'
> will atrophy... Many potentially satisfying leisure activities are off
> limits because they take too much time: participating in community
> theatre, seriously taking up a sport, or a musical instrument, getting
> involved with a church or community organization. In the leisure
> time available to us, there's less of interest to do.

Students of leisure have long argued that people who experience
dissatisfaction in paid employment look to leisure for enjoyment and
fulfilment. After all, this is the main assumption behind the compensatory

model of work–leisure. But we should be cautious in degrading the social importance of paid employment. Several points should be made:

1. There is no 'one size fits all' model of paid employment. The kind of emotional rewards one receives from work depend on the levels of autonomy, respect and trust in the workplace and the intrinsic interest in work tasks. Most studies show that workers experience dissatisfaction when levels of autonomy, respect and trust are low. But when these levels are high, work experience is a source of self-actualization and social bonding (Hochschild 1997). As such, paid employment offers *cultural* and *social* attractions, which imply that the 'post-work' scenario painted by writers like Aronowitz and Culler (1998) may be strongly resisted by workers.

2. High income is a source of pleasure and a key component in identity formation. Individuals voluntarily work long hours because they find work experience to be either a source of *intrinsic* reward or a means of *extrinsic* satisfaction. Intrinsic reward refers to the satisfaction that the individual derives from work experience. Beating the competition and designing a product to the best of one's abilities are examples of intrinsic rewards. Extrinsic rewards refer to the life options that high income delivers. By earning high surplus income the individual enjoys options to participate more fully in consumer culture, for example by long-distance travel, buying designer clothes or luxury apartments, and so on.

3. Paid employment is an important source of status in market society. Our social worth is judged by our contribution to society. Through paid employment we generate individual wealth, but also add to social wealth through taxation to fund education, policing, environmental protection and welfare.

4. Casualized labour patterns may enhance the significance of leisure practice as a means of status reward and status distinction. If work carries low intrinsic satisfaction for workers, leisure may become more important in developing a sense of meaning and supporting the experience of career development. Alternatively, casualized labour may correlate with casual forms of leisure in which immediate gratification and desultory traction between varieties of passive or low-attention forms of leisure become the norm (Stebbins 2001).

Regulative mechanisms: a summary

In this chapter we have examined the central regulative mechanisms that manage the twin circuits of production–consumption and the economy of aggressive–sexual energy. Central regulative mechanisms are understood to be the forces that govern the motion of everyday life, including leisure forms and practice. They are unintended, unplanned mechanisms which arise from the intended actions of individuals, that allocate economic resources and distribute prestige. They inscribe their influence on everyday life through institutions of normative coercion. For example, the state influences leisure forms and practice through licensing, taxation, policing and curriculum development in schools and universities. But the power bloc in which the state is situated conditions the various actions of the state over leisure forms and practice. The central regulative mechanisms that the power bloc uses to pursue its interests are the inequalities and relations of legitimation associated with class, gender, race and occupation.

Key points

- Regulative mechanisms service the circuit between production and consumption and the regulation of aggression and sexuality that all societies require to maintain social order.
- Regulative mechanisms structure the allocation of resources and the distribution of prestige.
- Regulative mechanisms operate at the level of context; normative institutions of coercion may be thought of as the local means through which axial functions are realized.
- Class, gender, race and occupation inscribe leisure forms with distinctive characteristics and pose specific forms of resistance.
- Leisure forms and practice expose the position of individuals and groups in relation to the question of scarcity.
- Ritualized leisure practice, especially in respect of relations of class, gender and race, reflects positions of disadvantage in resource allocation and the distribution of prestige.
- Leisure forms and practice rechannel frictions that derive from structures of inequality and often constitute significant bases of solidarity.
- Transformations in the allocation of paid labour, especially the outsourcing of work, are changing the old connotation of leisure as the reward for paid employment.

8
Location Principles

In this chapter you will be:

- Introduced to methodological issues pertinent to the study of location practice.
- Shown the difference between *indexical, homological* and *integral* levels of location research.
- Appraised of the distinction between *serious* and *casual* leisure.
- Invited to consider the relationship between leisure, social density and social capital and encouraged to assign the political dimensions of leisure forms and practice as a prerequisite of research.
- Shown the meaning of the concepts of 'escape', 'limit experience' and 'edgework' in leisure forms and practice.
- Offered a model of the abnormal forms of leisure.

How can we study leisure theory in practice? The question is relevant because the Action approach to leisure is committed to producing *testable* knowledge. A huge variety of research methods exist. Alan Bryman (2001) has produced the best guide to them that I know. Anyone interested in the techniques of social research and the pros and cons of different research methods should consult Alan's book. His technical advice and assessment of valid social research practice enable ready transference to more specialist fields like Leisure Studies.

In this chapter I confine myself to a discussion of location *principles*. This means addressing the primary considerations that students of leisure must apply in doing field research. Utmost amongst these is respecting the *sensuous* dimension of leisure practice. Embodiment draws attention to being-in-the-world and the various conditions and circumstances that go with it. This is not simply a question of recognizing that bodies have senses. Feminist contributions have done much to correct models of leisure that are overdependent upon a model of men and women as preeminently rational actors by insisting that the emotional character of practice must be acknowledged (Shaw 1994; Henderson *et al.* 1996). A consistent perspective on the sensuous character of the body requires the researcher to recognize the capacity of the body to 'write over' interpellation and the positioning of subjects. Interpellation and positioning provide the rules and resources for action. However, a characteristic of action is to reproduce and transform the conditions in which it is emplaced. If researchers are naturally drawn to embodied action, since it is the primary means through which individuals appear to realize desires and wants, the context of emplacement is also of indispensable importance.

Think of embodied action as the *manifest* dynamic in leisure practice. Factors of emplacement relating to class, gender, race, generation and locale may be less visible, but they nonetheless exert a *latent* force upon leisure practice since they condition life options of choice and self-determination. The dynamic nature of embodied action means that there is always a surplus beyond the reach of the discursive restraints associated with emplacement.

Vitally, a quality of humans is the capacity to reflect upon the courses of action and the contexts in which they are embedded. One purpose of the academic study of leisure practice is to elucidate trajectories of embodied action and the contexts of emplacement in which these trajectories unfold. This has produced informative theoretical propositions about the socio-historical matrix of embodiment and emplacement. Conversely, an unfortunate feature of theories of positioning is their tendency to bury leisure practice into pre-designated categories that neutralize the sensuous dimension of embodied action. The unfinished quality of action, which means that leisure trajectories are fundamentally *processes of becoming* since we possess the capacity to reflect upon the origins and causal sequence of leisure conduct and can therefore take steps to alter it if we feel we need to, is therefore erased. The same is true of ideologies of leisure. A central principle of location analysis therefore is to test pre-designated categories and the propositions that follow from them against embodied practice. In the words of Willis (2000: 37; emphasis in original):

> Whereas ideological and official linguistic forms seek to annex all lived meanings to their powerful constitution of meaning – good

citizen, worker, student, etc. – socio-symbolic practices stabilize alternative liminal, uncoded or residually coded identities and meanings. They are held sensuously and practically and therefore *outside* and resistant to dominant linguistic meaning.

Through articulation actors have the capacity to subvert discursive categories. In studying the margin of excess, the space that lies beyond the resources of rules and regulations, we may hope to gain a better appreciation of how ideology and interpellation operate in leisure practice. We may also learn more about how embodied action outflanks the precepts of theory and ideology. Willis's (1977) own best example is his study of 'the lads' in a school in the English Midlands. Through basic means of social resistance – 'the laff' and 'the crack' – they oppose the official routes of behaviour mapped out for them by school culture. They create areas of resistance and opposition, signalled above all through language (cursing, swearing, irony, the use of 'in-words', the cultivation of **anti-structures** of behaviour). In this way the lads create their own spaces of control in the midst of the regimented, rule-bound culture of school. Observe: the leisure or play cultures developed by the lads involve *using* free-time practice to fulfil all four functions of leisure – representation (of their distance from school protocol); identity (solidarity based around distance from school protocol); control (creating anti-school spaces for the cultivation of opposition); and resistance (practising opposition against the authority structures of the sanctioned school power regime).

The concept of **anti-structures** of behaviour is associated with the work of the anthropologist Victor Turner (1969, 1992). It refers to institutions and rituals of conduct that are the inverse of the institutions and rituals of normative coercion. These include oppositional cultures that are dedicated to the political transformation of normative order. But it is a portmanteau concept that extends to subcultures that exist in a state of resistance to normative order.

However, we should be aware of the danger of reading practice in relation to function in a *programmatic* way, that is, allowing the designation of practice in a functional category to be dictated by function. The sensuous, developing character of practice can only be plotted in relation to these general functional fields. That is, we may only determine if leisure practice is fulfilling one or a mixture of the four functions by examining it on location. For example, in the case of Willis's (1978) 'lads', the forms of swearing or the direct expression of emotions belong to the functional field of resistance, but they do not necessarily extend the area of opposition through which the lads seek to create spaces of control in which they may challenge the sanctioned values of school culture. On the contrary, because they do not generate a viable alternative, they are often directed at simply letting off steam or ventilating pressure. The relationship between leisure practice in a functional field and its functional effect depends on on-site relationships and must always be a matter of on-location analysis, it cannot be *predetermined* by theory. Effective analysis should ideally strive to achieve a constant dialogue between theoretical hypotheses relating to context and location research.

Willis's (1977, 1978) work profoundly questions essentialism by exposing the category errors between location practice and the discursive strategies of institutions of normative coercion. His work places the creative actor centre stage. Through the boldness, energy and intelligence of the actor, culture is made and changed. Of course, the conditions for action are not chosen by the actor, but imposed by spatial–historical context. However, the accumulation of actions upon these conditions through sensuous and rational practice transforms the context in which culture is situated.

So it is with leisure practice and trajectories. Embodied and emplaced sensuousness are always beyond the categories imposed upon them by schools, the police, the judiciary, manufacturers of leisure commodities and so on. Discursive strategies of control in leisure are resources for resistance, counter-representation and counter-identity. Judith Butler (1993: 218) has expressed this very well in her comment about the failure of the concept of 'female identity' to encapsulate the meanings of 'female experience':

> If 'women' within political discourse can never fully describe that which it names, that is neither because the category simply refers without describing not because 'women' are the lost referent, that which 'does not exist', but because the term marks a dense intersection of social relations that cannot be summarized through terms of identity.

If it is unsatisfactory to study experience exclusively through manifest narratives of identity, how should it be studied? The view submitted here is that location research should operate with the trinity of meaning, form and structure. To elucidate: first, research must focus on the meanings made through sensuous and rational leisure practice and articulated in narrative data. Second, the meanings in practice should be related to location factors arising through *forms* and *regulative mechanisms*. Third, leisure practice, forms and regulative mechanisms should be related to the social regime of power, that is, the twin circuits of production–consumption and aggression–sexuality, which constitutes the *context* in which leisure trajectories are pursued.

Although it is generally regarded to be a contribution to the sociology of culture and cultural studies, Willis's (1977, 1978, 1990, 1998) work is a valuable methodological resource for studying leisure. His ethnographic approach has always been committed to examine location practice in culture in a dialogic relationship with theory and context. Moreover, his was one of the first approaches to reject work-centred views of culture in favour of a perspective more sensitive to embodiment, emplacement and play. The importance of non-work relations and leisure forms are original features of his ethnographic work in the 1970s and remain paramount.

A variety of interesting research findings was harvested by taking this approach. For example, Willis's (1978) study of motorbike cultures explored how aggressive forms of masculinity were cultivated in leisure cultures and lifestyles for men who no longer found their primary meaning in work and family. Similarly, his (1990) sometimes rather overstated emphasis on creativity in culture demonstrated how ordinary leisure forms are used to resist dominant power regimes through music, fashion, poetry, literature and story-telling. Willis was always true to the roots of his training in the Birmingham School of Contemporary Cultural Studies in stressing that politics is integral to leisure practice. However, his articulation of the type of politics and society to which he aspires is relatively mute. His primary focus is always upon how action unfolds in concrete settings of culture and direct action rather than in the development of strategies and policies to achieve economic and political transformation. Transgressive action is inherently political in Willis's sociology. There is no need to make the wider ends of action explicit: it is enough to act against the grain of authority, conformity and habit.

Elsewhere, he (1978: 190–203) formulates a mixed (quantitative and qualitative) methodological framework for cultural analysis that can be readily adapted for location research into leisure. He distinguishes between indexical, homological and integral levels of cultural analysis:

1. *Indexical*

The term is borrowed from ethnomethodology (Garfinkel 1967). It refers to the quantitative relationships between external cultural and leisure items and personal or group formation. For example, how much leisure time a person or group spends in playing computer games or listening to pop music, when and where, provides data about group integration and personal identity. This level of analysis is mainly quantitative. It simply observes and records time usage and spatial location in relation to leisure commodities that are external to the individual or group, that is, supplied by the market, or sponsored by individual or group direct action. By examining how much leisure time is spent watching *Pop Idol*, *Big Brother* or *Who Wants to be a Millionaire?* on television, a map of behaviour can be constructed that can eventually be analysed as an index to social values. Warde and Martens (2000), operating in a very different research tradition, nonetheless apply principles of indexicality in their study of the social and cultural functions of eating out. They measured how many residents of each household cooked and dined out to gain insights into power relationships in private dwellings and the social values attached to eating at home and dining out. Not surprisingly, they found that women are the main providers of domestic meals. The proportion of income spent on eating out has risen since the 1960s. Dining out possesses social values of mutuality and reciprocity. For women, the additional value of breaking with domestic routine is important.

The concept of social values here has a twofold character. On one side indexical analysis of leisure and cultural maps of behaviour elucidate the beliefs and interests behind leisure practice. Conversely, the indexical mapping of group behaviour also reveals how the 'external' commodity world and power regime penetrate the lives of individuals and groups. In Willis's work, leisure cultures have primary ideological significance in organizing subjects. 'Through the medium of such relationships', writes Willis (1978: 190) 'the tyranny of the commodity form is enforced, and through which the slow drip of conventional daily habit, supported by institutions, state agencies and the systematic practices of others, wears in to subjectivity the shape of larger ideologies.'

2. *Homological*

Homological analysis investigates how far indexical maps are consistent with the structure, style, typical concerns, actions and narratives of the group. Objects of culture and leisure are used as external items for the representation of group values and prejudices. For example, Skeggs's (1997) study of working-class women provides a good example in the group attitude to pornography as a leisure resource. As with Shaw's

(1999) sample of Canadian women, the British working-class women that Skeggs researched generally disapproved of pornography. The response of 'Linda' is typical:

> I'm really not into pornography. I can be very straight sometimes. I think Page 3 degrades women, why are women expected to do that?. . . but if people don't like things they don't need to watch. I don't mind porn existing I just couldn't watch it in front of a man – I'd just laugh. My friend at work had video parties, all porn with animals and that. She's been told off for laughing. She laughs all the way through. (Skeggs 1997: 146)

Linda's attitude to pornography is doubly coded. She regards it as demeaning to women, but also as a source of male ridicule. Male production of pornography and male interest in pornography as a recreational form are redefined as ways of confirming female maturity. Laughing 'all the way through' ridicules pornography as a leisure form and mocks the credulity of men who are attracted to it as a representation of 'real sexuality'.

At the same time, Linda is typical in regarding censorship to be *more* objectionable than pornography. Censorship deprives consumers of the right to exercise choice and make up their own minds. For her, and the cohort of respondents to which she belongs, censorship smacks of condescension. It is an example of the 'we know what's best for you' mentality of rational recreation, which Skeggs (1997) relates to habitus, class control and class struggle.

Linda's stance on pornography as a leisure form and censorship as a cultural practice doubly differentiates her and the group to which she belongs from men whose immaturity allows them to be seduced by the dishonest representations of sexuality perpetuated in the genre and the joyless, feminist 'do-gooders' intent on controlling her choices (Skeggs 1997). The use of pornography as a way of gender *and* class differentiation is a deliberate strategy of *positioning*. It constitutes an immediate basis for recognizing social inclusion, representing solidarity and attributing social exclusion.

In this case a homology can be readily established between an artefact of leisure and a subcultural group because the group is *in situ* and easily identifiable. But homologies can also be established in groups that have what might be called a *virtual* existence. In consumer culture devotees of particular leisure forms may never share the same physical or cultural space, yet nonetheless constitute a formation. Simple questionnaires can establish an index between subjects like body piercing and values relating to work and leisure, or aesthetic interests in film or fashion and cultural interests in freedom, choice and self-determination. Other methods, such as observation, interviews, group discussions and recorded discussions can assist in building a map of leisure trajectories in relation to axial institutions of class, race, gender and work groups and general social variables.

3. *Integral*

Integral analysis relates indexical and homological analysis to social context. Ultimately, it is concerned with how homologies are generated. Interestingly, Willis's (1978: 201–2) work concentrates on the question of *control* to elucidate the influence of the integral. The capacity of the individual or group to creatively engineer freedom from cultural or leisure forms measures the strength or weakness of integral pressures that follow from the power regime. Integral analysis, then, seeks to place cultural and leisure practice into locations and contexts of power. To express it differently, it seeks to bridge the gap between location practice (that is often blind or at least not fully conscious of the force of regime and the precise role of axial institutions) and context (that is, the study of how the twin circuits of production–consumption/aggression–sexuality management are historically and concretely sustained). In this way a theory of the 'objective possibilities' of leisure forms and practice may, through achieving testable knowledge, be assembled.

Propositions should ideally be tested by using methods of cross-validation. For example, narratives of leisure trajectories supplied by actors in unstructured interview should be compared and contrasted with narratives generated through group discussion, questionnaires and comparative and historical analysis. This may not always be compatible with research time and financial budgets, hence the use of the adjective 'ideally'. Cross-validation provides a means of correction for problems of false memory, the embellishment of 'facts' and 'causes' in speech and strategies of deliberate deception. The researcher's own prejudices and partialities should be tested with those of leisure research subjects as an integral part of the research process. In addition, research findings should generally be made public and subject to academic and public commentary.

Serious and casual leisure

One of the core issues in location research is identifying the ends of leisure practice from the standpoint of the leisure actor. Expressed in polarized terms, leisure can be directed at letting off steam, having a laugh, engaging in conspicuous wasteful activity and breaking with routine, or it may be motivated by harnessing and extending personal skills though cultural reproduction, which is to say the confirmation of habitus.

An important contribution to location research in this regard is found in the writings of Bob Stebbins (1992, 2001). Centrally, he introduces the fruitful distinction between **serious** and **casual** leisure practice.

Serious leisure

- Amateur hobby or unpaid service activity which is based on the disciplined, systematic acquisition of knowledge and skills.
- The organization of this activity in the life course as a 'career' involving programmatic benchmarks of achievement.
- The employment of perseverance and 'deferred gratification' as a principle of voluntary time-budget allocation.
- Strong identification with the voluntarily chosen area of activity.

Casual leisure

- Amateur voluntary activity that is driven by a search for intrinsic reward, hedonism or opportunism.
- No systematic, disciplined organization is involved and participation is not dependent upon the concept of a programmatic career.
- Immediate gratification dominates the allocation of voluntary time-budget resources.
- Identification with a voluntarily chosen area of activity may be strategic and contingent.

Serious leisure and casual leisure can be mapped indexically by measuring the time allocated to specific activities in a designated leisure trajectory. Through time diaries and observation a map of practices can be constructed. Once flows of leisure activities have been established, analysis can turn to matching practice to the beliefs and values of individuals and groups to establish correlations and variance. This may be accomplished through interviews, group work, observational techniques or quantitative data analysis. Establishing homologies between practice, beliefs and values is the basis for taking analysis to the next level of mapping the contours of context, and determining if integral relations between leisure trajectories, beliefs and values and regimes of power can be disclosed.

Successful serious leisure practice involves durable benefits such as self-actualization, self-enrichment, enhancement of self-image and intensification of solidarity. As such it is a significant means of status acquisition and identity attainment and a strategy of resistance for individual and social integration and the generation of social capital. Participation in amateur operatic societies, drama groups, keep-fit networks, creative writing classes, bridge clubs and so on has the potential to augment the sense of belonging between individuals by reaffirming the interdependence between the individual and the group. It offers friendship networks that constitute the basis for reciprocity and mutual help in times of need. It presupposes regular, predictable activity and coherent leisure community networks. Serious leisure activity, then, is likely to correlate with stability in the domestic arrangements and time allocation of individuals and groups.

By contrast, casual leisure is typically opportunistic and desultory and focuses on hedonism and sensory stimulation as intrinsic sources of satisfaction. It is directed at short-term, intrinsically rewarding activities that require no training, skills acquisition or sense of career development. Examples include killing time, window-shopping, napping, strolling, smoking, games of chance, party games, sociable conversation, drinking, eating or deviant leisure activity such as joyriding, petty theft and trespass. Casual leisure correlates with contingency in domestic arrangements and spontaneity in time allocation. It is not typically directed at status acquisition or consolidation, but celebrates flexibility and acquiring satisfaction by switching between activities.

All of this points to a dismissive view of casual leisure. Stebbins takes a different view. He (2001: 65–7) warns of the dangers involved in rejecting casual leisure at face value. For one thing, he argues it provides an important source of identity and membership for individuals who feel at odds with the values of serious leisure, especially the claustrophobic connotations of 'community', 'discipline' and 'respectability', or who wish to compensate for the deprivations of work. Analogously, he (2001: 66) maintains that it is 'the main source of "serendipity" in modern life, the quintessential form of informal experimentation, accidental discovery and spontaneous invention'. It is also a major component of the modern economy.

Indexical research through observation, time diaries, group discussion or interviews maps leisure trajectories for individuals and groups.

Mapping according to casual or serious leisure distinctions may be used to reveal clusters of leisure practice organized around the evening, the weekend and the vacation. Even for workers who demonstrate a 'spillover' or 'extension' work pattern, the weekend is richly embroidered at the level of myth, as unfettered time in which individuals are released not merely from the quantitative restraints of work but also the qualitative controls. In studying working-class gendered leisure in the North of England, both Skeggs (1997) and Blackshaw (2003) allude to the importance of leisure activity in ritually sanctioned non-work time in developing escape and solidarity. The weekend with the lads or the girls creates space for recognizing belonging and refining a sense of collective identity. As such, it is not strictly speaking 'time off', but rather time in which the crucial work of maintaining a viable self-image and investing in personal substantiation, which is necessary to enable the individual to play a meaningful part in the community, is accomplished. In Black-shaw's (2003) study, the casual leisure practices of weekend drinking, arguing with each other and ogling and picking up girls are heavily ritualized forms of reaffirming working-class masculine youth group solidarity. In his view, casual leisure has serious effects in constructing a necessary functional milieu for articulating identity and resistance. For Blackshaw, the critical point is that while these leisure transactions are conducted in the spirit of defying the system and reaffirming narratives of belonging, they are conducted as *revolts into style* and, as such, do not challenge the fundamentals of the power regime. Incidentally, these leisure styles are ritually celebrated throughout the life cycle, but their form becomes ever more glossed with nostalgia as the participants bow to the ageing process and the responsibilities of family life. In maturity and old age, the lads' weekends and vacations become memorialized as a moment of carefree existence before marriage and fatherhood curtailed the pursuit of hedonism in leisure.

Because Stebbins (1992, 2001) connects serious forms with the notion of a career one might infer that leisure trajectories that reveal high indexical correlations with serious forms must exclude casual leisure practice. To do so would be a mistake. Leisure trajectories are seldom exclusively composed of either serious or casual forms. Indexical weighting may reveal that practice in given trajectories is weighted to one side or the other. Typically, both forms occur in a single leisure trajectory.

You can test this by using yourself as a resource for source of data for studying leisure. Keep a time diary of your leisure activities over a seven-day period, noting down the nature of activities, time spent on different forms of practice and whether the activities involved others or you alone. Typically, the standard leisure trajectory consists of a mixture of serious and casual forms. Your time diary will allow you to provide weightings of serious and casual leisure to your distribution of time and activities so that you construct a map of your leisure dispositions.

There are two reasons why variation in individual trajectories between casual and serious practice is commonplace. First, casual or serious forms are monotonous if they are selected as exclusive leisure life options. Few individuals are content with a diet of leisure activity that is *either* wholly disciplined, systematic and organized around deferred gratification *or* wholly opportunistic, desultory and driven by an attachment to immediate gratification. Second, the mobility of contemporary everyday life dislocates most individuals from adherence to a diet of serious forms. The hiatus between serious practice tends to be colonized by casual forms. For example, if one breaks from rehearsals for amateur dramatics, the mere insistence of consumer society draws one into casual leisure practice like window-shopping, killing time by people-watching, having a smoke and so on. Although both casual and serious forms carry strong connotations of escape – from household chores, work routines, habitus – the monotonous practice of each is likely to result in deadening engulfment. It is as if the channel of casual or serious practice that we navigate as a means of escape gradually descends into a bog of quicksand from which we seek new forms of escape.

Social density and social capital

Indexical analysis can establish the number of connections between individuals and leisure items and, crucially, the connections between *individuals* in leisure practice. The **social density** of leisure practice can therefore be revealed. Social density is conventionally understood in terms of physical contact between individuals attached to given leisure forms. However, clustered social density in leisure is not necessarily

---

Social density refers to the amount of physical contact between individuals attached to a particular leisure form. Clustered density is usually associated with serious leisure forms in which groups develop shared leisure careers. Atomized density is usually associated with casual forms in which individual leisure trajectories involve low levels of physical contact with others.

a matter of regular physical co-presence with others. You can have closer relationships with people on the net who live thousands of miles from you than with people with whom you go drinking and shopping every week. New forms of clustered social density may be emerging with the spread of the internet (Putnam 2000).

Social density is an important influence in the investment of **social capital**. Working and playing together is the basis for developing bonds of mutuality and sharing (Hemingway 1999). Reciprocity, mutuality

---

Social capital refers to informal, reciprocal obligations and expectations that support meaningful, civilized relations between individuals. It is like economic capital in that it is a variable asset, the value of which rises and falls over time. However, it is unlike economic capital in as much as its value is only realized through use. It cannot be deposited in a bank and left to accumulate value without practice. Social capital requires the regular voluntary investment of time and energy to prosper. (Rojek 2002: 22)

---

and companionship generally score highly in *quality of life* valuations (Rapley 2003). Through these means the individual's concept of self-esteem is enhanced and community solidarity strengthened. Serious leisure is a significant investment channel in the accumulation of social capital. Reciprocity, mutuality and companionship are frequently the by-product of making music together, playing sports and eating and drinking together.

However, critics of civic culture argue that several factors in the postwar period have combined to produce a serious debasement of social capital in the fabric of Western communities. Putnam (2000) is arguably the foremost advocate of this position. The picture he paints is of the steady erosion of community, the privatization of life, the unravelling of social density and declining rates of participation in politics, religion, civic culture, volunteering and philanthropy. Individualization and privatization express these trends centrally in leisure forms. Leisure practice based around group activity is losing its foothold. Individualized forms such as watching television, listening to music on personalized mini-disc players and computer games of combat and chance are gaining popularity. The development of leisure trajectories around atomized forms of social density diminishes social capital by transferring bonds of reciprocity and mutuality into contract ties of rights and responsibilities with the state, so much so that the communitarian movement in the United States has campaigned for the renewal of civic culture by increasing the donation of disposable time and income to voluntary charity work (Etzioni 1993).

However, the reversal of contract ties of rights and responsibilities with the state to bonds of reciprocity and mutuality has been fairly marginal. Economic inequality, cultural and political divisions and the mobility of populations have produced an uneven establishment of the communitarian impulse. Leisure forms may have an important part to play in strategies designed to reverse the situation. Putnam (2000) certainly thinks so. However, a discussion of his recommendations and the more general question of the role of leisure forms in civic renewal must be postponed to the next chapter.

Escape, limit experience and edgework

Freedom and choice are never absolutes in leisure practice. They are concomitant with boundaries and licences of behaviour that derive from location and context. However, precisely because location and context impose priority, externality and constraint over leisure practice they engender strong pressures for escape experience. Escape is an underdeveloped concept in Leisure Studies but it is commonplace in leisure practice. What we want to escape from varies in relation to how we are positioned in relation to scarcity and other groups which have differential claims on scarce resources. It may be unfulfilling work experience, the red tape of modern life, urban squalor or routine. Michel Foucault (1975, 1981) argued that identity and practice are *discursively* constituted. This is obviously the case with respect to the law which lays down rules of legal and illegal conduct and forces identity and practice to comply. But Foucault also pointed to models of good practice, designs for healthy living and programmes of self-improvement as examples of discursive control and regulation. His (1981) account of the history of sexuality argued that debates about sexual hygiene, campaigns against overpopulation and movements of sexual ethics cast codes of practice and identity types that shaped sexuality. It is in the nature of a code of discourse to be challenged and redefined.

Codes are the basis for individual freedom, but freedom can never be contained by codes. There is always an urge to go beyond boundaries and break codes. Foucault used the term 'limit experience' to refer to the tendency in human behaviour to reject discursive limits to identity and practice and search for new forms (Miller 1993: 29–31).

Limit experience is clearly demonstrated in the twentieth-century avant-garde where artists, dramatists and novelists have regularly tested discursive boundaries of culture and power regimes. We can think of these artistic forms of limit experience as artistic projects of escape designed to liberate creativity and energy from the conventions of the times and, in particular, the political and cultural oppression of power regimes. For most of us escape is a more prosaic matter. Tourism and travel are a common way of escaping from convention and routine. The motive for travel may be mere variation from habitual factors of location, or more grandly it may be interpreted as a 'quest for authenticity' denied by the conditions of everyday life (MacCannell 1999, Franklin 2003). In both cases escape is a powerful motive behind leisure choice and practice. Sexual promiscuity, taking narcotics and joyriding may all be studied as examples of 'escape attempts' (Cohen and Taylor 1993). Those of us who preach that rules are meant to be obeyed underestimate the pleasure gained by breaking them.

An elementary but often neglected principle of location analysis is to determine if the leisure form or practice involves illegal behaviour. Lyng (1990, 1991) introduces the concept of *edgework* to refer to forms of practice that operate around discursive and legal boundaries. The concept is not solely relevant to leisure practice since it has obvious implications for the study of crime, sexual relations and work practice. Even so, it is significant in the study of leisure. If we think of casual and serious forms as invoking boundaries around practice, much on-location behaviour can be examined as working along boundary edges to weaken or outflank discipline. Because the ludic or play element is institutionalized in leisure forms, leisure practice is a particularly rich social setting to explore edgework.

Again, your own experience is as good a resource as any to examine this. If you keep a time diary of leisure activities over a seven-day period try to isolate examples of edgework. Examples may include parking your bike or car in an illegal spot, taking banned drugs, introducing controversial topics to the social networks built around your leisure practice, trespass, computer-hacking and so on. By recording these activities in your own leisure trajectory and supplementing them with data from the trajectories of friends and relations you can assemble a map of edgework and limit experience. The exercise will also clarify switch-points in leisure trajectories where serious forms change tracks with casual forms and vice versa. Incidentally, don't worry if you find that a surprising amount of the time diary involves illegal activity. You should not necessarily draw the conclusion that you are a criminal! Western types of society celebrate individual freedom. However, as we have seen, individual freedom is heavily conditioned. It is all too easy to break a rule through inadvertent action.

Abnormal forms

The strong ideological connotation between leisure and freedom, choice and self-determination has resulted in a distorted perspective on the field of leisure forms that are appropriate for Leisure Studies. In particular, the voluntary donation of disposable time to abnormal practice has been neglected, so much so that abnormal leisure practice is often routinely defined as **pathology**. As such its diagnosis is usually assigned

A **pathology** is a biological or social illness that causes deviant behaviour. Pathologies are associated with malignant results in the individual and society.

to criminologists, psychoanalysts and medical/paramedical practitioners. The question is not that this procedure is inherently invalid, since many forms of abnormal leisure *are* caused by psycho-biological, cultural, economic and political factors. Rather, it is that pathologizing deviant leisure practice erases the ludic element in illegal leisure trajectories. As such, the contribution of Leisure Studies in elucidating abnormal leisure is preempted.

What is this ludic element? The question is more complex than it seems at first sight. Ideologically, leisure forms are positioned in culture as spaces in which the individual is interpellated to reinforce core social values. The defects of this position were examined in the second chapter in the discussion of the weaknesses of the systems approach to leisure and the critique of ideology made by Marxists and feminists. Leisure time and space involve the relaxation of rules and regulations. Various types of leisure practice are compatible with relaxation that involve the separation of the individual from society and the crystallization of anti-social attitudes and practices. Elsewhere (Rojek 2000) I argued that there are three main types of abnormal leisure in secular, urban–industrial society. At this juncture it is worth reviewing these again in order to show how the ludic element is central in abnormal types of practice.

Invasive

Relaxation may involve the individual in failing to build viable and enriching relationships with others. Greater freedom may signify greater solitariness, since the individual may experience a heightened sense of irretrievable difference from others. In such cases leisure may function as a place in the life course in which the individual seeks to bury the elements of the self which are experienced as invalid or cherish them in isolation from others. Invasive leisure practice may take the forms of outward conviviality and companionship. But these forms are experienced as a mask which conceals an inner world where the individual feels estranged from others and divorced from the conventions of performance that orthodox leisure forms require.

Typically, invasive leisure involves slowly withdrawing from a society that is regarded as inauthentic and unfulfilling or gradually abandoning that part of the self which is defined as no longer possessing the capacity for engaging in ordinary life. The individual may become depressed, neurotic and paranoid, especially if the retreat from social networks is replaced by increasing the diet of mass media output. Invasive leisure patterns are also associated with the development of dependency on alcohol or drugs in an effort to drown out a world that is perceived as too complex, hostile or false to engage with.

Mephitic

The term 'mephitic' derives from *mephisis*, meaning noxious emanation or foul-smelling stench. I use it judgementally, because mephitic leisure refers to forms and practices of leisure designed to harm either the self or others. Individuals transfer feelings of invalidity upon those elements of the self that are perceived as problematic or to others who are regarded as inauthentic. Some types of mephitic leisure practice may derive from the invasive form. The desire to extinguish problematic elements in the self through developing addictions to alcohol and drugs are examples. However, some mephitic types of practice are quite unlike invasive forms in that they are based in the violent engagement with others. The perception of others as invalid translates into the dehumanization of others as objects of gratification for aggressive or sexual impulses. This is institutionalized in the development of gang subcultures and sex tourism (Yablonsky 1997; Ryan and Hall 2001). But mephitic types of practice are also evident in relations between the sexes and same-sex friendship networks in leisure where forms of individual behaviour are ritually stereotyped as negative or where individuals are turned into the scapegoats for all that is perceived to be wrong about the relationship.

In extreme cases, mephitic types of leisure may lead to physical violence against others.

Wild

Wild forms of leisure consist of sporadic, opportunistic attempts to escape from social scripts that are perceived as limiting. For many, transgressing and doing wrong is inherently pleasurable, and for others the act of observing these performances voyeuristically is exciting (Katz 1988; Presdee 2000: 30). A mundane example in the British leisure calendar is 5 November. This is Bonfire Night, when fireworks are used to celebrate the failure of the Gunpowder Plot to assassinate the king and his ministers in 1605. This often involves illegal behaviour such as letting fireworks off in public streets, parks or recreation grounds. But the authorities generally turn a blind eye to it. Similarly, on New Year's Eve, disturbances through the use of whistles and horns, public displays of nudity and drunkenness or trespass into public recreation space such as fountains, pools and other waterways are treated with a degree of tolerance befitting the celebration of the New Year.

Wild forms possess a carnivalesque spirit, in which leisure practice denies the routine scripts of performance and the containment of the emotions. Writers like Katz (1988) and Presdee (2000) maintain that some types of crime can only be satisfactorily explained by referring to the emotional release and pleasure that follow rule-breaking. The shading between wild leisure forms and criminal activity can be very thin. Location analysis is likely to reveal how the momentum of wild forms can sometimes tip into breaking the law and the formation of criminal careers.

Key points

- Location analysis examines the dynamic interrelationship between motivation, location and context.
- Location analysis aims to relate three levels of investigation *à la* Willis: indexical, homological and integral.
- Location forms can be examined according to the division between serious and casual leisure made by Stebbins.
- On-location practice supplies data about social density.
- Transgression is the inevitable complement of leisure boundaries. Transgressive forms can be investigated in relation to invasive, mephitic and wild types of practice.

9
Central Problems

Students of leisure face many challenges. They range from devising positions and policies on deviant forms to determining the right balance between environmental protection, leisure and work activity. What criteria should we mobilize to determine our decisions? How can we choose between options? In this chapter we deal with the central problems facing Leisure Studies under two general headings: 'Disciplinary questions' and 'Interpretive challenges'. The former have to do with the basic issue of how the discipline is organized, and deal specifically with the questions of fact/value distinctions, the problems of multi-paradigmatic complexity and the question of professional independence. The second set of issues relate more generally to problems of empowerment, distributive justice and social inclusion in leisure forms and practice.

Disciplinary questions

As a discipline, Leisure Studies is composed of an interdisciplinary amalgamation of perspectives and research traditions, of which the most significant are Sociology, Psychology, Social History, Human Geography, Economics, Business Studies, Management Studies and Environmental Studies. Because of this it cannot avoid the methodological dilemmas that exist in these disciplines. In particular, the questions of fact/value distinctions, multi-paradigmatic complexity and professional independence are germane. Students of leisure must be encouraged to take a position on them.

Fact/value distinctions

Science makes judgements on the basis of factual knowledge. But because so many issues in the social sciences and Leisure Studies are constructed through interpellation and ideology the question of value judgement is constant and poses a range of problems. For example, the rational recreation movement which rose to prominence in Western Europe and North America after the 1860s developed a philosophy of self-help based on a version of muscular Christianity that was presented as a *scientific* model of leisure practice. Although many elements of this model have stood the test of time, notably the emphasis on the value of physical exercise and discipline and planning in the development of leisure careers, later critics have exposed much in it as gender, class and racial bias (Bailey 1978; Hunnicutt 1988, 1996; Cross 1993). How can we deal with the distinction between fact and value in Leisure Studies?

In the social sciences an influential answer to this question was given by the sociologist Max Weber (1949). He argued that social scientists can never exclude all value bias in their work. After all, if we have understood interpellation and ideology correctly, it will be clear that these processes often operate at the levels of the unconscious and subconscious, making it very hard to recognize, let alone manage, them. Weber proposed that if social scientists cannot exclude value bias they can at least attach themselves to the professional ideal of *value neutrality* by which their values, and the place of these values in their scientific labours, are made explicit. Weber maintained that social science can reveal facts about social and cultural life. However, at the current stage in the development of human knowledge it cannot settle the question of the *ultimate* values by which we should live. These values have to do with our deepest beliefs about what is right and wrong in social, cultural and economic practice. They always involve a struggle between ethical value positions. For example, in the area of Leisure Studies, science may reveal the best form of organization for a keep-fit community programme. But the question of whether it is best to pay for it by capping public funds to health and education or raising taxes is a matter of ultimate beliefs about questions of ethical propriety, economic efficiency and social justice. Neoliberals will see these matters differently to social democrats and socialists. That reflects the real world in which we live. From the Weberian vantage point, the correct course of action is to advocate policies on the basis of the transparency of political values and subject this process to democratic validation through the open debate.

Many things commend this approach to scientific enquiry in Leisure Studies. It requires students of leisure to treat their hypotheses and proposals as *provisional*. It calls upon them to make a vocation of *self-interrogation*, that is, always asking themselves to isolate the value component in their work and, wherever possible, to make it transparent. It urges them to *test* their work by empirical means and open debate.

Now, while these conditions may appear to be self-evidently worthy of support, the devil is in the detail. For example, leisure scientists may profess to honour the doctrine of provisionality but the power struggle between competing positions in the discipline may regularly cause them to abandon it in practice. This relates to the issue of multi-paradigmatic complexity and we will review it at greater length presently. Similarly, while few leisure professionals would dismiss the importance of self-interrogation, a great many take the view that analysing issues from a clearly defined value position and ensuring that this position carries the day is their professional and moral duty. Thus, Marxists would very likely insist that viewing problems in leisure from the standpoint of the victims of class domination is the only defensible, scientific position since they believe that other positions that call themselves 'scientific' merely collude with the ruling order, while feminists might well be expected to have difficulties with the concept of 'science', regarding it as riddled with masculinist and heteronormative presuppositions that marginalize gender and difference.

Turning to the question of testing, it sounds admirable to require hypotheses and proposals to be subject to empirical testing and open debate, but the doctrine falls at an obvious first hurdle. To begin with, public and private funding does not support effective across-the-board, empirical testing of leisure theories. Private funding is an option, but it is usually tied to direct business outcomes that tend to discount what might be called the pure questions of leisure research. Among the most important of these questions are: what is the meaning of leisure? How is leisure related to structures of power? From what interdisciplinary mix has the study of leisure emerged, and how do these origins enable and constrain theory and research? All of these questions are fundamental in the study of leisure, having to do with how researchers interpret forms and practice and how participants in leisure orient themselves to activities, beliefs and values. But none has direct business outcomes on the issue of raising the rate of return from investment in research into leisure activity.

Because there are funding and other resource issues in leisure research, informed, open debate does not really exist since there is no financial base to make it truly viable. Hence, much that we do in Leisure Studies is extremely speculative. This is not a reason to pack up our bags and go. It is the reality of our situation and it is important for students of leisure to believe and maintain that speculation has a virtue of its own.

By asking those awkward 'what if?' questions, that have no immediate practical solutions or business outcomes, we can throw the issue of how power influences leisure forms and practice into sharper relief and contemplate alternatives.

The sociologist, cultural critic and political activist Stuart Hall (1989a; 1989b) argues that these awkward questions are not confined to social theory. They are also explored in popular culture at the level of what Hall terms **the social imaginary**. The social imaginary poses a set of

> The **social imaginary** is a perspective that relates the facts and values of leisure forms and practice with speculation on the nature of different facts, more humane values and more enriching, satisfying forms and practice. It is a feature of public culture and derives from the active struggles of ordinary people to understand their institutions and practices and envision alternatives. The imaginary is a collective resource for developing what Bromley (2000) calls 'narratives for a new belonging'.

metaphysical challenges about the condition of being that we recognize as culture and leisure, and a set of political considerations designed to realize this condition in life experience. It is the stuff of legend, stories and images of a better life that emerge in the texture of everyday life.

Taylor (2000: 371–3) notes that it is a mistake to confuse the social imaginary with theory. To begin with, theory is a privilege of a minority, whereas the social imaginary is shared widely by large groups of people. Similarly, theory is expressed in a professional lexicon that requires training and which is often forbidding to strangers. In contrast the social imaginary is expressed and transmitted through popular vernacular devoted to exploring the way in which people imagine their social and political surroundings. The social imaginary may evolve in the same direction as social theory. Conversely, there may be a lag between the two. For example, the ideal of social order based on 'the mutual benefit of equal participants' was born in the seventeenth century of the state of nature and contract theory (Grotius and Locke) (Taylor 2000: 371). Yet it was not until the next century that it became part of popular vernacular. The political importance of the social imaginary is that it elicits 'common understandings which make possible common practices, and a widely shared sense of legitimacy' (Taylor 2000: 371). Thus, the French and American revolutions sprang from a common sense of, respectively, monarchical and colonial injustice that underpinned popular practices and bestowed upon the acts of revolution a higher sense of legitimacy.

Leisure is an important social institution in generating and disseminating the social imaginary through meetings, demonstrations, rallies, musical events, popular theatre and sport. It is the cultural material through which dreams of a better future are made. As such, it is a universal feature of social groups, but it possesses particular significance for the excluded and the marginalized.

Multi-paradigmatic complexity

Scientific communities are the same as all social groups. That is, they exist in a condition of unequal resource distribution in which some strata have more power to set the agenda of debate, and dismiss issues *before they even become relevant topics for 'open' debate*. Does this mean that we should discard Weber's advice? The answer is a qualified 'no'. The objections to value neutrality are well-taken. Nonetheless, the discipline of aspiring to this doctrine as an *ideal* of scientific activity probably produces more gains than losses. Thus, it sensitizes scientists to questions of *location* and *context* in their trajectories of scientific work. It encourages us to interrogate the partiality of our perspectives and expose unconscious bias. Perhaps above all, it disposes us to defend open discussion, even if it raises values that conflict with those of our own. This is difficult to do. It is painful to give floor-room to arguments that we see as faulty or self-serving. The temptation is to prevent them. But the consequences of doing this are much worse than hearing out the arguments and attempting to deal with them through rational discussion.

Leisure Studies will not prosper if a climate of intimidation and fear is permitted to prosper. The correct course of action is to encourage open debate, but also, of course, to criticize those positions that for one reason or another seem to be untenable. There are difficulties with this, not least in respect of the rifts and schisms between the various and diverse leisure perspectives that comprise the field.

The interdisciplinary origins of Leisure Studies, and the development of different positions within the dicipline, amount to a condition of **multi-paradigmatic** complexity. This raises a number of problems about the conduct of scientific research and the character of open debate. One can think of these issues in terms of A&B analysis. Think of one group of scientists as being a collection of As. In order to achieve the status of being an A, each A has to go through a period of recognized training to achieve a level of recognized accreditation. Accreditation takes the form of undergraduate and postgraduate degree awards, but it is also enhanced

> The term **'paradigm'** is associated with the work of the noted sociologist of science, Thomas Kuhn (1962). Kuhn argued that scientific activity is informed by agreement on a set of assumptions and procedures that provide unity and purpose to scientific activity. Agreement may be implicit in the doings of scientists, in that it consists of an uninterrogated unity of practice. That is, it is immediately recognized as being what scientists do, without being articulated into a system of articulated values and rules of practice. Or agreement may arise from a distinction between facts and values that has followed a programme of debate and research. According to Kuhn, scientific revolutions arise when a scientific finding or trajectory of debate makes the agreements on the set of assumptions and procedures that hitherto provided unity and purpose to scientific activity untenable. The main thrust of scientific activity during these revolutionary periods is devising concepts and procedures that have a more fruitful fit with the 'facts' as they are currently perceived.

through conference presentations, conducting research and publishing articles and books. The scientific values and procedures that provide unity to the group of scientists called As is a binding framework or *paradigm*. It is binding in the sense that the intrinsic worth of these values and procedures is recognized by all As. In some cases, recognition may take the form of a quite unconscious *conviction* in the importance of the defining values and assumptions. Supporting these values and procedures is not simply a matter of professional practice, it often involves an entire series of ritualized codes of behaviour relating to dress, speech and honorific distinctions that operate to integrate the group more closely with the paradigm to which they are attached.

Very few, indeed probably *no* types of science comply with this simple paradigm. There are good reasons for this. All As may be well-versed and skilled in understanding the values and procedures of the paradigm to which they are attached and this is a matter of verifiable fact through accreditation. But some As are more skilful than others, and this is reflected in their interpretation of theory and research questions that raise issues and challenges that have not occurred to other As in the group. Unless we make the improbable assumption that a paradigm is entirely stagnant, it is the duty of As to expand knowledge. It follows, *à la* Kuhn (1962), that far-reaching questions will, from time to time, produce a scientific revolution. Something of this sort occurred when Nicolaus Copernicus (1473–1543) defied Ptolemaic theory by proposing that planets orbit the sun; or when Charles Darwin (1809–92) published his theory of human evolution in *The Descent of Man* (1871); or when Albert Einstein (1879–1955) proposed his theory of relativity.

Another way in which this outcome is achieved is if the group of scientists attached to the A paradigm come into contact with a group of B scientists attached to a different set of values and procedures which have the effect of throwing A's set of values and procedures into disarray and crisis. When a scientific revolution occurs paradigms are bent out of shape. Some scientists will behave like ostriches and pretend that nothing fundamental has changed. Others will meet the revolution halfway by trying to embrace *some* of the new issues while retaining *essential* features of the old paradigm. Still others will become fully paid-up members of the scientific revolution and abandon the old paradigm.

This is how science works. One can infer that between scientific revolutions, Bs will articulate positions which conflict with the assumptions of the paradigm to which As adhere and, for this reason, these positions will be marginalized. Science does not merely operate by the strength of rational argument, it operates through politics as well. Political considerations certainly militate against open debate in Leisure Studies. One often attends conferences in which functionalists, Marxists, feminists and post-structuralists talk across each other, as if they are intrinsically disregarding the salience of one another's perspectives. Students of leisure need to be aware of the political dimension of scientific activity and to recognize it both in the work of others and in the paradigm to which they are attached. They should seek to cultivate **reflexive** forms of analysis.

Reflexivity is the capacity to recognize the pretext, location and context of an argument or theory. The personality and the presence of the research are recognized as important relative factors in the articulation of a position. An important precondition of reflexivity is the establishment of a climate of open debate in which positions can be freely debated.

Another paradigm problem, which is arguably unique to Leisure Studies, is the benign self-image that prevails in the discipline. Generally speaking, leisure is equated as an intrinsic social, economic and cultural benefit. Indeed, it is frequently elevated to a moral cause célèbre. For example, the São Paulo Declaration on leisure, issued in 1998 during the World Leisure and Recreation Association conference, declared that 'all persons have the right to leisure through economic, political and social policies that are equitable and sustainable', and further that 'all persons have a need to celebrate and share our diversity in leisure'.[1] In this way leisure activity and leisure professionals are presented as forming a virtuous circle and the institution of leisure is identified with the triumph of humanism. The consequence of this is to stifle critical thought. Those who try to further a *scientific* understanding of leisure by investigating how leisure forms and practice contribute to *harm* of the self or *injury* to others run the risk of being demonized.

Students of leisure must ask themselves whether the discipline's benign self-image is justified. Must we be barred from examining how leisure forms and practice contribute to self-mutilation or violence to others? Are we to continue with the cod celebration of leisure as an unequivocal social and economic benefit? Or is it time to subject leisure forms and practice to systematic cost–benefit analysis? As leisure theorists, we have no prior brief to be critical. Leisure theory has a constructive role in adding to empowerment, distributive justice and social inclusion. But nor should we flinch from asking difficult questions abut leisure forms and practice that are dysfunctional to the individual and society, even if it introduces clouds into the sunny self-image of leisure that prevails in the discipline. These brings me to the third disciplinary point.

Professional independence

Maintaining a climate of open debate is difficult to achieve. As Weber observed, people disagree about fundamental values. These disagreements are the basis for many versions of inclusion and exclusion in the scientific community. But if they are permitted to harden into dogmatism and cronyism, the vitality of our disicpline is imperilled.

The question is thrown into sharp relief in a context in which teaching and research are subject to state auditing and a mixture of central and private funding. Of course, it is right for leisure teachers and researchers to be accountable. However, especially in the area of leisure theory their work raises issues of empowerment, distributive justice and social inclusion that must not be dictated by business interests, the auditing objectives of the state, the imperatives of the political directorate or the virtuous self-image that many in the discipline cultivate. Of course, it is desirable for leisure professionals to work with business corporations and the state, because through these means, our ideas enter into society and politics. In doing so they must not compromise their professional independence which includes a duty to examine forms, practices and institutions *critically*.

Although many leisure professionals will not like the term, the leisure theorist is part of the intelligentsia. Bauman (1992) argues that there are two polarities of intelligentsia: legislators and interpreters. The former operate to provide knowledge for strategy and policy formation among the political directorate and business corporations. Interpreters are more concerned with asking awkward questions about resource allocation, the legitimacy of authority and ethical justice. In practice, most members of the intelligentsia in Leisure Studies are typically a mixture of legislator and interpreter. If you are using leisure theory in your work as a professor or park ranger you should try to form tenable policies and strategies for the enrichment of leisure forms and practice, but you also have a professional duty to ask awkward questions relating to power structures, their legitimacy and the value of leisure activities. There is a *moral* dimension to professional work in leisure. To put it concisely, the duty of leisure professionals is to enhance the prominence of the twin ethical imperatives of care for the self and care for the other in leisure forms and practice. In pursuing this, leisure professionals have an obligation to delineate and protect their responsibility to participate in public debate without surrendering their critical independence or ethical integrity. The *ethic of cognition*, which Gellner (1998: 183–4) identifies with freedom of thought and articulation, is what might be called a **domain** issue in Leisure Studies and it is the underlying theme behind all of the central interpretive problem issues that students of leisure face. This is because these problems typically challenge the regulative mechanisms that allocate economic resources and distribute prestige. It is likely that this activity will bring leisure professionals into conflict with the vested interests behind regulative mechanisms, whether they refer to the political, economic and cultural intermediaries that manage the twin axial circuits of production–consumption and the sexual–aggressive economy of emotions or the predatory strata to whom they are accountable.

Domains are the backgrounds, assumptions and professional convictions that demarcate a group. In part they are an aspect of *context* since they reflect the larger culture. However, they also constitute the professional bodies of knowledge constructed by a group in the course of its actions over generations.

We can now come to the question of the central interpretive challenges in the domain.

Interpretive challenges

Axiomatic to the Action approach is the proposition that leisure activity is not voluntaristic. Instead it is bound up with functions of representation, identity, control and resistance which position individuals and theme leisure trajectories. These functions directly pose questions relating to the regulative mechanisms, axial circuits and predatory strata that inscribe leisure forms and practice. The narrative of the actor is an essential building block in leisure theory. However, because leisure trajectories are always and already situated on location and in context it is insufficient to examine leisure forms and practice merely on the basis of narrative data supplied by individuals. Locations and contexts have narratives too. To fully explore them it is necessary to apply comparative and historical methods. Inevitably, this takes us far away from the individual's stated motives in following a particular form of leisure practice. For it requires us to examine how these motives are assembled and structurally supported; the course of their origins; and their implications for distributive justice, social inclusion and empowerment. Our field must therefore be unafraid to examine wider questions of power, again along comparative and historical dimensions, in order to elucidate how individual action, location and context are consolidated in particular trajectories of leisure behaviour.

Outwardly, this is certainly acknowledged in the profession. For example, the *Charter for Leisure* (2000), published by the World Leisure Board of Directors and adopted by the World Leisure and Recreation Association, stipulates a number of articles for leisure professionals that *imply* confronting economic, political and cultural power on many fronts.[2] The Charter builds on Article 27 of the Universal Declaraton of Human Rights which holds that all societies recognize the right to rest and leisure. It is worth listing its eight articles here:

1. All people have a basic human right to leisure activities that are in harmony with the norms and social values of their compatriots. All governments are obliged to recognize and protect this right of its citizens.
2. Provisions for leisure for the quality of life are as important as those for health and education. Governments should ensure their citizens a variety of accessible leisure and recreational opportunities of the highest quality.
3. The individual is his/her best leisure resource. Thus, governments should ensure the means for acquiring those skills and understandings necessary to optimize leisure experiences.

4. Individuals can use leisure opportunities for self-fulfilment, develop-ing personal relationships, improving social integration, developing communities and cultural identity as well as promoting inter-national understanding and co-operation and enhancing the quality of life.
5. Governments should ensure the future availability of fulfilling leisure experiences by maintaining the quality of their country's physical, social and cultural environment.
6. Governments should ensure the training of professionals to help individuals acquire personal skills, discover and develop their talents and to broaden their range of leisure and recreational opportunities.
7. Citizens must have access to all forms of leisure information about the nature of leisure and its opportunities, using it to enhance their knowledge and inform decisions on local and national policy.
8. Educational institutions must make every effort to teach the nature and importance of leisure and how to integrate this knowledge into personal lifestyle.

The Charter is a serious document that seeks to gain recognition for leisure forms and practice as fundamental quality-of-life issues. However, it is also a *pious* document. A *piety* is a virtuous, self-righteous, earnest expression of duties or obligations. The Charter *acknowledges* issues having to do with distributive justice, empowerment and exclusion, but it does not spell them out, nor does it raise the thorny questions that need to be asked in order to address them. Who amongst us will disagree with the view that 'citizens should have access to all forms of leisure information about the nature of leisure and its opportunities' or that 'governments should ensure their citizens a variety of accessible leisure and recre-ational opportunities of the highest qualities'? In some countries, notably Brazil with the imaginative leisure provision of SESC (Servico Social Do Comercio), impressive strides have been made to achieve these goals. But to *really* get to a stage in which the state recognizes leisure on an equal footing with education and health, and to provide access to all forms of information about the nature of leisure and its opportunities, requires a more profound commitment to tackling structural inequalities and the role of regulative mechanisms in allocating economic resources and distributing prestige. In this respect, the Charter begins from the wrong position by contending that 'because personal freedom and choice are central elements of leisure, individuals can freely choose their activities and experiences'. My discussion of axial circuits, regulative mechanisms, location principles and context in relation to trajectories of leisure experience does not discount the relevance of concepts of personal choice or freedom. That personal freedom and choice come with many strings attached is perhaps one of the chief lessons of this book. The Charter ought to have gone much further into the questions of distributive *injustice*, social *exclusion* and *disempowerment* and also the axial circuits and regulatory mechanisms that maintain this state of affairs. Inevitably, this raises the subject of the role of predatory strata and their grossly unequal share of control over economic assets and public influence.

Another weakness of the document is the overemphasis placed upon the part of the state in managing leisure rights, responsibilities, forms and practice. This misconceives the transformation in politics produced by the rise of active citizenship and wrongly excludes corporations from obligations and initiatives in enriching leisure forms and practice. A more productive way to conceptualize the enhancement of global leisure is to redefine social inclusion, distributive justice and empowerment as a set of responsibilities involving a *partnership* between active citizens (and their representation through various voluntary organizations), the state and the corporation. Partnership offers a better framework of checks and balances than the unregulated market or strong central control. It recognizes that active citizens must have rights, responsibilities and *power* in addressing the axial circuits and regulative mechanisms that inscribe leisure forms and practice. What then are the principal challenges facing leisure professionals today?

Social and economic exclusion

Social and economic exclusion is the systematic isolation of individuals from access to the material and cultural benefits produced by society. It is often based upon racial or sexual prejudice. However, it may also reflect distinctions of social hierarchy, as with the Indian caste system, or embodiment, for example in relation to the status of disability. Social exclusion can be studied *endogenously* (in relation to conditions within a given nation state) or *exogenously* (in relation to global conditions). With respect to the latter, the plight of populations in the Third World has been a long-standing example of social and economic exclusion, not merely from the right of access to leisure resources, but from an equitable, sustainable basis for subsistence. The United Nations Development Report (2003) makes uncomfortable reading for anyone in the West who believes that the **development gap** is closing. Despite some progressive development in improving natal and post-natal care, education, income and life expectancy in *some* Third World countries over

> The **development gap** is the difference in per capita income, life expect-
> ancy, levels of infant mortality and literacy between the advanced
> industrial nations and the emerging Third World.

the last decade, the general picture is appalling. Among the findings of
the report are:

- 54 countries experienced a *decline* in average income in the 1990s.
- 827.5 million of the world's population are defined as clinically
  undernourished.
- 500,000 women a year, one for each minute, die in pregnancy or
  childbirth.
- 13 million children died of diarrhoea in the 1990s, more than all
  the people killed in armed conflict over the same period.
- In Zimbabwe life expectancy *dropped* from 56 in the early 1970s to
  33.1 in the late 1990s; in the UK it increased from 72 to 78.2.
- The 1990s witnessed a drop of the world's percentage of people living
  on less than $1 per day from 30 per cent to 23 per cent. But the
  drop is mainly accounted for by improvements in China and India.
  In South Asia, 42 per cent still live on less than $1 per day; in East Asia
  and the Pacific, the number is 24 per cent; in sub-Saharan Africa,
  22 per cent; in Latin America and the Caribbean, 7 per cent; in the
  Arab states, 4 per cent; and in Central and Eastern Europe, 4 per cent.

The richest 1 per cent of the world's population (around 60 million)
now receive the equivalent income of the poorest 57 per cent. The income
of the richest 25 million Americans is equivalent to that of almost 2 billion
of the world's poorest. In Norway, top of the UN's table of human
development, average life expectancy is 78.7 years and annual income
is just below $30,000. At the bottom of the table, a newborn child in Sierra
Leone will be fortunate to reach 35, has a two-in-three chance of growing
up illiterate and an average annual income expectancy of $470.

The figures speak for themselves. As students of leisure we confront
vast, entrenched global inequalities. How can we reconcile our expenditure
on luxury, distraction and fun with the persistence of chasms of global
poverty that result in 30,000 children dying daily in 2003 from prevent-
able disease and hundreds of thousands not having enough food to eat?
What is the moral defence of a system of Western leisure, sourced by
low-pay workers in developing countries? How can we make care for the

other meaningful? Brand-name leisure multinationals like Levi Strauss, Nike, Reebok, Adidas, Wal-Mart, Ralph Lauren, Gap, IBM and Esprit manufacture their products in countries such as the Philippines, China, Mexico, Vietnam and Indonesia (Klein 2001; Smart 2003: 160–1). The unpalatable conclusion is that part of the context in which pleasure is pursued in the West is inextricably bound up with the suffering of others who are condemned to lives of want, hunger, illiteracy, and are statistically likely to come to a premature end.

Care for the other is an ethical imperative of active citizenship in the West. While it may commence with local issues and national circumstances, these are not sufficient. The local and the global are interdependent. The historical, social, political and economic context in which both are situated constitutes a single whole, although there is also much diversity and variation within this formation. Students of leisure must extend the scope of their study to include the questions of global inequitable resource distribution and the levers of global social and economic exclusion from leisure resources.

A start has been made at the endogenous level, through the analysis of the regulative mechanisms of class, gender, race and occupation. Access to leisure resources is preconditioned by relations of inclusion and exclusion with respect to distinct social formations within this regulative terrain. For the sake of simplicity, consider again the influence of but one regulative mechanism taken in isolation: class. A's parents are university-educated professionals. His mother is a chief executive of a national charity and his father is a lawyer specializing in international patent law. B's parents are first-generation immigrants. Both of his parents left school at 16. His father is a fireman who also works in a bar. His mother is a midwife who is studying at night school for a community care qualification.

Statistically speaking A is likely to have greater **life chances** than B. These reflect the material differences between A's and B's family of origin. A is likely to live in multi-roomed private accommodation, with a private garden situated in a desirable part of town. B is likely to live in either basic private dwelling space or rented property with, at best, communal

---

Life chances is a term invented by the sociologist Max Weber to refer to the material, political and cultural advantages or disadvantages that a typical member of a class receives as a condition of class membership.

garden space. A's family is likely to have at least two cars, whereas B's is statistically likely to rely on public transport. B's experience of international long-distance travel will probably be spare. A's will probably be extensive. A variety of cultural differences are concomitant with economic divisions that bear on leisure choice and orientation. Statistically speaking, it would be rare to find a well-stocked library in B's home, whereas A is likely to have wide access to books, magazines and serious newspapers. B's linguistic code, the cultural status of his or her leisure activities and social networks are likely to carry lower status than A's. Class life chances, then, structure access to leisure resources, participation in leisure forms and the quality of leisure experience. This holds good for gender, race and occupation divisions and, of course, the situation is rendered much more complex if one examines the cross-currents of relations and counter-relations between these regulative mechanisms.

The endogenous and exogenous levels of studying social and economic exclusion must address the context of the *capitalist* form of organization. Capitalism is an economic and social system based on the principles of private ownership of economic resources and individual freedom. The typical unit of production that it generates is a commodity carrying a price, rather than a service carrying a non-pecuniary obligation validated by habit and tradition. A good deal of social science is concerned with mapping the origins of capitalism, its distinctive mode of production and historical and comparative variations in its forms. These questions became especially salient after the collapse of the old Soviet command system in the early 1990s, since at that point capitalism regained its late nineteenth-century status as a system of organization in the industrial world *without* a viable alternative.

Here, I wish to focus upon but one aspect of the deeply rooted and ongoing discussion about the character of the capitalist form of organization, that is, the tendency for capitalism to replace human labour with automated processes. For unemployment is closely related to social and economic exclusion. The tendency of capitalism to shed labour is not a one-sided movement. Capitalist science and technology have combined to *create* jobs as well as *destroy* them. But here the student of leisure must concentrate upon the destructive power of capitalism, especially in relation to the benign neglect that capitalists have shown for many centuries in respect of issues of empowerment, social inclusion and distributive justice in relation to the Third World. In the words of Castells (1998: 344–5), in the contemporary capitalist system of production:

> a considerable number of humans, probably in a growing proportion, are irrelevant, both as producers and consumers, from the perspective

of the system's logic... What is happening is that the mass of generic labour circulates in a variety of jobs, increasingly occasional jobs, with a great deal of discontinuity. So millions of people are constantly in and out of paid work, often included in informal activities, and, in sizeable numbers, on the shop floor of the criminal economy. Furthermore, the loss of a stable relationship to employment, and the weak bargaining power of many workers, lead to a higher level of incidence of major crises in the life of their families: temporary job loss, personal crises, illness, drugs/alcohol addictions, loss of employability, loss of assets, loss of credit.

Obvious problems of social and economic exclusion are raised by this situation. Castells (1998: 346) invites us to consider the proposition that three new levels of social and economic cleavage are emerging at the endogenous and exogenous levels:

1. *Skills-based* – information and communication workers are positioned in a more advantageous position in the labour market than 'generic replaceable labour'.
2. *Surplus reserves of labour* – some sections of 'replaceable generic labour' are defined as surplus to requirements. Their relevance as producers and consumers has been superseded. Their value as people is ignored.
3. *Intensified alienation* – a division has emerged between the business and management logic of the system and the 'human experience of workers' lives'.

Students of leisure must devote their energies to ensure that *generic replaceable labour* does not translate into *generic replaceable citizens*. In part, this involves loosening the ties that make paid employment and capital ownership the precondition of respectable citizenship and establishing a guaranteed minimum wage. As we will see in more detail presently, in the section on 'post-work', the casualization of labour and part-time work patterns which have long been the norm in developing countries have a strong foothold in the advanced industrial economies and are unlikely to go away. On the contrary, the balance of evidence is that these systems of employment will become more prominent in Western civil society (Beck 2000; Giddens 2002). What can be done to inhibit the tendency towards social exclusion in economies that are no longer regulated by a moral commitment to full, permanent paid employment?

An important objective of leisure professionals is to elucidate the contribution of voluntary behaviour in cultivating social capital. Putnam (2000) identifies leisure as one of the key channels through which communities can be regenerated. In his manifesto for the enlargement of social capital in America he (2000: 410–11) declares:

> Let us find ways that by 2010 Americans will spend less leisure time sitting passively alone in front of glowing screens and more time in active connection with fellow citizens. Let us foster new forms of electronic entertainment and communication that reinforce community engagement rather than forestalling it ... Let us find ways to ensure that by 2010 significantly more Americans will participate in (not merely consume or 'appreciate') cultural activities from group dancing to songfests to community theatre to rap festivals. Let us discover new ways to use the arts as a vehicle for convening diverse groups of fellow citizens.

Putnam may be criticized for offering a somewhat one-sided view of leisure. After all playing together can accentuate the barriers associated with axial circuits and regulative mechanisms as well as contributing to their decline. It can enhance relations of mutuality and reciprocity that relieve the burden of caring and helping in the community from the shoulders of the state. But it can also revive prejudice, stereotyping and scapegoating and create new pressure points in the community that require state intervention.

Much depends on factors of location and context, and students of leisure should be wary of allowing abstract policies to determine how resources are allocated and what systems of legitimation are used to distribute them.

However, leaving Putnam's over-optimism about the potential for leisure to enrich individual and community life aside, an important point about voluntary activity and social capital is being made here. A new view of leisure that does not equate unemployment with social exclusion must begin by redefining the relationship between paid employment, capital ownership and respectability. The work ethic has dissolved these issues around the central question of the labour contract, so much so that the right to leisure is commonly construed as a condition of paid employment, capital ownership or marriage to someone occupying this status. The work ethic attributed idleness and opprobrium to those non-capital owners who elected not to work. In addition, it applied the category of the 'deserving poor' to those with aspirations to either acquire paid employment or improve their conditions of life. As a result, large numbers were excluded from the right to leisure. Similarly, voluntary activity that did not possess a pecuniary outcome or which could not be shown to reinforce the work ethic was seriously undervalued.

As we shall see in the section on 'post-work', a variety of changes in the labour market and lifestyle are combining to produce a reassessment of the work ethic and the categories of social inclusion and exclusion that it has generated. The debate around leisure and social capital highlights these issues by suggesting that the allocation of economic resources and the distribution of prestige must be re-geared. In particular, it must be redirected to offer economic rewards and social distinction to those individuals who elect to devote non-pecuniary, voluntary activity to enhancing social capital whose status is not preconditioned by occupying the ascription of paid labour, capital ownership or marriage to a paid labourer or capital owner. Establishing a minimum wage as a citizenship right is crucial in this respect. Leisure professionals must break the work ethic's long associations between leisure, hedonism and the reward for work. A revitalized model of leisure and the community is required, built around the principle of leisure as a primary source of social capital and voluntary activity in generating and defending social capital as a source of self-worth and distinction. The use of leisure in constructing social inclusion, distributive justice and empowerment must situate itself in relation to Third World poverty because local and national inequalities and global inequalities are interrelated.

This implies a bolder, more ambitious brief for leisure professionals. We must cease confining ourselves to questions of people's pleasure and expand our role to elucidating how our pleasures are built upon the pain and suffering of others globally. This does not mean putting an end to the traditional preoccupations of Leisure Studies. We must still study activities that give people pleasure and a sense of personal worth. In addition, we must expand this study critically to examine how pleasure in the West is interpellated and the ideologies that bracket out questions of global oppression, hunger and poverty. One aspect of this is to examine how the work ethic contributes to social exclusion, especially in rationing the right to leisure to individuals who are capital owners, working in paid employment, or their dependants. The other side of this is exploring the mechanisms which toss the mantle of 'idleness', 'eccentricity' and 'non-respectability' around the shoulders of those who *choose* not to engage in paid employment, cultivate capital ownership or become dependants of individuals who occupy these categories. For these are matters of interpellation too.

McDonaldization

The prominence of the corporation and the state in leisure provision has raised persistent anxieties that leisure forms and practice are subject to commercial and bureaucratic controls that produce mass conformity. The Frankfurt School articulated this cogently between the 1940s and 60s and related it to the culture industry and class domination (Adorno and Horkheimer 1944; Marcuse 1964; Adorno 1998). An adjacent case was made by mass society theory during the same period, but set more store on corporate manipulation and psychological technologies of organizing mass consent and docility (Riesman 1950; Packard 1957).

Today, perhaps the leading proponent of the standardization thesis is George Ritzer. His (2000, 2004) work on McDonaldization and globalization holds that spontaneity is being systematically replaced throughout the globe with standardization, freedom with control, choice with regimentation and self-determination with self-policing. Expressed formally, McDonaldization is the process through which the principles of the fast-food restaurant industry are generalized throughout society. It utilizes four principles:

- *Efficiency* – the satisfaction of demand by the quickest means of delivery. When the founder of the McDonald's food chain, Ray Kroc, founded the company he developed a 'three-minute rule'. This laid down that it should take no more than three minutes for the customer to order his food and beverage and be served. Efficiency encourages the stream-lining of services by breaking down production and delivery.
- *Calculability* – the quantification and monitoring of production and consumption. In McDonald's this involves placing ultimate emphasis upon the value for money of the quantity of food and drink delivered in a regular meal and the turnaround of service.
- *Predictability* – the standardization of products, settings and services. The McDonald's chain boasts that it delivers the same food, in the same settings, to the same standard of delivery throughout the world. Standardization is achieved by through staff training systems, the routinization of delivery flows and uniform architecture.
- *Control* – the mechanization of labour with non-human technologies. In McDonald's sensors are employed to dispense the correct volume of soft drink per order, thus minimizing waste or delay. French fries are prepared by an automated system. Computerized cash registers have been developed which tally the price of food and drink when the employee presses the relevant icon, thus reducing the risk of human miscalculation.

The thesis is actually an imaginative overhaul and retooling of Weber's (1968) theory of rationalization. Weber maintained that the application of **rational systems of authority** and **bureaucratic types of organization** produced higher standards of efficiency in human life but resulted in dehumanization. Among the miscellaneous evocative phrases that he coined to describe the process, 'the iron cage of bureaucracy' and the 'disenchantment of the world' have passed into the heritage of the social sciences. Ritzer takes over many aspects of Weber's theory but modernizes them by showing how rationalization and bureaucracy permeate consumption and leisure forms and practice.

Rational authority refers to a modern type of decision-making under which rule is based on actions and policies that are legally accountable. Accountability is ultimately referred to the national electorate, but in the sociology of organizations it refers to businesses, hospitals, schools, prisons and the other central institutions of normative coercion. Rational authority replaces *charismatic* rule, which is based on the perceived qualities of an individual; and *traditional* authority, which is a system of rule based on custom and habit. Bureaucracy is a type of organization based upon the principles of limited, positional responsibility, impersonal rules and the rational–legal legitimation of authority.

As with all terms that purport to sum up the character of an era, McDonaldization involves a condensation of meanings. It points to the predominance of branding in everyday life and therefore the importance of multinational companies in influencing the context in which life options and leisure choices are exercised. By extension, it alerts us to the high degrees of quantification and rationalization in consumer culture. It also emphasizes that if we are to understand branding and rationalization correctly we must examine them at the global level. McDonaldization is a global process that is slowly making the whole world in its image. It underlines that choice and freedom occur within a context of programmed options. Finally, it presents global standardization and regimentation as the unplanned consequence of planned initiatives in business and culture. There is not a strong political dimension in the McDonaldization thesis, because Ritzer generally presents standardization and regimentation, in the long run, as inevitable.

Ritzer means us to understand that the defining feature of our world is nothing less than the relentless onslaught of efficiency, predictability, calculability and control into every aspect of life, burning away variety and destroying the possibility of escape. In a later work he (2004) refers to 'the globalization of nothing'. This rather bleak phrase refers to the replacement of content with nullity, that is, settings of consumption and leisure that possess no binding force. The distinction between something and nothing in Ritzer's sociology is reminiscent of McLuhan's (1964) categories of 'hot' and 'cold' media of communication. A hot medium requires concentration and background knowledge to be appreciated. Examples include reading literature or listening to classical music. A cool medium is a comic strip, a tabloid newspaper or a reality TV show. It is highly accessible because it requires little concentration or background knowledge. Hot and something and cool and nothing go together. McLuhan and Ritzer see the world as moving towards the globalization of cool media and nothing cultures. Ritzer provides many examples in his account of McLeisure:

- *Shopping centres/malls* – provide an 'assembly line' experience of shopping based on predictability, uniformity and standardization.
- *Convenience foods* – offer a streamlined, predictable, efficient experience of food consumption. Microwave foods 'mechanize' and 'quantify' the process of food preparation by timing the process of cooking.
- *Theme parks* – control and monitor the consumption of leisure space and time. Theme parks employ systems of queuing that are akin to a 'conveyor belt' system. Seeing sights is based on the principle of efficiency which discourages lingering or wandering off on your own.
- *Television* – schedules and increasingly programme content are driven by the ratings war. This involves the predominance of calculability and quantitative over qualitative criteria.
- *Sports* – measuring and monitoring sports performance is now a standard feature of sports organization. Sports stadiums increasingly utilize standards of predictability as features of design. For example, domes and artificial turf aim to minimize disruption caused by the weather. Processes of queuing and seating adopt 'assembly-line' standards of efficiency and predictability.

Although Ritzer does not expand the point systematically, he clearly regards the development of McDonaldization in leisure as dehumanizing. The frequent comparison of contemporary leisure experience with an 'assembly line' and a 'conveyor belt' suggests that he sees parallels between the processes of mechanization and deskilling at work and the development of routinization and passivity in leisure.

The irrationality of rationalization became a signature theme in Weber's mature writings. He questioned the ultimate value of a system of administration that he believed reduced workers to robots and consumers to cyphers. Ritzer's discussion of McDonaldization reaches the same conclusions. Both writers emphasize the ultimately irrational consequences of rational–bureaucratic systems of control.

One difficulty with Ritzer's approach is that it privileges context over location. The McDonaldization thesis presents rationalization as the process that defines the context for McLeisure. As a result of privileging factors of context, the place of location and the role of social and cultural interests, and the contradictions and tensions between them, are underdeveloped. Of course, interaction between local social and cultural interests and the spurt towards rationalization occurs at every stage of this process. However, in the long run the logic of McDonaldization is to negate resistance.

Students of leisure will easily find much to support this somewhat gloomy conclusion. Consider again the example of P2P downloads. Internet companies like Napster began as populist bandit organizations intent on providing free music for anyone with the capacity to download. They valued spontaneity and sharing since anyone with a record collection could copy recordings and make them available on the net. They also incensed record companies who regarded the intellectual property that they controlled to be hijacked. The result has been a lengthy series of court cases in which the record companies and their affiliates have sought to eliminate free P2P downloads. Since P2P technology cannot be disinvented the strategy of the plaintiffs has been to subject it to rational control that rations access to music and imposes a fee for downloading. It is a classic example of the McLeisure process.

Conversely, if the long-term drift of efficiency, predictability, calculability and control is to advance, or, at the very least, solidify dehumanization in society, how are the improvements in leisure experience of the last century to be explained? Creating public parks, propagating leisure and sport in schools and local communities, combating racism and sexism in leisure and sport, pursuing the links between leisure and health, preserving heritage space and striving to increase leisure time have qualitatively improved leisure experience for many. All make use of the principles of efficiency, predictability, calculability and control, but they do so to enhance leisure forms and practice. Evidently, the effect of these principles depends upon the uses to which they are being put. If bureaucracy and rationalization have a tendency to McDonaldize humanizing principles and systems of organization, they are also the pretext for resistance. The flow between resistance and rationalization is not as unilinear as the McDonaldization thesis suggests. One goal for leisure professionals is to devise checks and balances to prevent rationalization and bureaucratization from dehumanizing leisure and culture.

Post-work

The twinning of leisure with work reflects the power of the work ethic in the organization of personal identity and everyday life. The work ethic elevates paid labour as the central life interest and, along with family life and religious devotion, as a primary means of self-realization. Max Weber (1930) argued that the roots of the work ethic lie in the quest for religious salvation. In Puritan belief systems the doctrine of predestination held that one's fate in the afterlife is predetermined. Every Puritan is faced with the agonizing dilemma of never knowing in this life if he or she is one of the elect or destined for damnation. The psychological and social mechanism that they develop to cope with this burden is work-style. Devotion to work is interpreted as adding to the glory of God and the wealth that it creates is presented as a sign of God's favour. Why would God grant you favour unless he intended to call you unto him when you die? Weber presents a compelling argument, not least in providing a basis for understanding the irrational commitment to the work ethic. For, as Schor (1992) demonstrates, overwork is associated with various physical, mental and social maladies and premature death. By following Weber's logic, we can see that the excessive devotion to work may be inspired by a subconscious religious quest for salvation.

For her part, Schor (1992) places a different perspective upon the work ethic. She argues that in secular society it is unconvincing to analyse devotion to work as the reflection of the religious quest for salvation. Instead, she contends that overwork is related to the uncontrollable desire to participate in consumer culture. The rise of part-time work and the general casualization of the labour process obliges individuals to subject themselves to multi-work contracts in order to consume.

Students of leisure must certainly confront the persistence of the work ethic. In social and welfare policy, the *a priori* of citizenship rights and economic entitlements has been taken to occupy the status of paid employment or the dependants thereof. Moral censure has been directed at members of the community that choose not to engage in paid employment. This was often veiled under the more general preoccupation with *respectability*. The model citizen is constructed as someone who voluntarily enters into paid employment. His taxes help to fund the welfare state and his contributions provide entitlements for himself and his dependants. Traditionally, those who emphasize hedonism over labour, or shun paid employment for some version of self-sufficiency, have been regarded as problematic citizens and their entitlement to leisure has been questioned. Although moral censure has been especially strong in respect of the poor, it also applies to the rich. Veblen (1899) regarded the leisure class to be morally repugnant because they devoted themselves to leisure and conspicuous consumption and therefore flaunted the prudent values of industry and discipline cultivated by the artisan class.

A variety of processes are combining to weaken the work ethic. The deregulation of the labour market has contributed to the casualization of the labour process. Interrupted work patterns and part-time paid employment have repositioned the citizen in relation to welfare and insurance entitlements. The pressure on the state to guarantee postwar health and pensions entitlements has been intensified by the success of medicine and technology in prolonging life. The result has been the revision of welfare discrimination and the revival of political ideologies of welfare prudence and self-reliance. Their effect is to leave the citizen more exposed and to seek to enhance welfare cover through private health insurance and pension schemes. However, the latter are subject to the vagaries of the stock market which may not perform according to expectations. The inequality between men and women in the job market and the tendency for women to be preeminent in the child-rearing process and hence abandon work expose women to higher risks of inadequate health insurance and pension provision. As a result women are more subject to state audits of *respectability* and less able to fulfil the doctrine of self-reliance.

The deregulation of the labour market has contributed to the decline of full-time, permanent work opportunities. The ideal of the model citizen has had to be repositioned. It can no longer be based on the combination of the work ethic with paid employment. This is one reason why there is currently so much interest in reviving the concept of social capital and exploring how personal dignity and worth can be generated from voluntary activity assigned to care for the self and care for the other. The renewed interest in establishing a minimum wage also reflects state and civil reassessments about the character of working life and the opportunities for contributing to health, pension and welfare entitlements.

A parallel development has been the revival of critical interest in moderating the work ethic, reducing work time and lowering the age of retirement. Gorz (1978, 1983) argues that most people today are not ruled by the work ethic. They do not expect to experience self-realization or to attain salvation through work. Rather they position themselves *instrumentally* in relation to paid employment. Work provides the wherewithal to follow their desires in leisure and consumption. Schor (1992) mirrors this analysis in her conclusion that self-realization is now explored in leisure and consumer culture rather than paid labour. There appears to have been a shift in social values, in which the personal and social costs of the work ethic are now more widely recognized and respectability and paid employment are no longer bound together by iron.

Aronowitz and Cutler (1998) have developed a 'post-work manifesto' which envisages radical revisions in the concept and practice of work and leisure. The post-work manifesto envisages the eclipse of work as the central life interest and the enlargement of the role of the active citizen through leisure and the revival of community. Voluntary activity in caring and environmental protection envisages a retreat from the concept of the privatized citizen and the concentration of social responsibilities in the hands of state personnel. The active citizen recognizes organic links with the community and regards voluntary labour to increase social capital as a prime responsibility of citizenship. Leisure and recreation are identified as a primary area in social life for implanting and propagating the central values of care for the other and preservation of the environment. The active citizen practises civic virtue, but this does not mean that private leisure experience is eradicated. On the contrary, in post-work society the individual will have the time and space to address the central questions of existence concerning the purpose of education, the character of economic and social distribution and what

---

Chief features of the post-work manifesto

- Substantial reduction of working hours
- Guaranteed income plan
- National health and education provision
- Progressive taxation system
- Expansion of civic responsibilities to increase social capital, for example, voluntary care for the elderly and children, protection of environment
- Dramatically increased life options for all strata

it means to be human. In the words of Aronowitz and Di Fazio (1994: 354):

> Space and time themselves become objects of knowledge and ... of personal and social exploration. Consequently, lifelong learning, travel, avocations, small business, and artisanship take on new significance as they become possible for all people, not just the middle and upper classes.

Of course, the transition to post-work society is never going to be smooth. The work ethic is deeply etched into our social institutions and recasting it to embrace the voluntary enhancement of social capital as a laudable basis for self-worth and collective benefit will nettle many vested social interests. In particular, the predatory class has little interest in an exchange of paid labour for the voluntary enhancement of social capital, since that would undermine a long-standing foundation of social control. Against this, the long-term tendency in manufacturing and the service economy to progressively displace labour from full, permanent paid employment, even during cycles of economic growth, suggests that there are practical limits in modern capitalism to retaining the work ethic as a source of personal worth and collective benefit. The establishment of a minimum wage and a system of economic and social reward for voluntary activity designed to enhance social capital may be the price required to maintain social order. Without it the drift into illegal activity and deviant leisure forms and practice is likely to accelerate, since these are the means of attaining a sense of personal worth and collective identity in a system that has defined some citizens as *generically replaceable*.

Risk

A decade ago, many working in the field of Leisure Studies would have scoffed at the notion that students of leisure must address the risk of terrorism. So far from the habitual study of self-realization, pleasure, companionship and conviviality, the subject of terrorism might have seemed to be outlandish and irrelevant. In the USA, 9/11 decisively changed that. The al-Qaida attack on the World Trade Center destroyed the myth of American exceptionalism with respect to terrorism. More widely, it dramatically exposed the globalization of risk. The Trade Center towers included ground-level leisure space in which public sculptures were displayed, seating was provided and public concerts were regularly staged. The attack was not merely directed against potent symbols of

American capitalism, it struck at what John Kelly (1987) called people's 'freedom to be'. One result is that it produced a 'homeland security' strategy in the USA that has vastly enhanced civil defence measures and police surveillance in public spaces, transport links and other sensitive spaces.

Alas, the postwar activities of the Irish Republican Army in England provided Britain with a longer history of terrorist violence in public space. The pub bombings in Birmingham city centre (1974) and Guildford (1974); the explosions in the major tourist attraction of the Tower of London (1974); the Hyde Park massacre (1982); the bombing of major sites of consumer culture such as Harrod's department store (1983), Warrington shopping centre (1993) and the Arndale shopping centre in Manchester (1996) were all cases in point.

There are several reasons why terrorists target public space. To begin with, it symbolizes civil society's commitment to order, progress and companionship. Parks, tourist sights and shopping areas are also locations in which citizens feel free and invulnerable. The al-Qaida bomb in a Bali disco which killed 202 (2002) was intended not merely to kill and maim but to intimidate citizens by threatening civil liberties of play. The same is true of the terrorist attacks on tourists in Cairo which killed 18 (1996), Luxor in which 68 tourists died (1997) and Mombasa, Kenya in which over a dozen were slaughtered (2002). By exposing the vulnerability of citizens in locations like these, terrorists hope to propagate a climate of civil distraction and paranoia that destabilizes government and discourages public support for policies of which the terrorists disapprove.

Similarly, public spaces are locations of mobility and freedom. The 1995 attack on the Tokyo subway system involving sarin gas that killed 12 and the 2004 attack on the railway system in Madrid that killed 190 struck at the capillaries of modern civil order. Without a safe and effective public transport system, citizens become immobilized and frustrated. Work and play activities are disrupted. A pernicious bunker mentality may be cultivated. The West has set great store by the freedom of movement as a symbol of progress. Not to be in possession of it creates discord, unrest and pressure upon governments.

Terrorist campaigns are frequently compared to wars. But the analogy is unsound. Terrorists do not possess standing armies in the accepted sense of the term. That is, their combatants live and work in civil society rather than being confined to barracks and uniformed as professional attack-and-defence specialists. Their assaults typically take the forms of sporadic outbursts, rather than the continuous war of attrition of orthodox armed military combat. Leisure professionals must come to terms with terrorist risk as an ordinary part of civic culture. Because public spaces are frequently locations for leisure and recreation, students of leisure must explore ways of securing them against attack while implacably honouring traditional civil liberties. Because terrorists live, play and work among us, we must be vigilant about suspicious behaviour without encouraging intolerance of racial, religious or subcultural difference. The challenge is formidable, because the essence of effective terrorism is that it remains invisible until it bursts asunder in the form of a physical attack. The problem again illustrates the need for leisure professionals to cease viewing leisure sentimentally as a charmed realm of individual freedom and collective harmony. We need to be responsive to the threats posed in leisure settings and the benefits that terrorists identify in disrupting them. This calls upon leisure professionals to take the political and religious context of location forms and practice far more seriously than has hitherto been the case.

Terrorism provides a virulent example of contemporary risk, but it hardly exhausts the category. Ulrich Beck's (1992) mould-breaking book emphasized the alarming varieties of global risk. Environmental pollution, HIV infection, drug addiction and biochemical catastrophe recognize no national boundaries. These forms of risk already exert formidable global influence over lifestyle and the life cycle. For example, the US Census Bureau's (2004) projections for world population trends estimate that Aids, which has already killed 20 million in the past twenty years, will lower the average life expectancy at birth in some countries in sub-Saharan Africa, Asia and Latin America to around 30 years by 2010 (www.census.gov). Barring major medical breakthroughs, it is predicted that 45 million people known to have HIV will die by 2015. The evidence is that in these countries, despite public awareness campaigns, the risk of being infected with a sexually transmitted disease through casual sex has been normalized.

Similarly, the recreational use of Class A drugs, especially cocaine and ecstacy, has increased over the past decade (Parker *et al.* 1999; Hammersley *et al.* 1999). This tendency is related to the growth of the party-clubbing scene. There is some evidence of cultural accommodation to the recreational use of non-Class A drugs, especially cannabis. Parker *et al.* (2002: 949) refer to a 'blurring' in social attitudes between the use of licit (for example alcohol) and illicit (for example cannabis and cocaine) substances in 'going out'. This is reinforced by routine references to drug-taking in television dramas, serials and comedy shows and public disclosures by celebrities and politicians that they have 'dabbled'. With respect to non-Class A drugs, there are now strong pressures of decriminalization. The old reaction of blanket moral condemnation has been replaced by one of relative neutrality.

Conversely, the recreational use of Class A drugs is confined to relatively small groups and is subject to widespread censure and prohibition. There is some evidence that this social reaction increases the glamour of using Class A drugs for recreational purposes and diminishes risk awareness in these groups (Parker *et al.* 1999). The loosening of inhibitions associated with participation in recreational drug cultures may increase social pressures to be 'adventurous' or 'experimental', with potentially fatal consequences. The uncertainty and risk that derive from the casualization of the labour market are likely to be 'managed' by greater recreational use of illicit drugs. The result of this is that it is probable that greater numbers of people will be exposed to risk through Class A drug use.

Global risk has the potential to unite nations because it poses common threats to life. Leisure professionals must endorse the traditional connotation of pleasure and life satisfaction with leisure in Western civilization. But they must also develop a geometry of leisure risk assessment to counterbalance strategies and methods developed by the police and surveillance forces. Among other things, this must explore risk potential in leisure settings, the symbolic power of leisure forms as terrorist targets, the dynamics of psychologies of transgression that identify play as a *legitimate* target of attack, safe sex and drug education in family and school relations, and mechanisms of monitoring environmental pollution. Central to this geometry should be the principle that the pursuit of personal pleasure involves trajectories of action that have consequences for others. Leisure as an *end in itself* is a bogus concept. It must always be situated in relation to the motivation of individuals and factors of location and context.

The dilemmas of post-identity thinking

The confluence between the three streams of post-feminism, post-colonialism and post-structuralism in social and cultural theory produces specific dilemmas of **post-identity thinking** for students of leisure. The question of *Othering*, that is, the categories of difference denied by

---

Post-identity thinking condenses a number of nuances: (1) recognizing that personal and cultural substance is always and already a result of hybrid forms; (2) acknowledging the political reality of multiculturalism; (3) understanding that forms of identity organized around nation, race, gender and religion constitute an incomplete horizon.

colonialism, patriarchy and religious fundamentalism, must be embraced as a core component of leisure theory. This is fully compatible with the Action approach because it focuses upon how individuals are embodied and emplaced through relations of power. As Edward Said (1995), Stuart Hall (1992, 1993c) and others propose, until recently the history of the West is a history of erasing or 'writing over' cultural difference. Othering is closely related to empowerment, distributive justice and social inclusion because it seeks to expose the partiality of group perspectives and widen the horizon of collective life.

An important task for leisure theory is to identify a role for leisure in progressive identity politics and active citizenship. How can we destabilize confining forms of identity without eliminating the sense of place and personal substance that we all need in order to feel secure? What forms of new belonging can be forged from the many intersections of cultural difference? What part can leisure play in securing the conditions for the effective representation of difference and unity? These are difficult questions raising new issues relating to the form of active citizenship and the meaning of care for the self and care for the other. That we do not currently have answers to them presents Leisure Studies with one of its most urgent and biggest tasks.

Post-identity thinking may offer a solution to the problem posed by multi-paradigmatic complexity. For regardless of the divisions between Marxists, feminists, critical theorists, figurational sociologists, post-structuralists and postmodernists, they are united around a profound distaste for essentialism. Post-identity thinking simply dismisses essentialism as an option. It is extraordinarily sensitive to issues of embodiment and emplacement, regarding both to reflect factors of context, location and the motivation of social actors rather than the mechanics of fate. The refusal to regard identity as defined or finished offers the opportunity to develop collaboration between traditions that hitherto have regarded one another to be polarized. But it would be premature to predict an imminent *entente cordiale* between paradigms. In general, differences do not arrive without reasons. The antagonisms and divisions between paradigms in leisure theory derive from different perspectives on questions of leisure and power, scarcity and solidarity and reality and the imaginary. The challenge for critical positions in leisure theory is to set their divisions against the mutilating politics of ethnocentric colonial, patriarchal, religious and national forms of authoritarianism. Capitalism recognizes differences between people and exploits them to augment profit margins. Generic replaceable labour and generic replaceable citizens are contemporaneous accomplishments of the capitalist system. While critical theorists in leisure squabble among themselves, the juggernaut of capitalism rolls on and threatens to create a world of leisure without an alternative. This is exactly what Ritzer (2000, 2004) alludes to in his presentation of the processes of standardization and regimentation associated with McDonaldization and the globalization of nothing.

If it is to have meaning in people's lives, leisure theory must address the dilemmas of leisure forms and practice as they are expressed in leisure trajectories, but must also grasp the mettle of the social imaginary to posit leisure relations built around empowerment, distributive justice and social inclusion. This means confronting the question of post-identity and pitting it against the various demoralized versions of leisure identities constructed by primitive capitalism. Consumption as mass conformity, women as *only* sexual objects, the individual as primarily devoted to self-interest, race as inherently antagonistic, the various crude and limited images of personhood presented in tabloid journalism and pornography, and all of the other essentialist phantoms conjured by the magic of capitalism may be dispelled by recognizing that we are all embodied and emplaced at the intersections of cultural difference and that the purity of identity is an illusion.

Post-identity thinking is an enormous resource for hope, in the sense articulated by the late Raymond Williams (1989), that is, an asset that ordinary men and women can share to construct a world of leisure which is less troubled, less stressed and less divided. Despite the various points made about the role of ideology, interpellation and power, made in relation to situating individuals in relation to leisure, students of leisure must defend their field as having great potential for personal enrichment and collective growth. Leisure may not be the *freedom to be* in John Kelly's (1987) sense of the term. But it is a zone of engagement wherein questions of liberation, fulfilment, mutuality and reciprocity may be exchanged more unconditionally than in other areas of social and cultural life. Recognizing this should be a distinguishing characteristic of *what we do* as students of leisure and leisure professionals, but always with a critical, reflexive perspective.

Conclusion

The ambition of the interpretive challenges set out here is no small thing. It is testimony to the strides made by leisure theory in producing sharper, more relevant knowledge about voluntary activity and the representation and theming thereof. In part our knowledge has improved because leisure is now more central in the lives of ordinary people. The ethic of care for the self identifies leisure as a necessary part of a balanced lifestyle and reveals work-driven existence to be associated with an assortment of social and physical ailments and morbidities. The ethic of care for the other raises the consciousness of those in the West about the delusions of hedonism and global inequalities of access to leisure resources. Active citizenship encompasses both ethical imperatives.

There is a long way to go before we can claim victory in globalizing active citizenship. But, crucially, a start is well under way. One responsibility of the leisure theorist is to disseminate these new ideas, test them in the field and assimilate new information relating to leisure forms, trajectories and practices. This may not produce knowledge that will enable us to adjudicate between competing models of leisure. Most certainly, the struggle between *atomistic individualism* and *romantic organicism* has not been exhausted (Gellner 1998). Building leisure forms, trajectories and practices must always be a *political* process in which the leisure theorist is but one of many partners. Leisure theory may set out the advantages and disadvantages of life options in leisure, but it cannot tell the individual what to do; it can expose regulative mechanisms in leisure relations, but it cannot compel states and corporations to change their spots; it can demonstrate how some types of religious belief distort difference and reinforces ethnocentricity, but it cannot force people to change their religious belief. To these faults one should add Gellner's (1998: 184) criticism, that the *ethic of cognition* is unable to generate a 'gratifying sense of belonging', or a basis for obligation and cooperation or a set of consolations for tragedy. Yet by insisting on the significance of the ideal of unencumbered thought and research, developing new knowledge often *against* the grain of privilege, testing it against the evidence in order to establish its validity, and remaining open to new developments in leisure forms, trajectories and practice, we accentuate the stock of *testable knowledge* upon which advances in human well-being ultimately depend.

These advances frequently test public morality. For example, for most of the twentieth century, smoking in leisure became prevalent in all socioeconomic sectors for both men and women. However, after the 1970s, the recreational use of cigarettes became subject to increasing criticism and censure. Scientific knowledge was the catalyst in this, since medical research established unequivocal causal links between smoking and cancer and coronary disease. However, far from precipitating an immediate transformation in leisure habits, the move to ban smoking in public places provoked a passionate counter-argument that the initiative constituted an intolerable infringement upon civil liberties. This argument remains powerful, especially in countries like the UK, where no ban is currently in force. Yet the probability is that it will not prevail. Knowledge about the physical damage to care for the self and care for the other (through the medical effects of secondary smoking and environmental pollution) is likely to outweigh the moral liberty to smoke in public places. Already, there are strong pressures to restrict public space for smoking and there is some evidence that in many social circles smokers are now routinely stigmatized as 'anti-social'. Granted these changes have taken a long time and more time is needed before the issue is resolved. But the trend is unmistakable.

We are in the midst of a parallel moral shift in the West with respect to recreational drug use. The consumption of illicit Class A drugs, particularly cocaine and ecstacy, in the recreational activity of the young, employed and educated has grown steadily during the past decade (ESPAD 1997, 2001). The evidence suggests that otherwise 'law-abiding' adults have developed informal networks of friends and 'friends of friends' who supply drugs as a 'normal' part of leisure lifestyle, thus establishing physical and symbolic distance between themselves and drug dealers (Parker *et al.* 2002: 960). The moral reaction to this development is complex. The recreational use of Class A drugs in public is primarily related to the 'semi-private' party-clubbing scene. While some evidence exists that illicit drug use in these settings has been 'normalized', it appears to be confined to relatively small numbers of regular users (Measham *et al.* 2000). Even within these settings there is significant moral disapproval about the recreational use of cocaine and ecstacy. Levels of public disapproval to the recreational use of Class A drugs outside these settings remain high.

Conversely, public attitudes to the recreational use of cannabis have relaxed considerably during the past two decades. In the UK cannabis is currently being declassified so that possession is no longer an arrestable offence. Calls for a review of the drug laws in respect of cannabis frequently mobilize the argument that the drug is 'safer' than alcohol. Be that as it may, the weight of evidence supports the conclusion that the 'sensible' recreational use of cannabis is already tolerated.

Leisure practice is fraught with moral battles because it constantly raises the question of what is good for you and others. In traditional society this question was answered by the facts of privilege and social hierarchy. You give unto Caesar that which is Caesar's. In our society, where all types of *ascribed* authority are queried and citizens are encouraged to rank each other according to their *achievements*, questions of good and bad leisure forms and practice are more contentious. Those who enter the lion's den of leisure theory seldom escape controversy. For in our type of society who is anyone to tell anyone else about the proper use of 'free' time?

In the light of the moral minefield of the nature of voluntary action and the causality behind human choice, it is right to end with another rationale to add to the foregoing for *doing* leisure theory (see pp. 197–99). An advocacy of leisure theory must relate it to a task of utmost importance and interest for human beings: the enhancement of democracy. By producing better knowledge about *why* people make the leisure choices that they do, *how* these choices are related to location and context and *what* the probable consequences of these choices will be, leisure theorists will contribute to more fulfilling leisure experience. Or at least, they stand an even chance of doing so.

Notes

Introduction

1. The original version was adopted by the International Recreation Association in 1970. It was revised by its successor the World Leisure and Recreation Association in 1979.
2. The question of the practical institutional, economic and political arrangements for realizing global planning is signally neglected in the document. This rather weakens the practical force of the document.

1 Narrating Leisure

1. The Sapir–Whorf thesis is a relativist doctrine which holds that language is conditioned by the habits of our community and predisposes certain choices of interpretation.
2. Priority, externality and constraint are the three conditions specified by Durkheim in the identification and classification of social facts.
3. The suggestion was made from the floor of the annual Leisure Studies Association conference at the University of Sussex in 1984.
4. 'There is no such thing as society' is one of the many *bon mots* of the arch atomistic individualist (who nevertheless held steadfast an unattractive streak of primitive nationalism): Margaret Thatcher.

2 Action Analysis

1. A fuller version of this model of emplacement and embodiment and its significance for research into society and culture can be found in Turner and Rojek (2001).

3 Primary Functions

1. A questionnaire of a sample of Londoners by the market solutions company CACI reported the following top hobbies in the city:

	%
Eating out	32
Reading	25
Foreign travel	22
Pub	21
Cookery	20
Gardening	16
Fashion	15
DIY	15
Cinema	13
Gym	12
Theatre/arts	12

Bingo	9
Health club	6
Birdwatching	4
Current affairs	4
Gourmet food	4
Charity work	3
Yoga	2

5   The Life Course and Generations

1. Jonathan Swift anticipated this state of affairs in *Gulliver's Travels* (1735). He recounts the plight of the Struldbruggs who are granted perpetual life, but pass it accumulating all the usual disadvantages that old age brings with it.

6   Power and Leisure

1. A methodological problem that students of leisure face in researching predatory strata is that, despite their great influence upon society, economy and culture, they are well-concealed from the public and relatively insulated from critical scrutiny.
2. Historically in Britain, the Estates of the Realm were divided into three divisions of Parliament: the Lords Temporal (peers), the Lords Spiritual (bishops) and the Commons. The Fourth Estate was a term to denote any additional group with power in the land, chiefly the press. The power of the press is proportionate to their independence.

9   Central Problems

1. The Sao Paulo Declaration was issued in October 1998 by delegates to the 5th World Leisure Congress of the World Leisure and Recreation Association in conjunction with Servico Social Do Comercio (SESC), Sao Paulo, and the Latin American Leisure and Recreation Association (ALATIR). It consists of ten articles:

    1. All persons have the right to leisure through economic, political and social policies that are equitable and sustainable.
    2. All persons need to celebrate and share diversity in leisure.
    3. All governments and institutions should preserve and create barrier free environments e.g. cultural, technological, natural and built, where people have time, space, facilities and opportunity to express, celebrate and share leisure.
    4. Collective and individual endeavours should be permitted to maintain the freedom and integrity of leisure.
    5. All governments will enact and enforce laws and policies designed to provide leisure for all.
    6. All private and public sectors consider the threats to diversity and quality of leisure experiences caused by the local, national and international consequences of globalization.
    7. All private and public sectors consider the threats to the abuse and misuse of leisure by individuals i.e. by deviant and criminal behaviour, which results from local, national and international forces.

8. All private and public sectors ensure that policies are implemented to provide leisure education, curricula and programs for school and community systems, as well as programs to train related voluntary and professional human resources.
9. Efforts be made to understand better the consequences of globalization for leisure through a coherent program of ongoing research.
10. Efforts be made to disseminate information on the costs and benefits to leisure from the several and profound forces of globalization.

2. Policy and strategy implications are seriously underdeveloped, thus raising questions about the practical viability of the document.

Bibliography

Adorno, T. (1991) *The Culture Industry*. London, Routledge.
——(1998) *Critical Models*. New York, Columbia University Press.
Adorno, T. and Horkheiner, M. (1944) *Dialectic of Enlightenment*. London, Verso.
Aitchison, C. (2000) 'Poststructural Feminist Theories of Representing Others', *Leisure Studies* 21(1): 57–74.
Aitchison, C., MacLeod, N. E. and Shaw, S. J. (2000) *Leisure and Tourism Landscapes*. London, Routledge.
Althusser, L. (1971) *Lenin, Philosophy and Other Essays*. London, New Left Books.
——(1977) *For Marx*. London, Verso.
Anderson, B. (1983) *Imagined Communities*. London, Verso.
Andrew, E. (1981) *Closing the Iron Cage*. Montreal, Black Rose Books.
Appadurai, A. (1990) 'Disjuncture and Difference in Global Political Economy', in M. Featherstone (ed.) *Global Culture*. London, Sage: 295–310.
——(ed.) (1995) *Globalization*. Durham, NC, Duke University Press.
Argyle, M. (1996) *The Social Psychology of Leisure*. Harmondsworth, Penguin.
Armesto (2000) *Civilizations*. Basingstoke, Palgrave Macmillan.
Aronowitz, S. and Di Fazio, W. (1994) *The Jobless Future*. Minneapolis, University of Minnesota Press.
Aronowitz, S. and Cutler, J. (eds) (1998) *Post-Work*. London, Routledge.
——(2003) *How Class Works*. New Haven, CT, Yale University Press.
Bailey, P. (1978) *Leisure and Class in Victorian England*. London, Routledge.
Bakhtin, M. (1968) *Rabelais and His World*. Cambridge, MA, MIT Press.
Barrett, M. (1980) *Women's Oppression Today*. London, Verso.
Baudrillard, J. (1981) *For a Critique of the Political Economy of the Sign*. St Louis, Telos.
Bauman, Z. (1992) *Intimations of Postmodernity*. Routledge, London.
——(1998) *Work, Consumerism and the New Poor*. Buckingham, Open University Press.
Beck, U. (1992) *Risk Society*. London, Sage.
——(1999) *World Risk Society*. Cambridge, Polity Press.
Beck, U. (2000) *The Brave New World of Work*. Cambridge, Polity Press.
Beck-Gernsheim, E. (2002) *Individualization*. London, Sage.
Becker, G. (1965) 'A Theory of the Allocation of Time', *Economic Journal* 75: 493–517.
——(1979) 'Economic Analysis and Human Behaviour', in L. Levy-Garbona (ed.) *Sociological Economics*. London, Sage: 7–24.
Becker, H. (1953) 'Becoming a Marijuana User', *American Journal of Sociology* 59: 235–42.
Bell, D. (1974) *The Coming of Post-Industrial Society*. London, Heinemann.
Bindel, J. (2003) 'Rape Is Never Glamorous', *Guardian*, 2 October: 25.
Blackshaw, T. (2003) *Leisure Life*. London, Routledge.
Blok, A. (1974) *The Mafia in a Sicilian Village*. Oxford, Blackwell.
Boal, A. (1979) *Theatre of the Oppressed*. London, Pluto.
——(1995) *The Rainbow of Desire*. London, Routledge.

Bouchard, C. (1988) 'Genetic Basis of Racial Differences', *Canadian Journal of Sports Science* 13(2): 104–8.

Bourdieu, P. (1984) *Distinction*. London, Routledge.

Braverman, H. (1974) *Labour and Monopoly Capital*. New York, Monthly Review Press.

Briffault, R. (1965) *The Troubadours*. Bloomington, Indiana University Press.

Brightbill, C. (1961) *Man and Leisure*. Englewood Cliffs, NJ, Prentice-Hall.

Brohm, J. (1978) *Sport: A Prison of Measured Time*. London, Interlinks.

Bromley, R. (2000) *Narratives for a New Belonging*. Edinburgh, Edinburgh University Press.

Bryman, A. (2001) *Social Research Methods*. Oxford, Oxford University Press.

Bunce, M. (1994) *The Countryside Ideal: Anglo-American Images of Landscape*. London, Routledge.

Burfoot, A. (1992) 'White Men Can't Run', *Runner's World*, August: 89–95.

Butler, J. (1990) *Gender Trouble*. London, Routledge.

——(1993) *Bodies That Matter: On the Discursive Limits of 'Sex'*. London, Routledge.

Cabinet Office (2002) *Women's Earnings over the Lifetime*. London, HMSO.

Cannadine, D. (2001) *Ornamentalism*. London, Penguin.

Cashmore, E. (1982) *Black Sportsmen and Society*. London, Routledge & Kegan Paul.

Castells, M. (1996) *The Rise of Network Society*. Oxford, Blackwell.

——(1997) *The Power of Identity*. Oxford, Blackwell.

——(1998) *The End of the Millennium*. Oxford, Blackwell.

Cheek, N. and Burch, W. (1976) *The Social Organization of Leisure in Human Society*. New York, Harper & Row.

Clarke, John and Critcher, Chas (1985) *The Devil Makes Work*. Basingstoke, Macmillan.

Clements, P. (2003) 'The Arts, Culture and Exclusion', PhD thesis, *Department of Arts Policy and Management*. London, City University.

Cohen, S. (1972) *Folk Devils and Moral Panics*. London, Paladin.

Cohen, S. and Taylor, L. (1993) *Escape Attempts*. London, Routledge.

Cross, G. (1993) *Time and Money: The Making of Consumer Culture*. London, Routledge.

Csikszentmihalyi, M. (1990) *Flow: The Psychology of Optimal Experience*. New York, Harper & Row.

Csikszentmihalyi, Milhay (1997) *Creativity*. Harcourt Brace Jovanovich, New York.

Csikszentmihalyi, Mihlay (1998) *Finding Flow: The Psychology of Engagement With Everyday Life*. Harcourt Brace Jovanovich, New York.

Cunningham, Hugh (1980) *Leisure in Victorian Britain*. London, Croom Helm.

Dahl, Robert (1961) *Who Governs?* New Haven, Yale University Press.

Daniels, B. C. (1995) *Puritans at Play: Leisure and Recreation in Colonial New England*. New York, St Martin's Griffin.

De Grazia, Sebastian (1964) *Of Time, Work and Leisure*. Doubleday, New York.

Deem, R. (1986) *All Work and No Play*. Milton Keynes, Open University Press.

Department of Health (2002) *Tackling Health Inequalities: Cross Cutting Review*. London, Department of Health.

Ditton, J. (1977) *Part-Time Crime: An Ethnography of Fiddling and Pilferage*. London, Macmillan.

Donnelly, P. (1986) 'The Paradox of the Parks: Politics of Recreational Land Use Before and After the Mass Trespasses', *Leisure Studies* 5(2): 211–32.

Douglas, M. and Isherwood, B. (1996) *The World of Goods*. London, Routledge.

Dower, M. (1965) *The Challenge of Leisure*. London, Civil Trust.

Dumazedier, J. (1967) *Towards a Society of Leisure*. New York, Free Press.

Duncan, J. (1990) *The City as Text*. Cambridge, Cambridge University Press.

Dunning, E. and Sheard, K. (1979) *Amateurs, Barbarians and Players*. Oxford, Martin Robertson.

Dunning, E., Murphy, P. and Williams, J. (1988) *The Roots of Football Hooliganism*. London, Routledge & Kegan Paul.

Dworkin, A. (1978) *Right-Wing Women*. New York, Coward-McCann.

Eames, Penny (2003) *Creative Solutions and Social Inclusion: Culture and the Community*. Arts Access, Aoterea.

Edwards, H. (1973) *The Sociology of Sport*. Homewood, IL, Dorsey Press.

Eisenstein, Z. (1977) 'Constructing a Theory of Capitalist Patriarchy and Socialist Feminism', *The Insurgent Sociologist* 7(3): 3–17.

Elias, N. and Dunning, E. (1986) *Quest for Excitement*. Oxford, Blackwell.

Elias, Norbert (1978a) *The Civilizing Process. Vol 1: The History of Manners*. Oxford, Blackwell.

Elias, Norbert (1978a) *What Is Sociology?* London, Hutchinson.

Elias, Norbert (1982) *The Civilizing Process. Vol 2: State Formation and Civilization*. Oxford, Blackwell.

Entine, J. (2000) *Taboo: Why Black Athletes Dominate Sports and Why We're Afraid to Talk About It*. New York, Public Affairs.

ESPAD (1997) *Alcohol and Other Drug Use Among Students in 26 European Countries*. Stockholm, Swedish Council on Alcohol and Other Drugs.

——(2001) *Alcohol and Drug Use Among Students in 30 Countries*. Stockholm, Swedish Council on Alcohol and Other Drugs.

Estes, R. and Wilensky, H. (1978) 'Life Cycle Squeeze and the Morale Curve', *Social Problems* 25: 277–92.

Etzioni, A. (1993) *The Spirit of Community: Rights, Responsibilities and the Communitarian Agenda*. New York, Crown.

Ewen, Stuart (1988) *All Consuming Images*. New York, Basic Books.

Eysenck, H. (1971) *The IQ Argument: Race, Intelligence, Education*. New York, Library Press.

Featherstone, M. (1987) 'Leisure, Symbolic Power and the Life Course', in J. Horne, D. Jary and A. Tomlinson (eds) *Sport, Leisure and Social Relations*. London, Routledge & Kegan Paul.

Ferguson, H. (1992) 'Watching the World Go Round: Atrium Culture and the Psychology of Shopping', in R. Shields (ed.) *Lifestyle Shopping*. London, Routledge.

Flaubert, G. (1983) *Flaubert in Egypt*. London, Michael Haag.

Foucault, M. (1975) *Discipline and Punish*. Harmondsworth, Penguin.

——(1980) *Power/Knowledge: Selected Interviews and Other Writings 1972–77*, edited by Colin Gordon. Hemel Hempstead, Harvester.

——(1981) *History of Sexuality*. Harmondsworth, Penguin.

Foucault, Michel (1970) *The Order of Things*. London, Tavistock.

Frank, R. and Cook, P. (1995) *The Winner Takes All Society*. New York, Penguin.

Franklin, A. (2003) *Tourism*. London, Routledge.

Freire, P. (1970) *Pedagogy of the Oppressed*. Penguin, Harmondsworth.

Freud, S. (1936) *Civilization and Its Discontents*. London, Hogarth.

Freysinger, V. (1999) 'Life Span and Life Course Perspectives on Leisure', in E. Jackson and T. Burton (eds) *Leisure Studies: Prospects for the Twenty First Century*. T. State College, PA, Venture: 253–70.

Friedman, Milton (1980) *Free to Choose*. Harcourt Brace Jovanovich, New York.
Friedman, Milton (1984) *The Tyranny of the Status Quo*. Harcourt Brace Jovanovich, New York.
Frisby, D. (1985) *Fragments of Modernity*. Cambridge, Polity Press.
——(2001) *Cityscapes of Modernity*. Cambridge, Polity Press.
Fullagar, S. (2002) 'Narratives of Travel: Desire and the Movement of Feminine Subjectivity', *Leisure Studies* 21(1): 57–74.
Garfinkel, H. (1967) *Studies in Ethnomethodology*. New York, Prentice-Hall.
Gartman, D. (1994) *Auto-Opium*. London, Routledge.
Gellner, E. (1981) *Muslim Society*. Cambridge, Cambridge University Press.
——(1985) *Relativism and the Social Sciences*. Cambridge, Cambridge University Press.
——(1998) *Language and Solitude*. Cambridge, Cambridge University Press.
Gershuny, J. (1978) *After Industrial Society?* London, Macmillan.
——(2000) *Changing Times: Work and Leisure in Postindustrial Society*. Oxford, Oxford University Press.
Gerth, H. *et al.* (1948) *From Max Weber*. London, Routledge.
Giddens, A. (1991) *Modernity and Self Identity*. Cambridge, Polity Press.
——(1998) *The Third Way*. Cambridge, Polity Press.
——(2000) *The Third Way and Its Critics*. Cambridge, Polity Press.
——(2002) *Runaway World: How Globalization is Reshaping Our Lives*. London, Profile Books.
Gilroy, P. (1987) *There Ain't No Black in the Union Jack*. London, Hutchinson.
——(2000) *Against Race*. Cambridge, MA, Harvard University Press.
——(2004) *Between Camps*. London, Routledge.
Gilroy, P., Grossberg, L. and McRobbie, A. (2000) *Without Guarantees: Essays in Honour of Stuart Hall*. London, Verso.
Girard, R. (1988) *Violence and the Sacred*. London, Athlone.
Gitlin, T. (2002) *Media Unlimited*. New York, Owl Books.
Goldman, R. and Papson, S. (1998) *Nike Culture*. London, Sage.
Goldstein, Paul (2003) *Copyright's Highway,: From Gutenberg to the Jukebox*. Stanford, Stanford University Press.
Goldthorpe, J., Lockwood, D., Bechhofer, F. and Platt, J. (1968) *The Affluent Worker*. Cambridge, Cambridge University Press.
Goodale, Thomas and Godbey, Geoff (1988) *The Evolution of Leisure*. State College, PA, Venture.
Goodman, F. (1997) *The Mansion on the Hill: Dyman, Young, Geffen, Springsteen and the Head-on Collision of Rock and Commerce*. London, Pimlico.
Gorz, A. (1978) *Farewell to the Working Class*. London, Pluto.
——(1983) *Paths to Paradise*. London, Pluto.
Gottdiener, M. (1997) *The Theming of America*. Boulder, CO, Westview.
Gottdiener, M. (ed.) (2000) *New Forms of Consumption*. Lanham, MD Rowman & Littlefield.
Gramsci, A. (1971) *Selections for Prison Notebooks*. London, Lawrence & Wishart.
Gray, R. (1981) *The Aristocracy of Labour*. London, Macmillan.
Green, E. (1998) 'Women Doing Friendships', *Leisure Studies* 17(3): 171–86.
Green, E., Hebron, S. and Woodward, D. (1990) *Women's Leisure, What Leisure?* London, Macmillan.
Greenblatt, S. (1992) *Marvellous Posessions: The Wonder of the New World*. Chicago, IL, University of Chicago Press.

Gruneau, R. (1983) *Class, Sports and Social Development*. Amherst, University of Massachusetts Press.

Habermas, J. (1962) *The Structural Transformation of the Public Sphere*. Cambridge, Polity Press.

Hall, S. (1970) 'Leisure, Entertainment and Mass Communication', *Society and Leisure* 2(2): 28–47.

——(1973) 'Encoding and Decoding in Media Discourse', Occasional Paper, Birmingham Centre for Contemporary Cultural Studies.

——(1979) *Drifting into a Law and Order Society*. London, Coden Trust.

—— (1985) 'Authoritarian Populism: A Reply to Jessop et al.', *New Left Review* 151: 115–24.

——(1988) *The Hard Road to Renewal*. London, Verso.

——(1989a) 'The "First" New Left: Life and Times', in R. Archer (ed.) *Out of Apathy*. London, Verso: 11–38.

——(1989b) 'Then and Now: A Re-evaluation of the New Left', in R. Archer (ed.) *Out of Apathy*. London, Verso: 68–82.

——(1991) 'Old Identities and New Identities; Old and New Ethnicities', in A. D. King (ed.) *Culture, Globalization and the World System*. London, Macmillan: 41–68.

——(1992) 'The West and the Rest: Discourse and Power', in S. Hall and B. Gielen (eds) *Formations of Modernity*. Milton Keynes/Cambridge, Open University Press/Polity Press: 275–332.

——(1993a) 'Culture, Community, Nation', *Cultural Studies* 7(3): 1–13.

——(1993b) 'Reflections Upon the Encoding/Decoding Model: An Interview with Stuart Hall', in J. Cruz and J. Lewis (eds) *Viewing, Listening, Reading: Audiences and Cultural Reception*. Boulder, CO, Westview: 253–74.

——(1993c) 'Minimal Selves', in A. Gray and J. McGuigan (eds) *Studying Culture*. London, Arnold: 134–8.

——(1996) 'Introduction: Who Needs Identity?', in S. Hall and P. Du Gay (eds) *Questions of Cultural Identity*. London, Sage.

——(1999) 'Unsettling "the Heritage": Re-imagining the Post-nation', in *Whose Heritage?*, London, Arts Council of England.

Hall, S. and Du Gay, P. (eds) (1996) *Questions of Cultural Identity*. London, Sage.

Hall, S. and Jefferson, T. (eds) (1975) *Resistance Through Rituals*. London, Hutchinson.

Hall, S., Critcher, C., Jefferson, T., Clarke, J. and Roberts, R. (1978) *Policing the Crisis*. London, Macmillan.

Hall, S., Hobson, D., Lowe, A. and Willis, P. (eds) (1980) *Culture, Media, Language*. London, Unwin Hyman.

Hammersely, R., Ditton, J., Smith, I. and Short, E. (1999) 'Patterns of Ecstacy Use by Drug Users', *British Journal of Criminology* 39(4): 625–47.

Hannigan, J. (1998) *Fantasy City*. London, Routledge.

Haraway, D. (1991) *Simians, Cyborgs and Women*. London, Free Association Books.

Hardt, M. and Negri, A. (2000) *Empire*. Cambridge, MA, Harvard University Press.

Hargreaves, J. (1994) *Sporting Females*. London, Routledge.

Harvey, D. (1989) *The Condition of Postmodernity*. Oxford, Blackwell.

Hayek, Friedrich (1944) *The Road to Serfdom*. London, Routledge.

Hayek, Friedrich (1976) *Law, Legislation and Liberty. Vol II: The Mirage of Social Justice*. London, Routledge.

Hayek, Friedrich (1979) *Law, Legislation and Liberty. Vol III: Political Order of a Free People*. London, Routledge.

Haywood, L. and Henry, I. (1986) 'Policy Developments in Community, Leisure and Recreation', *Leisure Management* 6(7): 25–9.

Hebdige, D. (1988) *Hiding in the Light*. London, Routledge.

Hemingway, J. (1999) 'Leisure, Social Capital and Citizenship', *Journal of Leisure Research* 31(2): 150–62.

Henderson, K., Bialeschki M., Shaw, S. and Freysinger, V. (1996) *Both Gains and Gaps: Feminist Perspectives on Women's Leisure*. State College, PA, Venture.

Hernstein, R. and Murray, C. (1994) *The Bell Curve: Intelligence and Class Structure in American Life*. New York, Free Press.

Hill, J. (2002) *Sport, Leisure and Culture in Twentieth Century Britain*. Basingstoke, Palgrave Macmillan.

Hill, J. O. and Trowbridge, F. L. (1998) 'Childhood Obesity: Future Directions and Research Priorities', *Pediatrics*, Supplement: 571.

Hobbes, Thomas (1651) *Leviathan*. Harmondsworth, Penguin.

Hochschild, A. (1989) *The Second Shift: Working, Parents and the Revolution in the Home*. London, Piatkus.

——(1997) *The Time Bind: When Work Becomes Home and Home Becomes Work*. New York, Metropolitan Books.

Hoggart, R. (1957) *The Uses of Literacy*. Harmondsworth, Penguin.

Hollands, R. (1995) *Friday Night, Saturday Night*. Newcastle, University of Newcastle.

Hooks, B. (1983) *Ain't I A Woman*. London, Pluto.

Horna, J. (1994) *The Study of Leisure*. Oxford, Oxford University Press.

Huizinga, J. (1947) *Homo Ludens*. London, Routledge & Kegan Paul.

Huizinga, Johann (1948) *Homo Ludens*. London, Routledge.

Hunnicutt, B. (1988) *Work Without End*. Philadelphia, PA, Temple University Press.

——(1996) *Kellog's Six Hour Day*. Philadelphia, PA, Temple University Press.

Inglis, T. (1997) 'Empowerment and Emancipation', *Adult Education Quarterly* 48(1): 3–17.

Institute for Fiscal Studies (2002) *Briefing Note 19*. London, Institute for Fiscal Studies.

Iso-Ahola, S. (1980) *The Social Psychology of Leisure and Recreation*. Dubuque, William Brown.

Iso-Ahola, S. (1989) 'Motivation for Leisure', in E. Jackson, and T. Burton (eds) *Understanding Leisure and Recreation: Mapping the Past, Charting the Future*, State College, Venture Publishing, 247–80.

Jameson, F. (1991) *Postmodernism or the Cultural Logic of Late Capitalism*. London, Verso.

Jensen, A. (1969) 'How Much Can We Boost IQ and Scholastic Achievement?', *Harvard Educational Review* 39: 1–123.

Johnson, K. (1998) 'Rape Statistics Not Crystal Clear', *USA Today*, 19 November.

Jones, S. G. (1986) *Workers At Play*. London, Routledge & Kegan Paul.

Kamin, L. (1974) *The Science and Politics of IQ*. Potomac, MD, Erlbaum.

Kammen, M. (1999) *American Culture, American Tastes*. New York, Basic Books.

Kaplan, M. (1960) *Leisure in America*. New York, Wiley.

——(1975) *Leisure: Theory and Policy*. New York, Wiley.

Katz, J. (1988) *Seductions of Crime*. New York, Basic Books.

Kellner, Doug (2002) *Media Spectacle*. London, Routledge.

Kelly, J. R. (1983) *Leisure, Identities and Interactions*. London, Allen & Unwin.
Kelly, J. R. (1987) *Freedom to Be: A New Sociology of Leisure*. New York, Macmillan.
Kelly, J. R., Steinkamp, M. and Kelly J. R. (1986) 'Later Leisure Life', *The Gerontologist* 6: 531–7.
Kennett, L. (2001) *Sherman: A Soldier's Life*. New York, HarperCollins.
Kerr, C., Dunlop, J. T., Harbison, F. H. and Meyers, C. (1973) *Industrialism and Industrial Man*. Harmondsworth, Penguin.
Kershaw, Ian (1998) *Hitler: 1889–1936, Hubris*. London, Penguin.
King, A. D. (1998) *The End of the Terraces: The Tranformation of English Football in the 1990s*. Leicester, Leicester University Press.
Kingsmill Review (2003) *Women's Employment and Pay*. London, HMSO.
Kipnis, L. (1999) *Bound and Gagged: Pornography and the Politics of Fantasy in America*. Durham, NC, Duke University Press.
Klein, N. (2001) *No Logo*. London, Flamingo.
Kracauer, S. (1995) *The Mass Ornament*. Cambridge, MA, Harvard University Press.
——(1998) *The Salaried Masses: Duty and Distraction in Weimar Germany*. London, Verso.
Kubey, R. and Csikszentmihalyi, M. (1990) *Television and the Quality of Life*. Hillsdale, NJ, Lawrence Erlbaum.
Kuhn, T. (1962) *The Structure of Scientific Revolutions*. Chicago, Chicago University Press.
Lacan, J. (1977) *Ecrits*. London, Routledge.
Laclau, E. and Mouffe, C. (1985) *Hegemony and Socialist Strategy*. London, Verso.
Langum, D. J. (1994) *Crossing over the Line: Legislating Morality and the Mann Act*. Chicago, IL, Chicago University Press.
Lasch, C. (1984) *The Minimal Self*. London, Picador.
Linder, S. (1970) *The Harried Leisure Class*. New York, Norton.
Linklater, A. (1998) *The Transformation of Political Community*. Cambridge, Polity Press.
Long, J. and Hylton, K. (2002) 'Shades of White: An Examination of Whiteness in Sport', *Leisure Studies* 21(2): 87–104.
Lowenthal, D. (1985) *The Past is a Foreign Country*. Cambridge, Cambridge University Press.
Lowenthal, L. (1961) 'The Triumph of Mass Idols', in *Literature, Popular Culture and Society*. Palo Alto, CA, Pacific: 109–40.
Lyng, S. (1990) 'Edgework: A Social Psychological Analysis of Voluntary Risk Taking', *American Journal of Sociology* 95: 887–921.
——(1991) 'Edgework Revisited: A Reply to Miller', *American Journal of Sociology* 96: 1534–9.
MacCannell, D. (1999) *The Tourist*, 3rd edn. Berkeley, University of California Press.
MacKinnon, C. (1993) *Only Words*. Cambridge, MA, Harvard University Press.
Malina, R. M. (1988) 'Racial/Ethnic Variation in the Motor Development and Performance of American Children', *Canadian Journal of Sports Science* 13(2): 136–43.
Maloney, E. (2002) *A Secret History of the IRA*. London, Penguin.
Mannheim, K. (1952) 'The Problem of Generations', *Essays on the Sociology of Knowledge*. London, Routledge & Kegan Paul: 276–322.
Marcuse, H. (1955) *Eros & Civilization*. London, Abacus.
——(1964) *One Dimensional Man*. London, Abacus.
——(1978) *The Aesthetic Dimension*. London, Macmillan.

——(2001) *Towards a Critical Theory of Society*. London, Routledge.
Marx, K. (1964) *The Economic and Philosophic Manuscripts 1844*. New York, International Press.
Marx, K. (1977) *Capital*, 3 vols. London, Lawrence & Wishart.
Marx, K. and Engels, F. (1965) *The German Ideology*. London, Lawrence & Wishart.
Matza, D. (1969) *Becoming Deviant*. Englewood Cliffs, NJ, Prentice-Hall.
May, L. (2000) *The Big Tomorrow: Hollywood and the Politics of the American Way*. Chicago, IL, University of Chicago Press.
McGuigan, J. (1992) *Cultural Populism*. London, Routledge.
——(1998) 'Cultural Populism Revisited', in M. Ferguson and P. Geliny (eds) *Cultural Studies in Question*. London, Sage: 140–5.
McLuhan, M. (1964) *Understanding Media*. New York, McGraw-Hill.
McRobbie, A. (1978) 'Working Class Girls and the Culture of Feminity', in Women's Studies Group (ed.) *Women Take Issue*. London, Hutchinson: 96–108.
——(1982) 'Jackie: An Ideology of Adolescent Femininity', in B. Waites, T. Bennett and G. Martin (eds) *Popular Culture: Past and Present*. London, Croom Helm: 262–83.
——(1993) 'Shut Up and Dance: Youth Culture and Changing Modes of Femininity', *Cultural Studies* 7(3): 406–26.
Measham, F., Aldridge, J. and Parker, H. (2000) *Dancing on Drugs: Risk, Health and Hedonism in the British Club Scene*. London, Free Association Books.
Merton, R. (1968) *Social Theory and Social Structure*. New York, Free Press.
Miller, D. (1987) *Material Culture and Mass Consumption*. Oxford, Blackwell.
Miller, D. (1998) *A Theory of Shopping*. Ithaca, NY, Cornell University Press.
Miller, J. (1993) *The Passion of Michel Foucault*. London, HarperCollins.
Mills, C. W. (1953) 'Leisure and the Whole Man', *New York Herald Tribune*, 25 October.
——(1956) *The Power Elite*. Oxford, Oxford University Press.
Moore, D. (1990) 'Anthropological Reflections on Youth Drug-Use Research', *Drug and Alcohol Review* 9: 333–43.
Moorhouse, H. F. (1983) 'American Automobiles and Workers' Dreams', *Sociological Review* 31(3): 403–6.
——(1989) 'Models of Work, Models of Leisure', in C. Rojek (ed.) *Leisure For Leisure*. London, Macmillan: 15–35.
Mumford, L. (1967) *The Myth of the Machine*. London, Secker & Warburg.
——(1970) *The Pentagon of Power*. New York, Harcourt Brace Jovanovitch.
Murdock, G. (1989) 'Class Stratification and Cultural Consumption: Some Motifs in the Work of Pierre Bourdieu', in F. Coalter (ed.) *Freedom and Constraint*. London, Comedia/Routledge: 90–101.
Nerval, Gerard (1851) *Journey to the Orient*. London, Michael Haag.
Neulinger, John (1974) *The Psychology of Leisure*. Springfield, Charles Thomas.
Neulinger, John (1990) *To Leisure: An Introduction*. Boston, Alyn & Bacon.
Nosow, S. and Form, W. (eds) (1962) *Man, Work and Society*. New York, Basic Books.
Office for National Statistics (2001) *UK 2000 Time Use Survey*. London, HMSO.
Olszewska, A. and Roberts, K. (eds) (1989) *Leisure and Life-Style*. London, Sage.
Osgood, N. J. and Howe, C. Z. (1984) 'Psychological Aspects of Leisure: A Lifecycle Developmental Perspective', *Leisure & Society* 7(1): 175–96.
Packard, V. (1957) *The Hidden Persuaders*. London, Longman.

Pahl, Ray (1995) *After Success*. Cambridge, Polity.

Parekh Report (2000) *The Future of Multi-Ethnic Britian*. London, Runnymede Trust.

Parker, H., Aldridge, J. and Measham, F. (1999) *Illegal Leisure: The Normalization of Adult Recreational Drug Use*. London, Routledge.

Parker, H., Williams, L. and Aldridge, J. (2002) 'The Normalization of "Sensible" Recreational Drug Use: Further Evidence from the North West England Longitudinal Study', *Sociology* 36(4): 941–64.

Parker, S. (1971) *The Future of Work and Leisure*. London, MacGibbon & Kee.

——(1983) *Leisure and Work*. London, Allen & Unwin.

Peirce, C. S. (1992) *Reasoning and the Logic of Things*. Cambridge, Cambridge University Press.

Perkins, H. C. and Cashmore, E. (eds) (1993) *Leisure, Recreation and Tourism*. Auckland, Longman Paul.

Phillips, K. (2002) *Wealth and Democracy: A Political History of the American Rich*. New York, Broadway.

Pieterse, J. N. (2004) *Globalization and Culture*. Boston, MA, Rowman & Littlefield.

Popper, K. (1945) *The Open Society and Its Enemies*. London, Routledge & Kegan Paul.

——(1957) *The Poverty of Historicism*. London, Routledge & Kegan Paul.

Pountain, D. and Robins, D. (2000) *Cool Rules*. London, Reaktion.

Presdee, Mike (2000) *Cultural Criminology and the Carnival of Crime*. London, Routledge.

Putnam, R. (2000) *Bowling Alone*. New York, Touchstone.

Rapaport, R. and Rapaport, R. (1975) *Leisure and the Family Life-Cycle*. London, Routledge & Kegan Paul.

Rapley, Mark (2003) *Quality of Life Research*. London, Sage.

Riesman, D. (1950) *The Lonely Crowd*. New York, Doubleday.

——(1964) *Abundance For What?* London, Chatto & Windus.

Rigauer, B. (1981) *Sport and Work*. New York, Columbia University Press.

Rimini, A. (2001) *The Life of Andrew Jackson*. New York, HarperCollins.

Ritzer, G. (2000) *The McDonaldization of Society*, Millennium edn. Thousand Oaks, CA, Pine Forge.

——(2004) *The Globalization of Nothing*. Thousand Oaks, CA, Pine Forge.

Roberts, K. (1999) *Leisure in Contemporary Society*. Wallingford, CABI Publishing.

Robinson, J. and Godbey, G. (1999) *Time For Life: The Surprising Ways Americans Use Their Time*. University Park, PA, Penn State Press.

Rojek, C. (1985) *Capitalism and Leisure Theory*. London, Tavistock.

——(1993) *Ways of Escape: Modern Transformations in Leisure and Travel*. London, Macmillan.

——(1995) *Decentring Leisure*. London, Sage.

——(2000) *Leisure & Culture*. Basingstoke, Palgrave Macmillan.

——(2001a) *Celebrity*. London, Reaktion.

——(2001b) 'Leisure and Life Politics', *Leisure Sciences* 23(2): 115–26.

——(2002) 'Civil Labour, Leisure and Post Work Society', *Society and Leisure* 25(1): 21–35.

——(2003) *Stuart Hall*. Cambridge, Polity Press.

Ryan, C. and Hall, M. (2001) *Sex Tourism*. London, Routledge.

Rybczynski, W. (1991) *Waiting for the Week-end*. New York, Viking.

Said, E. (1995) *Orientalism*. Harmondsworth, Penguin.

Sanjek, R. and Sanjek, D. (1996) *Pennies from Heaven: The American Popular Music Business in the Twentieth Century*. New York, De Capo.

Schor, J. (1992) *The Overworked American*. New York, Basic Books.

Schor, J. and Holt, D. B. (eds) (2000) *The Consumer Society*. New York, New Press.

Scraton, S. (1989) 'Boys Muscle in Where Angels Fear to Tread', in F. Coalter (ed.) *Freedom and Constraint*. London, Comedia/Routledge: 149–74.

Scraton, S. and Talbot, M. (1989) 'A Response to "Leisure, Lifestyle and Status: A Pluralist Framework for Analysis" ', *Leisure Studies* 8(2): 155–8.

Scraton, S. and Watson, B. (1998) 'Gendered Cities', *Leisure Studies* 17(2): 123–38.

Seiler, C. (2000) 'The Commodification of Rebellion', in M. Gottdiener (ed.) *New Forms of Consumption*. Lanham, MD, Rowman & Littlefield: 203–26.

Seltzer, M. (1979) 'The Older Woman: Fact, Fantasies and Fiction', *Research on Aging* 1: 139–54.

Sennett, R. (2003) *Respect*. New York, Norton.

Shaw, S. (1968) *Sinatra*. London, Hodder.

——(1994) 'Gender, Leisure and Constraints: Towards a Framework for the Analysis of Women's Leisure', *Journal of Leisure Research* 26(1): 8–22.

——(1999) 'Men's Leisure and Women's Lives', *Leisure Studies* 18(3): 197–212.

Skeggs, B. (1997) *Formations of Class and Gender*. London, Sage.

——(1999) 'Matter out of Place: Visibility and Sexualities in Leisure Spaces', *Leisure Studies* 18(3): 213–32.

Slater, D. (1997) *Consumer Culture and Modernity*. Cambridge, Polity Press.

Slotkin, R. (1973) *Regeneration Through Violence: The Myth of the American Frontier 1600–1860*. Norman, University of Oklahoma Press.

——(1985) *The Fatal Environment: The Myth of Frontier in the Age of Industrialization 1800–1890*. Norman, University of Oklahoma Press.

——(1998) *Gunfighter Nation: The Myth of Frontier in Twentieth Century America*. Norman, University of Oklahoma Press.

Smart, B. (1992) *Modern Conditions, Postmodern Controversies*. London, Routledge.

——(2003) *Economy, Culture and Society*. Buckingham, Open University Press.

Smith, R. B. (1991) 'The Leisure Experience of Post-Parental Attitudes'. Calgary, University of Calgary thesis.

South, N. (ed.) (1998) *Drugs: Cultures, Controls and Everyday Life*. London, Sage.

Spengler, O. (1926) *The Decline of the West*. Oxford, Oxford University Press.

St Louis, B. (2003) 'Sport, Genetics and the "Natural Athlete" ', *Body & Society* 9(2): 75–96.

Stebbins, R. (1992) *Amateurs, Professionals and Serious Leisure*. Montreal, McGill-Queen's University Press.

——(2001) *New Directions in the Theory and Research of Serious Leisure*. New York, Mellen Press.

Stedman Jones, G. (1971) *Outcast London*. London, Penguin.

Sullivan, O. (1996) 'Time Co-ordination, the Domestic Division of Labour and Affective Relations', *Sociology* 30: 79–100.

Suttles, G. (1968) *The Social Order of the Slum*. Chicago, IL, University of Chicago Press.

Taraborrelii, J. R. (1997) *Sinatra*. London, Mainstream.

Taylor, C. (2000) 'Modernity and Difference', in P. Gilroy, L. Grossberg and A. McRobbie (eds) *Without Guarantees: Essays in Honour of Stuart Hall*. London, Verso: 364–74.

Thompson, B. (1994) *Sadomasochism: Painful Perversion or Pleasurable Play?* London, Cassell.

Thompson, E. P. (1978) *The Poverty of Theory.* London, Merlin.

——(1991) *Customs in Common.* London, Penguin.

Thompson, F. M. L. (1988) *The Rise of Respectable Society.* London, Fonatana.

Thornton, S. (1995) *Club Cultures.* Cambridge, Polity Press.

Todorov, T. (1982) *The Conquest of America.* New York, HarperCollins.

Tomlinson, J. (1991) *Cultural Imperialism.* London, Francis Pinter.

——(1999) *Globalization and Culture.* Cambridge, Polity Press.

Touraine, A. (1971) *The Post Industrial Society.* New York, Random House.

Turner, B. (2003) 'Warrior Charisma and the Spiritualization of Violence', *Body & Society* 9(4): 93–108.

Turner, B. and Rojek, C. (2001) *Society and Culture: Principles of Scarcity and Solidarity.* London, Sage.

Turner, V. (1969) *The Ritual Process.* Chicago, IL, Chicago University Press.

——(1992) *Blazing The Trail.* Tucson, University of Arizona Press.

Turow, J. (1997) *Breaking Up America: Advertising and the New Media World.* Chicago, IL, University of Chicago Press.

United Nations (2003) *UN Development Report.* New York, United Nations.

Urry, J. (1995) *Consuming Places.* London, Routledge.

——(2002) *The Tourist Gaze,* 2nd edn. London, Sage.

Van Hoorebeek, M. (2003) 'Napster Clones Turn Their Attention to Academic E-Books', *New Library World* 104(1187/8): 142–8.

Van Moorst, H. (1982) 'Leisure and Social Theory', *Leisure Studies*: 2: 3: 157–69.

Veal, A. J. (1987) *Leisure and the Future.* London, Allen & Unwin.

Veblen, T. (1899) *The Theory of the Leisure Class.* London, Unwin.

Veblen, Thorstein (1904) *Theory of the Business Class.* Transaction, London.

Walby, S. (1990) *Theorising Patriarchy.* Oxford, Blackwell.

Warde, A. and Martens, L. (2000) *Eating Out: Social Differentiation, Consumption and Pleasure.* Cambridge, Cambridge University Press.

Wearing, B. (1998) *Leisure and Feminist Theory.* London, Sage.

Weber, M. (1930) *The Protestant Ethic and the Spirit of Capitalism.* London, Allen & Unwin.

——(1949) *The Methodology of the Social Sciences.* New York, Free Press.

——(1968) *Economy and Society,* (3 vols). New York, Bedminster Press.

Whatmore, S. (2002) *Hybrid Geographies.* London, Sage.

Wheatcroft, A. (2003) *Infidels: The Conflict Between Christendom and Islam 638–2002.* London, Viking.

White, Kevin (2001) *Sociology of Health and Illness; An Introduction.* Sage, London. www.lowpayunit.org.uk

Whyte, W. (1956) *The Organization Man.* Harmondsworth, Penguin.

Wilensky, H. (1960) 'Work, Careers and Social Integration', *International Social Science Journal* 12: 145–50.

——(1964) 'Mass Society and Mass Culture', *American Sociological Review* 29(2): 173–97.

Williams, L. (1989) *Hard Core: Power, Pleasure and the 'Frenzy of the Visible'.* Berkeley, University of California Press.

Williams, R. (1961) *The Long Revolution.* London, Chatto & Windus.

——(1989) *Resources of Hope: Culture, Democracy, Socialism.* London, Verso.

Willis, P. (1977) *Learning to Labour.* London, Saxon House.

——(1978) *Profane Culture*. London, Routledge & Kegan Paul.

——(1990) *Common Culture*. Milton Keynes, Open University Press.

——(1998) *The Youth Review: Social Conditions of Young People in Wolverhampton*. Aldershot, Avebury.

——(2000) *The Ethnographic Imagination*. Cambridge, Polity Press.

Wilson, B. (2002) 'The Canadian Rave Scene and Five Theses on Youth Resistance', *Canadian Journal of Sociology* 27(3): 373–412.

Wilson, Elizabeth (2002) *Bohemians*. London, I. B. Tauris.

Wimbush, E. and Talbot, M. (eds) (1988) *Relative Freedoms*. Milton Keynes, Open University Press.

Wyllie, R. (2000) *Tourism and Society*. State College, PA, Venture.

Yablonsky, L. (1997) *Gangsters*. New York, New York University Press.

Yeo, S. (1976) *Religion and Voluntary Organisations in Crisis*. London, Croom Helm.

Yeo, S. and Yeo, E. (eds) (1981) *Popular Culture and Class Conflict 1590–1914*. Brighton, Harvester Press.

Author Index

Subject Index